In the Lands of the
Christians

In the **Lands** of the **Christians**

ARABIC TRAVEL WRITING IN THE SEVENTEENTH CENTURY

EDITED AND TRANSLATED BY
NABIL MATAR

ROUTLEDGE
New York and London

Published in 2003 by
Routledge
29 West 35th Street
New York, NY 10001

Published in Great Britain by
Routledge
11 New Fetter Lane
London EC4P 4EE

Library of Congress Cataloging-in-Publication Data

In the lands of the Christians: Arabic travel writing in the seventeenth century / edited and translated by Nabil Matar.
        p. cm.
    Includes bibliographical references (p.)
    ISBN 0-415-93227-0 (alk. paper)—ISBN 0-415-93228-9 (pbk: alk. paper) 1. Traveler's writings, Arabic—Early works to 1800. 2. Arabs—Travel—Early works to 1800. I. Matar, N. I. (Nabil I.), 1949–
G227.I5 2002
910'.88927—dc21   2002069885

In Memoriam
Salim Kemal (1947–1999)
Unforgotten traveler

Contents

Acknowledgments

I AM GRATEFUL to many people who made this project possible, but foremost is Marilyn Goravitch, for her tireless dedication and unwavering commitment at the Humanities and Communication Department of the Florida Institute of Technology. Marilyn has been of great help to me in locating references, finalizing the text for publication, and compiling the index. To her, and to the other secretaries, Sue Downing (who was especially helpful in locating biblical references) and Suanne Powell, I am deeply thankful. I also wish to thank, as always, Victoria Smith and Linda Khan of the Evans Library at Florida Tech; and Anne Mercante and Laura Baade for their linguistic assistance.

Dr. Jane Patrick, former Humanities and Communication Department head at Florida Tech, was kind enough to read the initial proposal; and Dr. Mohja Kahf made some valuable comments and corrections, for which I am grateful. Thanks are also due to Yolanda Corey for responding to all my queries about South and Central American history, and to Marcia Denius, who proofread part of the text. I also wish to thank Drs. Muhammad Shaheen and Muhammad Asfour of Jordan University and Sharjah University respectively for their generous hospitality in Amman, Jordan and for sharing with me their vast knowledge of Islamic history and Arabic literature. I am very grateful to Dr. Khalid Bekkaoui of Sidi Mohammed University in Morocco for his close reading of the introduction and his helpful comments and insights. I also want to thank Dr. Anouar Majid of the University of New England for helping me with many of the Moroccan references and for always sending encouraging notes. And of course, in the final stages, there was G. Y.

I am grateful to the dean of the College of Science and Liberal Arts at Florida Tech, Dr. Gordon Nelson, who always encourages research; and to Dr. Andrew Revay, vice president for academic affairs (now in joyous retirement), who supported both my participation in the conference at the Temimi Foundation in Zaghouan, Tunisia (March 20–25, 2001) and my research at the National Library of Tunis. I am grateful to the librarians there for their kindness, and to Dr. Mohamed Habib El Hila for providing me with the proper library introduction and for clarifying some bibliographical entries.

I will be ever thankful to Dr. Abdeljelil Temimi for inviting me to the conference on Great Britain and the Maghreb: the State of Research and

Cultural Contacts at his quasi-monastic and stunningly evocative *Fondation* in Zaghouan. The five days of intensive presentations and discussions were invaluable to me. I also wish to thank Mohamed-Salah al-Omari of Exeter University for coordinating the conference and overseeing it to perfection. Dr. Khalid b. Srhir was extremely generous in sharing with me his vast knowledge of Moroccan and North African history. Many other scholars who attended the conference also have been of help. To all of them, I am deeply grateful.

Parts of the introduction were presented at different national conferences: the University of Arkansas, Fayettville, invited presentation at the King Fahd Center for Middle East and Islamic Studies (February 10, 2001); South-Central Renaissance Conference, College Station, Texas (April 4–7, 2001); and the annual conference of the Modern Language Association, New Orleans (December 26–29, 2001). To all the respondents in these conferences, especially to Dr. Donald Dickson and Dr. Vincent Cornell, I am deeply grateful.

This book is dedicated to a man who was the most powerful inspiration in my life—a man who was a traveler in the lands of Christians and indeed, in the whole lands of mankind: Salim Kemal.

Although we both went to Cambridge University at the same time, we did not meet until I was introduced to him, the new faculty member in the philosophy department, in Nicely Hall at the American University in Beirut in 1981. Salim proved a fiery teacher: *hami* ("hot") was the word that students used about a man who brilliantly awakened their curiosity in the midst of the cruelty of war. He was disarming and approachable, and possessed a gentle smile, but behind it was a mind that was devastatingly sharp. Once Salim got started, he was relentless, logical, unperturbed, unstoppable. Many members of faculty disliked that quality in him, but I knew how much he was driven by a brutal quest for truth, a Socratic devotion to ideas. During the Israeli siege of Beirut in the summer of 1982, we used to meet, alone among the remnants of the university, in the lower floor of Nicely, safe (or at least so we hoped) from the naval and aerial horrors that were visited upon us. We huddled under the stairwell, having brought coffee with us, and it was in those afternoons that I encountered the full range of his fearless curiosity. In those terrifying hours, he taught me about Walter Benjamin and Theodor Adorno, Abu Al-Nasr al-Farabi and Abu Ali al-Hussain Ibn Abdallah Ibn Sina, David Hume and Immanuel Kant, and in those hours began a friendship that will never end.

To Salim I owe my initiation into the fascinating world of translation. I had never thought of doing any translation until he suggested that I work on al-Farabi's treatise of poetry. I did, and discovered in the process the excitement of words.

Salim Kemal died of a heart attack on a grim Friday night, November 19, 1999, leaving behind him ground breaking publications on European and Islamic philosophy. He also left behind a deeply saddened wife and children, Jane, Sarah, and Rahim in Dundee, Scotland; aging parents in India; and his brother, Fahim, in London. May you rest in peace, dear friend, and unforgotten traveler.

كُلُّ نَفْسٍ ذَآئِقَةُ ٱلْمَوْتِ وَنَبْلُوكُم

بِٱلشَّرِّ وَٱلْخَيْرِ فِتْنَةً وَإِلَيْنَا تُرْجَعُونَ

[Every soul shall taste death. We will prove you all with evil and good. To Us you shall return. (21:35, Dawood translation)]

Introduction

ARAB TRAVELERS AND EARLY MODERN EUROPEANS

Safir, ta'rif al-nas.
[Travel, and you will learn about people.]
—Medjdoub, *Les quatrains de Medjdoub*
le sacrastique

God almighty said to Moses, peace be upon him: take an
iron staff and wear iron sandals, and then tour the earth until the staff is broken and the shoes are worn out.
—Muhammad bin al-Sarraj, *Uns al-Sari wa–al sarib*

WESTERN HISTORIANS, cultural analysts, and literary critics have viewed the
record of early modern travel and exploration as exclusively Euro-Christian,
demonstrative of modernity, superiority, and advancement. Englishmen traveling to the Ottoman Empire, Italians to Palestine, Germans to Egypt, the
Portuguese to Arabia, and Frenchmen to Morocco have been presented as
the harbingers of the intellectual and economic forces that prepared for the
Renaissance and for western European power and domination. Meanwhile, a
total dismissal of Arab-Islamic travel has prevailed, one that recalls the com-
ment by a Dutchman to the Moroccan envoy, Ahmad bin Qasim, in 1611,
"We are amazed at you: you know languages, read books, and have traveled in
the cities and countries of the world. And yet, you are a Muslim!"[1] For the
Renaissance interlocutor, totally ignorant of the Arab-Islamic heritage of geography and cartography, a well-traveled Muslim seemed an anomaly.

Such an opinion has persisted into modern scholarship. In Anthony Pagden's two-volume collection of articles, *Facing Each Other: The World's Perception of Europe and Europe's Perception of the World*, there was not a
single entry about the "perception" *of* or *by* any of the civilizations of Islam,

whether in the Mediterranean Basin, Central Asia, or the Indian Subcontinent. It is as if Arabic and Ottoman Islam, with which Europe had been interacting since the Crusades, did not exist at all. Earlier, Bernard Lewis had claimed in his *Islam and the West* (1993) that the Arabs "showed the same lack of interest [about Europe] as in medieval times"; and in his *The Muslim Discovery of Europe*, he accused Muslims of a total lack of "curiosity" toward Europeans.[2] Lewis so totally discredited Renaissance Muslims' curiosity that when the Ottoman Empire opened up to Western institutions in the nineteenth century, he compared that opening to a discovery not unlike Christopher Columbus's of America. Echoing Lewis, Khalid Ziyadah contended that there was nothing "to suggest that the Muslims exerted any effort to build a good knowledge about the Europeans."[3]

But the Ottomans had a history of travel and cartography,[4] and many Arab authors who studied their history found themselves reading about the variety of European peoples with whom the Ottoman conquerors had come in contact and conflict.[5] Mohammad bin abi al-Surur (al-Bakri al-Warithi, b. 1676) wrote about the history of the Romans and Byzantines ending with the advent of Islam, after which he (rightly) recognized that history was made in the Muslim rather than the Christian world:[6] the rest of his treatise focused on Ottoman rulers and their conquests. In the course of learning about the early Arab and then Ottoman Empires, he read about the Christian and European empires that had preceded them. At the same time, the Tunisian, Hussayn Khujah (d. 1732), translated Turkish and Persian sources into Arabic, as he announced at the opening of his *Kitab bashair ahl al-iman bi-futuhat Al Uthman* (finished c. 1726). In order to praise the Ottoman sultans, he wrote about their forays into Europe and their encounters with European armies, peoples, and cultures. Khujah wanted to compile information about the world into which the Ottomans had settled and the populations they had confronted or defeated. In writing about the Ottoman victory over Crete in 1669, for instance, he listed information about the conquerors and the conquered:

    1,833: the [number of] infidels who converted to Islam
    1,895: infidel spies who were seized
    1,895: infidels who were killed
    1,880: Muslims who were freed from captivity
  37,435: Martyrs from among the Muslims
     300: Number of churches in the city.[7]

Clearly, there was no sudden "discovery" of Europe among the Arabs. For as these and other Arabic writers reveal, information about the lands and peoples of Christendom was available and transmittable and was based on translation, research, and travel. Indeed, it was in the area of travel that much of that information made its way into the Arabic-speaking world of North Africa and the Levant. Travelers, merchants, envoys, ambassadors, and clergymen journeyed to London and Rome, Cadiz and Malta, Madrid and Moscow. In the 1590s, Mulay al-Mansur's scribe, Abu Faris al-Fishtali, wrote to the Algerian ruler to thank him for assisting the numerous envoys who were traveling to Venice "during the winter season when the waves of the sea make the pathways dangerous."[8] The autobiography of Ahmad bin Ghanem shows the extent of the author's travels, and the range of information which he collected about Spanish (and European) technology:

[After being expelled from Granada] I lived in Seville and started sailing the ocean. I crossed it many times, and sometimes I sailed the big ships, called galleons in the foreign tongue, which bring silver from the faraway Indian west. They used to sail as a fleet, as was their custom, with soldiers and technicians trained in artillery. They used to meet with their superiors to discuss that technology, often turning to some of the many books written about that topic. Many books have been written because authors and experts realize that their kings hold such books in high esteem. I used to sit with them and learn by heart what they discussed. I also worked on the cannons, without anybody suspecting that I was an Andalusian. At the time when the Sultan of the Christians ordered the expulsion of everybody from the Andalus, I was in jail because of some disagreement with Christians over courage. I had friends in high places, however, and I was released from jail. So I decided to emigrate to the lands of the Muslims, and join the Andalusians. But I was prevented from so doing, and nobody could help me. So I spent some money in bribes and I left and went to Tunis, may God protect it . . . Yusuf Dey ordered me to Halq al-Wadi fort where I learned about cannons, working on them as well as reading about them in European languages. When I noticed that the *tai'fa* of the cannon men was ignorant, unable to load or to shoot accurately, I decided to write a book because cannons are expensive, and if they are not used properly, they can be destructive.[9]

The result was a book, *Kitab ul 'Izz wal Rifa'*, which he wrote in Spanish and which was later translated into Arabic by Ahmad bin Qasim.

Between 1611 and 1613, Qasim traveled to France and Holland. He fell in love with a French woman, dined with princes and scholars, hobnobbed with the nobility, engaged in disputations and debates, and conducted delicate negotiations about a possible Dutch-Moroccan alliance against Spain. He wrote an account of his journey (now lost) and repeatedly told his story until decades later, on a visit to Egypt, he began writing a summary of the longer account, which he completed in Tunis. His account became so popular that even a writer from faraway Sudan asked him for a copy. In that same decade, an Egyptian copt came to Europe and traveled in the "republic of letters."[10] Indeed, there was as much travel to and exchange with Europe from the Levant as from the Maghreb. All communities that feared Ottoman encroachment or sought assistance against Ottoman hegemony sent envoys and delegations to European Christendom. In 1613, the anti-Ottoman Druze leader, Fakhr al-Din II, accompanied by his wife and seventy attendants, sailed to Leghorn and then Florence. An account was written about his journey by Ahmad bin Muhammad al-Khalidi al-Safadi whose purpose, as he stated at the outset, was to describe "the wonders in the lands of the Christians." Fakhr-al-Din's journey, which was to last five years, started with his arrival in Leghorn on October 25, 1613. As in the account by another Levantine fifty years later, Ilyas al-Mawsuli, travelers from the Levant always found themselves in quarantine because European ports feared the arrival of the plague on ships. Alone, Fakhr-al-Din was taken to a house where he removed all his clothes, amidst the burning of incense and herbs. Later, permission was granted for his entourage to join him, and after a few days' rest, they went to Pisa, with its "three huge bridges and leaning minaret."

Al-Safadi gave a detailed description of the city, its defenses, taxation system, and religious festivities, when the inhabitants "wore colored masks, and then removed the yoke from eggs and filled them with rose water and playfully threw them at each other and at the women." His attitude, as was the attitude of the refugees, was full of admiration for the wonders they saw. All engaged the Christianity of the Italian cities, and al-Safadi elaborately described the "Old Church" of Pisa with its statues of the disciples and followers. From Pisa the Lebanese refugees went to Florence, and then to the Vatican where Fakhr-al-Din met Pope Paul V. In 1615, they moved to Sicily where they stayed until 1618 when they returned to Lebanon. The journey opened Fakhr-al-Din's eyes to the marvels in "the lands of the Christians." In

1623, the Maronite Patriarch Jirjis Maroun went to Spain (having gone to the Tuscan court a decade earlier). In 1630, he wrote to Tuscany requesting an architect, a physician, a carpenter, a sculptor, a baker, and six farmers and their families to come to Lebanon and teach Tuscan biscuit-making and agricultural techniques to the local populace. The Europeans stayed in Lebanon until 1633 and influenced Lebanese house architecture. As a result of the journeys to Europe, some historians have argued for a subsequent dramatic change in the character of Lebanon's community and history.[11]

In 1654–55, an Orthodox priest from Aleppo accompanied his patriarch on a trip to "the Country of the Christians," Russia, and wrote about the churches, strange customs, and politics along with the various foreigners he encountered there, including those who told of dog-faced tribes that practiced cannibalism.[12] Just about the same time, two "Arabians" who had converted to Protestantism arrived in Paris, and lodged at a "Protestant house" where they assisted in the conversion to Christianity of a Turk by the name of Yusuf.[13] In 1663, there was still, surprisingly, a group of free (not enslaved) Muslims living in San Sebastián (in Madrid)—they were subsequently baptized.[14] A few years later, a Syriac Catholic priest from Iraq, Ilyas Hanna al-Mawsuli, arrived in Venice on an English ship from Iskandarun and for the next seven years wandered in the "lands of the Christians" (*bilad al-nasara*) from Italy to Spain, and from Portugal to Sicily. In 1675, he boarded a Spanish ship from Cadiz to South America and wrote the first account of the New World in Arabic. In 1681–82, a certain Butros al-Halabi (Pierre Dipy) settled in France and served as translator for North African envoys and visitors, as did another Aleppan who served as translator in Spain during the visit of the Moroccan ambassador al-Ghassani in 1690. The latter, accompanied by a retinue of fifteen to twenty men, visited Madrid and described the palace of the Escorial, royal hunting, river skating, hospitals, laws of inheritance, Lent fasting, Palm Sunday and Easter celebrations. He recorded contemporary events, such as the death of the pope, and commented on women's social and religious roles. The visit to Spain was a window on the rest of European affairs.

A year earlier, in 1689, Khujah went on a visit to the "lands of the *ifranj*" (probably Italy) where he met many doctors and learned from them some treatments with quinine, which he took back with him to his native Tunis. After his return, he wrote to the European doctors and to others whom he had known, asking them for a historical account of this medicine. In the short treatise that he wrote, *Al-Asrar al-kaminah* (*The Hidden Secrets*), Khujah reiterated how he had met with the physicians both in the lands of the Franks as well as "in our city Tunis" and how much he had benefited from them.[15] The account gives a history of quinine, with an emphasis on the facts that it had not been mentioned by Galen or any of the subsequent Arab physicians, and that its origin lay clearly in "India" (America).

A few years later, the Moroccan ambassador, Abdallah bin Aisha, went to France, established lasting friendships with members of the French court and trading companies, and fell in love. Upon his return to Morocco, he told his family and friends about France and gave very detailed reports about the whole journey to his ruler, Mulay Ismail, and to members of the court.[16] In 1736, a Levantine who fraudulently pretended to be a Prince of "Mount Libanus" traveled through Italy and France and raised contributions in Holland toward "recovering his Territory." Upon being discovered as a fraud, he was executed.[17] Other Muslims also visited Europe and told about it: "Hadge Lucas," who traveled to England twice, "has been a great Traveller," wrote the English captain John Braithwaite in 1729; he "speaks the Spanish perfectly well, and is very courteous to all strangers." Indeed, Braithwaite repeatedly noted Moroccan familiarity with Christendom: "[S]everal Moors frequented our House, that had been in England with their late Embassador."[18] In 1747, Mahmud Maqdish traveled to the European East and went into a church where he saw a painting that depicted a battle between Spanish ships and ships from his native Sfax.[19]

Although the very concept of "Europe" did not exist among either the Christian Arabs or Muslims, there was curiosity about the *ruum* (the Qura'nic name for the Byzantines and other Europeans), the *ifranj* (Franks), and the *ajam* (Spaniards) if only because from the Crusader invasion on, there had been conflict, exchange and a two-way trade with them. Merchants from the Maghreb and Andalucia, as well as from the Levant, boarded Genoese or Venetian ships and traveled across the Mediterranean to ply their trades.[20] Others reached as far as England in their ransom mediations on behalf of captives: "it hath pleas'd God," wrote a father about his captured son in a petition in Plymouth, 1688, "soe to order, that an Algerine Merchant being in this town of Plymouth aforesaid hath promis'd to pursue his redemption."[21] While many Maghariba such as this Algerian visited European lands for purposes of trade and business, others had military intent: in 1573, as the Algerians prepared to attack Tunis, they sailed to Malta and explored the coastline until they were able to cut down timber for siege operations.[22] At the same time, Moriscos in Spain inquired about European cities and travelers' routes in order to escape via France, Germany (as with

Ricote in Miguel de Cervantes's *Don Quixote*, 2:53) and Italy to North Africa and Turkey.[23] For the Christian population in the Levant, linguistic and educational reasons motivated their travel to European countries: from 1584 on, an average of fifteen Christian boys went to Rome every year to study at the Maronite College, after which they returned to their communities with an extensive knowledge of European history, art, theology, and Catholic doctrine.[24] Other Christians went on pilgrimages to centers of ecclesiastical authority: Catholics to Rome and the Orthodox to Moscow. As a result, the genre of *rihla* (travel writing) flourished in Arabic.[25]

After the 1609 expulsion from Spain, many Moriscos kept in touch with compatriot merchants who were settled on Malta, or in Palermo, Marseilles, Leghorn, and other European port cities to which they traveled frequently. One of the main reasons for such contact was to establish financial centers for money transfers, whether to pay off debts to European bankers; to pay for the purchase of small pinks and ships manufactured by French, Dutch, or Italian shipbuilders; or to finalize ransom payments for captives. An important commodity that motivated Muslims to travel to Europe or to the European-held presidios in North Africa was tobacco. The tobacco trade was so widespread that Muslim jurists condemned it for introducing Muslims to nefarious European habits, and for depleting national resources of much-needed hard currency. Abu Salim Ibrahim al-Kallali described at length the travels of Muslim merchants and their exchanges with their European counterparts, showing how frequently traders went in search of tobacco and how much they learned about the *nasara* (Christians), and about their own coreligionists too:

> The most degenerate of merchants travel to the lands of war, and enter under the authority of rulers there. . . . They take pure gold, pure silver, various kinds of weapons to use in payment for herbs which they call fire and smoke. . . . After I had asked about the whereabouts of the gold which the Muslims used in trade, and whether it was kept hidden by people or was spent, I heard the strangest tale from some of our friends the merchants. One said . . . that the gold was with the *nasara*, may God destroy them, because of the trade in that cursed tobacco. I asked him to explain. So he said, "I will tell you the truth. I traveled to the city of Ceuta, may God return it to the house of Islam, and I stayed there twenty days awaiting the merchandise from India in the hope of buying some. But I found nothing. While we were waiting

for the [Indian/American] merchandise, a ship arrived from the land of the Christians. I rejoiced but when I went to check on its contents, it had nothing but tobacco. By the next morning, all bundles had been bought, all 1,500 *qintars*. And they were all paid for in pure gold. I continued in the city for fifteen more days, hoping to do some purchases. I was not successful so I returned to Tetuan where I found that all the tobacco that had reached it had been sold, and that the revenue had gone to those whom God had cursed.[26]

No wonder, thus, that just as in England King James I denounced tobacco in his *A counterblast to Tobacco* (1604) as an imported alien herb used by "pocky Indian slaves," so did Mulay Ahmad order that "that insidious herb, which is in the possession of the Christians in New Fez, be burnt."[27] In 1607, the Moroccan rebel Abu Mahali denounced the "tree that came from the lands of the infidels," while the jurist Ali bin Ahmad denounced tobacco in 1617 as an import from the "land of the unbelievers."[28] The Europeans and the North Africans frequently encountered each other in the context of "taba," or *tabgh*; thus the "two Moors taking tobacco" at the beginning of Thomas Dekker's play *Lust's Dominion* (c. 1599–1600).

In light of their visits, "Moors," "Arabians" and "Mahometans" became prominent figures in European literary and artistic (portraiture) imagination and widely informed the verse and prose of the Renaissance: William Shakespeare's Moroccan Prince in *The Merchant of Venice*, Thomas Middleton's Moors (converted to Christianity by English traders) at the court of King James I in *The Triumphs of Truth*, the "Turqueries" of Spanish literature, and the many Moors of Miguel de Cervantes's and Lope de Vega's plays and novels.[29] The Moor, wrote an anonymous English versifier in 1682,

> who long inclosed had been pent
> Within parch't Africa's dull Continent,
> Whose untaught Hands did seldom ply the Oar,
> And trembling always crept along the Shore,
> Fir'd at the noise of the fam'd British Land,
> His active Soul disdains the Lazy Sand,
> And lanching forth, he plows th' Atlantick Main,
> Does boldly strive the Northern Pole to gain,
> And reach those wondrous Magazins of Hail & Rain.[30]

Despite the pomposity of his claim, the English writer recognized that the Moors were traveling and learning.

From the Mashriq and the Maghreb, Muslim and Christian Arabs read about, translated, and wrote from firsthand experience about the world around them. There was curiosity in their travel. In his account of his journey to Mecca between 1630 and 1633, Ibn al-Sarraj advised the prospective traveler in "the lands of God" to "observe and reflect on the differences in landscape, between mountains and valleys and wilderness, the sources of rivers and their courses, the ruins of ancient peoples and what happened to them and how they have become news of past history, after they had been seen and admired. He should also observe the differences in peoples, skin colors, languages, foods, drinks, clothes, customs and wonders."[31] Although Ibn al-Sarraj was traveling to a religious destination, he was open to new impressions, ideas, observations, smells, tastes, and colors—to novelties and differences. He was to satisfy his curiosity during his travel, the kind of travel that many of his contemporaries cherished. Shihab al-Din al-Maqqari, for instance, shows the extent of early modern Arab wanderlust: in 1600, he went to Fez, then returned to Tlemsan, then went back to Fez; in 1618, he headed to Egypt, then Hijaz, then returned to Cairo in 1623; then he traveled to Jerusalem, Cairo, Hijaz, back to Cairo and Jerusalem, and finally to Damascus, where he died in 1631.[32] Unlike his European counterparts, who had to be careful when traveling in neighboring countries of different Christian confessions, an Arab (or Turk) from North Africa and the Levant had access to a vast Ottoman empire ruled by the Istanbul-based Prince of the Faithful. While Europeans were frequently confined by their national borders and denominations and often feared crossing Protestant or Catholic lines, the Arabs (and the Turks, as in the famous case of Eleya Chelebi) had an empire to explore.

In January 1682, the Moroccan ambassador Mohammad Temim and seven members of his retinue visited France and discovered the social, artistic, and intellectual innovation of the country. The ambassador attended an opera, De Lully's *Atys*, where he "showed much surprise," probably at the amazing stage scenery that included "vne Motagne consacrée à Cybele" (a mountain consecretated for Sybil) along with a temple, palace, and gardens. He also attended a ballet at the Royal Academy of Music. A week later, he went to Notre Dame Cathedral and listened to an organ recital, and then went to an observatory and to the apartment of a professor of astronomy where he admired models of the globe and maps of the spheres, telescopes, and pendulums.[33] "Cet ambassadeur," commented one of the Frenchmen who accompanied him, "estant curieux de tout ce qui regarde les sciences et les arts."[34] The visit was such a success that when the ambassador left on February 25, he and his retinue received glamorous farewell gifts from the French monarch.[35]

This element of curiosity was again noted about Abdallah bin Aisha, and about the Tunisian delegation that visited France in 1743. "It is our pleasure to visit a kingdom we have long wanted to see," said the top envoy, Ali Agha, in the presence of his assistant, Mohammad Khujah, and the seven other members of the delegation (including an imam, a cook, three guards, and two servants). The French hosts thus became very eager to satisfy the guests' curiosity: they took them to the opera, explained to them the difference between the Copernican and Ptolemaic astronomy systems, and invited them to ceremonies that satisfied their "curiosité," according to the French observers.[36]

As the writings in this volume reveal, travelers, envoys, ambassadors, traders, and clerics were eager to ask questions about *bilad al-nasara* (the lands of the Christians) and to record answers—and then to turn their impressions into documents. They all wrote with precision and perspicacity, producing the most detailed and empirically based information about the way in which non-Europeans viewed Europeans in the early modern period. No other non-Christian people—neither the American Indians nor the sub-Saharan Africans nor the Asiatics—left behind as extensive a description of the Europeans and of *bilad al-nasara*, both in the European as well as the American continents, as did the Arabic writers.

The translations herein are taken from the following writers:

Ahmad bin Qasim, an Andalusian Morisco, went to France and Holland in 1611–13. The title of his account is *Nasir al-Din ala al-Qawm al-Kafirin* (*The Protector of Religion against the Unbelievers*). It is his own abridgment of a longer account he had written, *Rihlat al- shihab ila liqa' al-ahbab* (*The Journey of the Meteor to Meet the Loved Ones*).

Ilyas Hanna al-Mawsuli went to Italy, France, Spain, and Portugal in 1668, and in 1675 crossed to South America. The title of his account is *Kitab Siyahat al-Khoury Ilyas bin al-Qissees Hanna al-Mawsuli* (*The*

Book of the Travels of the Priest Ilyas, son of the Cleric, Hanna al-Mawsuli).

Mohammad bin Abd al-Wahab al-Ghassani went to Spain in 1690 to negotiate the release of Moroccan captives. The title of his account is *Rihlat al-Wazir fi iftikak al-Asir* (*The Journey of the Minister to Ransom the Captive*).

Abdallah bin Aisha was the Moroccan envoy who went to France in 1699 and left behind him numerous letters addressed to members of the French court and their families.

All of these accounts saw print only in the twentieth century, since the press did not come into use in the Middle East and North Africa until the early nineteenth century. But the fact that the texts were not published does not mean that they were not known or used. While print was central to European travel culture, Arab society had a rich oral tradition that transmitted news, episodes, histories, and biographies across the Arabic-speaking community from Fez to Jerusalem and from Aleppo to Mecca. There was also a vast trade in manuscripts (although Arabic writers in this period, like their European counterparts until the mid-sixteenth century, did not distinguish between "book" and "manuscript"). The Moroccan traveler Ali bin Mohammad al-Tamjarouti, who stopped in Algiers on his way back from Istanbul in 1590, noted how the city had more books in it than all the rest of the region, and the "wandering [*jawwal*] scholar" Mohammad bin Ismail acquired many books while visiting Istanbul in 1653.[37] Written material circulated so widely that Moroccan traveler Abu Salim al-Ayyashi reported that an Algerian he met owned over 1500 books.[38] In 1683, the poet-traveler Mohammed bin Zakour again noted the abundance of books in Algiers.[39] Meanwhile, attached to every major mosque were the *nassakheen* or *kataba* (scribes), who copied books in preparation for sale in the market. Until the mid-twentieth century, these *nassakheen* were still part of the mosque institutions in North Africa.[40] One of the *souks* (markets) near the central mosque in many Islamic cities is that of the scribes where books are still sold (those in Damascus, Cairo, and Tunis are fine examples).

Interest in books also prevailed among the Orthodox and Catholic minorities who composed their own texts and translated material into Arabic from Greek and Latin for the use of congregations and clergy.[41] Books also played a major role in Arabic dealings with the Europeans: both al-Ghassani and the Moroccan envoy to Spain in 1766, Ahmad bin al-Mahdi al-Ghazzal, were ordered by their rulers to bring back with them all the books in Arabic they could rescue from Spain. (The books that they failed to rescue, but which survived the fires, constitute part of the Escorial collection of Arabic manuscripts). The absence of print did not diminish the importance of books, nor did it prevent the circulation of manuscripts in Arab society. There is not a more monumental work in early modern bibliography than *Kashf al-Zunun 'an Asami al-Kutub wal-Funun*, the collection of 15,007 titles of predominantly Arabic, but also Turkish and Persian, writings that the Turkish scribe and traveler Haji Khalifah (1609–57) recorded in alphabetical order, with a separate unit on the books that circulated in the Maghreb. After inheriting money from a relative, Khalifah traveled in Syria, Egypt, Iraq, Iran, Arabia, Afghanistan, and other regions, writing down titles of books he found at the *warraqeen* (paper makers) and in the libraries. He produced the equivalent of the *Short Title Catalogue* of Arabic manuscripts in a large part of the Islamic world.[42]

The travel accounts vary in length between a few pages and whole treatises. While al-Mawsuli wrote two dozen pages about Europe, he wrote a vast unit on America along with lengthy translations from Spanish accounts about America. Paul of Aleppo wrote the longest travel account in early modern Arabic, and it was one of the most detailed descriptions of seventeenth-century Russia in any language. Such accounts constituted the chief source of information about Europeans, which was circulated in royal courts and ecclesiastical enclaves, discussed by rulers and their strategists, and used in diplomatic and commercial negotiations. Governors disseminated their information by letters that were proclaimed in Friday sermons, read by Sufi masters in their lodges, and communicated orally from village to village and tribe to tribe. Meanwhile, rulers listened to their envoys and queried them in great detail, while others looked at drawings of the lands of Christians. When the Tunisian envoy Yusuf Khujah visited Versailles in October 1728, he was overwhelmed by the grandeur around him. After he apologized to his hosts that he would not be capable of describing adequately to his compatriots the majesty of the palaces he had seen, he requested pictures, "perspectives en estampes," to show the Tunisian bey (Ottoman official), Hussein bin Ali, and other members of the Diwan (council of government) and the populace. Two weeks later, the French king ordered that pictures be made of all royal houses, gardens and ponds, and be given to the envoy—who took them back with him as evidence of the beauty and "richesses de la France."[43] News and pictures of the Europeans that the travelers brought back spread across the Arabic-speaking world, opening up venues for information, exchange, and dialogue.

Numerous as the travelers were, there is little doubt that there would have been more accounts written about Christendom had not specific factors militated against travel. While Bernard Lewis attributed the paucity of Arabic travel in Europe to Islamic lack of "curiosity," other scholars have invoked the Maliki injunction against travel.[44] But the evidence reveals that there were very practical reasons, neither necessarily theological nor intellectual, that deterred Arabs from traveling to Europe. First was the absence of Islamic religious sites in Europe. Prior to the modern period, all travel was either motivated by faith or commerce: given the dangers of travel, no early modern man or woman, whether Christian or Muslim, went on a journey to satisfy "curiosity," but to fulfill a religious, commercial or diplomatic mission.[45] The majority of medieval or early modern Europeans who traveled to the Levant wanted to see Christian holy sites; others went for trade and/or diplomatic exchange. Among the Muslim Arabs, the second motivation was widely applicable, but not the first. The absence of those sites, however, did not mean an indifference to travel and an absence of curiosity: the same reasons that motivated Christians to travel within Europe—the quest for knowledge—also motivated Muslim Arabs to travel within the world of Islam. The famous Moroccan jurist Al-Hasan bin Masood al-Yusi included various chapters in his *Canons* encouraging Muslims to travel in quest of learning.[46]

Furthermore, Arab travelers faced the difficulty of having to rely for their transportation on European ships—ships whose crew were not always willing to take "Mahumetans" on board. When the Moroccan delegation to England in 1600 desired to return home, English sailors and captains refused to transport "infidels";[47] in February 1628, John Harrison, the English representative in Morocco, reported that two Moorish agents "sent from Barbarie . . . have been here a Long tyme," and would not be able to return unless the king furnished them with means of transport.[48] A century later, the situation had not changed and the Moroccan ambassador to England complained how he "stood in need to Transport my self into my country" but was "deprived of the Necessary Means."[49] On many occasions, North African rulers wanted to send ambassadors and other emissaries to Europe, but were delayed or prevented by the unavailability or resistance of European carriers. Meanwhile, the relentless captivity of Magharibi seamen by European corsairs and privateers precipitated a shortage in manpower and a resultant decline in Magharibi naval capacity so that by the eighteenth century all trade and travel from and to North Africa was carried out by European ships.

But the most important reason that militated against travel was fear—fear of the Europeans who had invaded, terrorized, burned, expelled, and enslaved Muslims. The lands of Christians were lands of danger and violence, from which ships and soldiers repeatedly appeared to threaten and attack. Since the early fifteenth century, Portugal and Spain had been extending the *reconquista* onto Mediterranean and Atlantic Islam. In 1406, the Spaniards occupied Tetuan; in 1415, the Portuguese captured Ceuta, and in 1458 Kasr al-Saghir, whereupon the Portuguese king, Alphonso V, was given the title "the African" by the pope, in recognition of his anti-Muslim conquests; in 1471, Asilla and Tangier fell to the Portuguese, followed in 1497 by Melilla. The peoples of North Africa were haunted, as Ahmad Bucharb wrote, "par l'omnipresence de la peur" caused chiefly by the "infidels" who had well-fortified presidios, superior armaments, and mastery of the seas.[50] The Portuguese description of the establishment of Santa Cruz (Agadir) in 1505 recalls the European "discovery" and "conquest" of the Americas: the Portuguese viewed Muslim North Africa as a land of savage unbelievers to subdue and natural resources to pillage—just as they viewed Brazil. In 1506, the Portuguese occupied Mogador; in 1508, Hajar Badis and Safi; in 1514, Mazagan; and in 1515 al-Ma'mura. From 1537 to 1573, the Spaniards occupied Tunis and built there "une ville européene"[51]; in 1614, al-Ma'mura fell to Spain.

Throughout the seventeenth century, European ships of war besieged and bombarded the North African and Atlantic port cities. From 1621 on, Algiers was attacked by the English (1621, 1661, 1665, 1669), and by the French (1665, 1672, 1682, 1688)—the last destroying 9200 of the city's 10,000 buildings.[52] There were also intermittent attacks and blockades by Danish, Spanish, Flemish, Genovese, Neopolitan, Papal, Portuguese, and Sicilian fleets, and from 1662 until 1684, Tangier was in the hands of the British. All these attacks revealed the vulnerability of coastal cities, which forced Moroccan rulers to move their capitals inland—to Marrakesh and Meknes. The attacks led not only to European domination of Muslims but to the de-Islamicization of the region as churches and cathedrals and seminaries were built, often on the sites of desecrated mosques. Coastal cities such as Asfi, Mazagan, and Azammur (which had been occupied by the Portuguese) became, according to Busharb, "a foreign element hostile to the world around them," one filled with obtrusive architecture.[53] Such *presidios* severed the organic links between communities and market towns, both on land and by sea, creating fear and anxiety—similar to the fear Europeans would have felt had Algerians established a base near Plymouth or the Moroccans near Cadiz. The traveler Ibn Abid al-Fasi was on his way to the Moroccan Atlantic coast when he was warned, "The infidels are still hunting the Muslims there; they have harbors in which they dock their ships and from where they fan out and capture the Bedouins who graze their cattle around the harbor."[54] This traveler, who was able to reach Aden, was unable to reach the Atlantic shore of his own country. It is not surprising that as a result of fear, a special "Prayer of Fear," based on the Qur'an 4:102–4, was used at times of danger and Christian invasion.[55]

Fear was the most powerful deterrent to travel into the lands of Christians. The "anatomy of fear" that has been conducted on the inhabitants of the Spanish Mediterranean littoral should also be conducted on the North African population. Western historians find that the only fear in the early modern period was of innocent Europeans who feared the rapacious "Mahometans," completely ignoring the fear the Muslims had of the European *nasara*, whose legacy was not only of warfare but of religious persecution.[56] The psychological impact of the arrival, from 1609 to 1614, of hundreds of thousands of frightened and embittered men, women, and children who had been driven out of their European homes because of their Islamic faith, or the racial residues of that faith, permanently changed Arab and Islamic views of Europeans. After their expulsion, the Moriscos settled in Tunisia, Algeria, and Morocco and told the local inhabitants about the burnings, rampages, tortures, and exile they had suffered at the hands of the Christians. The first chapters in Ahmad bin Qasim's *Kitab* describe the dangers of life in Spain and his fears as a secret Muslim after witnessing the cruelty of the *harraqeen* (the burners). *Al-Anwar al-Nabawiyya fi Akhbar al-Bariyya*, by Mohammad bin abd al-Rafi' al-Andalusi, *Kitab ul-Izz wal Rifa'*, by Ahmad bin Ghanem, and *Nur al-Armash fi Manaqib sidi abi al-Ghaith al-Qashash*, by Abu Lihya al-Qafsi, all written in the wake of the expulsion, describe not only the persecution, robbery, and brutality that befell the Moriscos at the hands of the Christians, but repeatedly report the burnings of compatriots that survivors witnessed. *Al-Anwar al-Nabawiyya* has the word *burn* on every page of its conclusion. Clearly, the memories of the Europeans, along with the attacks that continued to be carried out against the Mediterranean and Atlantic coasts, frightened the Magharibi and dulled their "curiosity" about the Euro-

Christians. That Muslim travelers in Spain repeatedly wished for the destruction of the Christians (thus the repeated invocation for God to destroy or
shame them, *damarahum al-Lah* and *khadhalahum al-Lah*) was not a result
of structural hostility to Christians, but of the violence, expulsion, and autos
da fé committed by the Christians against the Muslims and their forefathers.

The fear of Europeans prevailed on the high seas too, especially as a fear
of the more seaworthy English, Maltese, or Spanish pirates who, as both
Arab and European travelers complained, including the famous French ori-
entalist Laurant D'Arvieux, indiscriminately attacked and kidnapped merchants and emissaries.[57] As early as the 1580s, such sea danger threatened
Magharibi travel. In his account of his journey to Istanbul from Tetuan, al-
Tamjarouti describes the dangers he encountered. He mentions how his ship
sailed close to the coast in order to avoid the Christian corsairs, and as soon
as they drew near Tunis, he heard sailors say that "he who crosses the Adar
tip will pay his ransom at home," signifying the danger of captivity for Muslims crossing that region.[58] Similarly, al-Safadi wrote about the Maltese pirates that accosted Fakhr-al-Din and interrogated the Flemish captain, and
only released the ship after they were assured that the travelers were "going
from the East to our country."[59] Over a century later, in 1731, the Moroccan
minister, Abu Muhammad al-Ishaqi, recalled while passing near a village in
Libya that the location had been famous for the capturing and selling of
Muslim travelers and pilgrims to Christians.[60] As Christians feared the Barbary corsairs, Muslims feared the European corsairs.

Despite peace treaties with European rulers, North African merchants
were afraid to sail to Marseilles, Genoa, or Leghorn, where there was either
open hostility or outright danger. The assassination/massacre of the Algerian
delegation, consisting of the ambassador and forty-five companions in Marseilles on June 18, 1620 (celebrated in print by one French author) is just
one of many dangerous cases in point.[61] In 1640, a Moroccan ambassador
who had just arrived in Cadiz to negotiate a treaty with Philip IV became so
afraid he would be taken captive by the Spaniards that he refused to continue to Madrid. He deserted his royal mission and hastened back home—to
certain punishment.[62] Although danger beset all ambassadors in the early
modern period, in Muslim as well as in Christian lands, there were, in the
late seventeenth and early eighteenth centuries, repeated humiliations for
the North African ambassadors, whose countries did not have the military
and naval power to retaliate when European hosts broke diplomatic protocol. Between 1727 and 1728, a Tunisian embassy was held hostage at

Chalon-Sur-Soane, and in June 1744, the Libyan ambassador, al-Hajj Ibrahim Agha, asked somebody to translate/write a petition to his "Grace," in which he complained how his (Jewish) servant, Moses Moravir, had been taken into custody

> (for Debt) of the said Sheriffs . . . in Contempt of the Law of Nations, and Your Grace's orders to them, which, I highly resent, in the Offenders, as a Reflection, & Reproach, on the King and the Countrey I represent, whom I, intent to acquaint with the Affair, unless my said Servants, are both immediately discharged, from out of their Confinement, which, I absolutely insist upon, without any Regard, or Reference had to your English Laws, which I do not understand. . . . I will forthwith, withdraw out of the Kingdom being Ashamed to appear Abroad, and hear it said, I have suffered my Servants to be imprisoned, and Confined, which is an affront, that has not been Offered to any Ambassador but myself.[63]

The humiliation of the ambassador was a humiliation for his country, not only among Europeans, but among fellow North African rulers and communities. Even worse, the Europeans could not be trusted to abide by the law of nations.

While European travelers-cum-traders could often establish bonds with merchant families and participate in civic and even religious activities, Muslims could not even find a place of residence in a European city. The European city did not have the variety of peoples and ethnicities that Aleppo, Cairo, Tunis, or Algiers had; nor did it have spaces such as the *caravanserais*, *khans*, *funduks* (travelers' lodgings/hostels), or even cemeteries that were designated for peoples from other lands and religions. The numerous funduks for Christians that existed in Moroccan cities in the sixteenth century—as Diego de Torres confirmed in his *Relacion del origen y svcesso de los xarifes* (c. 1574)—and the "English house" which was established in Alexandria as early as 1586, and the funduk built for the French "nation" in 1660 in Tunis (near the English funduk) attest to a willingness on the part of Muslim society to ensure an architecturally-appealing residence for European traders, diplomats, and visitors.[64] The survival of three gravestones belonging to three Britons and bearing the dates "MDCLXI," "MDCXLVIII," and "1667," which stand outside St. George's Church in Tunis, suggests a settled residence (and resting place) of European traders and travelers in the

Islamic city in the early modern period.[65] In 1736, Henry Boyde described
the French-run hospital in Algiers, which served all residents and local inhabitants, and the Christian cemetery, which was on a spot of land that had
actually been bought by a Christian for that purpose.[66]

Despite their fear and anxiety, Muslims still went to Europe, driven by
their familiarity with what the Qur'an designates as *al-nasara*. Both the Arab
Muslim and Christian writers used this term to refer to European Christians,
thereby situating the "foreign" European Christians within the accessible
context of the Qur'anic worldview: *al-nasara* were a religious community with
a scriptural revelation recognized by Muslims as "People of the Book." As a
result, rarely did Muslim travelers become confused or disoriented during
their visits because the lands of the European Christians, while new and
strange, were lands of a community they had known in their devotion as well
as in their daily lives. This was one of the paradoxes that travelers faced: the
fear of the *nasara* and, at the same time, the familiarity with the Eastern
nasara who lived in their midst from Baghdad to Jerusalem, and from Jaffa to
Alexandria to Meknes. Fakhr-al-Din II cooperated with the Maronite Christians in Lebanon who shared in his anti-Ottomanism, while al-Mawsuli's account shows the interaction between western Europeans and the Levant
through the activities of Catholic missionaries.[67] Al-Mawsuli met a few Europeans who had relatives in Syria and Iraq whom he had known and admired,
and while he was in Europe, he met Christians, including his nephew, Yunan,
who was receiving an education he would utilize when he returned to his
community (taking with him the necessary school supplies). Al-Ghassani
compared the "Eastern" Christians with the Christians of Spain, and showed
his familiarity with the Arabic names of Christian feasts; while he did not
know Arabic words for archbishop or procession (terms that derive from the
Catholic tradition), he knew the names for Easter and Palm Sunday. On many
occasions, he mentioned how he and his delegation found themselves among
Christians who proudly introduced themselves to them as descendants of Andalusian Muslims, with family names that were the same as those in North
Africa. So Islamic was their demeanor that they were urged by the ambassadors to emigrate to the lands of Islam—which they politely declined to do.
The Moroccan ruler Mulay Ismail reminded Louis XIV that Heraclius, whom
he thought the ancestor of the French monarch, had received a letter from
the prophet Muhammad which, the Moroccan believed, was still in French
possession. He believed that there was a millennium of exchange and communication between Muslims and the *ifranj* of France—which encouraged

him to propose to the King that he convert to Islam.[68] In Morocco, Franciscan fathers taught literacy to Catholic captives: on many occasions, Moroccans of noble families forced their way into those classes in order to learn foreign languages.[69] The Tunisian Ramadan Bey became so enchanted with European music that he purchased an organ from France, "which gave him great joy" (tarab).[70] As travelers therefore wandered among al-nasara, whether in France or Spain, Holland or England, they felt that despite being in foreign lands, they knew something about the host religion and culture. The Europeans were not total others beyond understanding or engagement.

The travelers wrote informative accounts that stand in contrast to many of the European descriptions of the Muslim world in the same period. Travelers from Europe to North Africa and the Levant, whether they came from countries with an extensive medieval history of contact (such as Spain and France) or countries of Renaissance interaction (such as England and Holland) often carried with them ideological and polemical baggage that burdened their accounts. They claimed to see what they never encountered, and interpreted authoritatively to their readers what they never understood: some claimed to meet Prester John, others claimed cannibalism among Muslims, and up until the end of the seventeenth century, there were writers who still declared that Muhammad's tomb was hanging in midair. Some travelers went to the regions of Mediterranean Christianity and Islam with a sense of Western superiority and denounced all that was "Mahumetan" and "oriental." Because Islam, in their view, was a false religion, the people, culture, and history of Islam could not but be perverse and debased: the errors of theology produced a failure in civilization. "The people [of Tunis]," wrote the Englishman John Weale in 1656, "do and act everything contrary to Christians as writing, sowing, cutting and feeding."[71] Muslims were structurally separated from Christians.

Meanwhile, Arab writers of the same period described what they saw, carefully and without projecting unfounded fantasies. They did not invent information because most of them were writing to governmental and ecclesiastical superiors who, if not accurately apprised, could blunder in their dealings with their European counterparts. Even Paul of Aleppo wrote his account "with accuracy" because his friend wanted to "verify, in general and in particular, what [the friend had] heard of them from the details of history."[72] The purpose of writing an account of a journey was to describe the lands, customs, religion, and social organization the traveler had seen—and

which another wanted to confirm. Authors therefore invested themselves
with an exemplary self in which their "I" was collective of all their coreligionists,[73] thereby telling more about the outer world they visited and the discussions and exposures they had than the inner world they experienced. The
Moroccan ambassador, Ahmad bin al-Mahdi al-Ghazzal, wrote in 1766 about
his mission to free Moroccan captives, but the first hundred pages of his account describe the topography, geography, and history of the parts of Spain
through which he traveled—all from personal (and reliable) observation. As
he noted at the outset of his account, "I was ordered by his highness [Mulay
Mohammad bin Abdallah, reg. 1759–90] may the heavens elevate him, to
write down during this auspicious journey all that I heard, saw, noted and
learnt; and to tell about the cities and villages and describe all that I experienced during my travels and stay."[74]

The travelers did not frame their encounter with the Europeans within
the "particular myths, visions and fantasies" that characterize many (if not
necessarily all) European texts.[75] The Arabic travel accounts cannot therefore be approached through the theoretical models with which European accounts have been studied by writers as different as Stephen Greenblatt,
Edward Said, and Gayatri Spivak.[76] They belong to a tradition that is different not only in its history but in its epistemology: the travelers were not harbingers of an Islamic imperialism compelled to alterize and to present, in the
words of Mary Louise Pratt, the "redundancy, discontinuity, and unreality" of
the Christians.[77] Rather, they wrote empirical accounts about Europe with
the same precision that many of their coreligionists used to describe their
journeys within the world of Islam, and in the case of the Christian travelers,
within the world at large. Furthermore, and unlike the European travelers
who used classical or biblical sources as their guides, the Arabs did not have
previous models with which to compare or contrast Europe and America.
They went with an open mind and a clean slate. And even when a traveler
such as al-Ghassani went with anger and antipathy—repeatedly denouncing
the *nasara* for having expelled his forefathers and coreligionists from
Spain—he still admitted, on the first page of his account, that he had kept
himself open to the wonders and innovations of the *nasara*.

Despite being in what Mary Louise Pratt defines as "contact zones,"[78] the
writers viewed travel as a means of experiencing rather than denouncing that
which was culturally and socially different. Al-Mawsuli enjoyed the bullfight
and described it without judgment, but, a century later, al-Ghazzal did not
enjoy it because he felt that "people should not torture animals"; still, he did

not seize the opportunity to generalize about Christian cruelty. Mohammad bin Uthman al-Miknasi, a Moroccan envoy who went to Spain a quarter of a century later, enjoyed the bullfight but was offended by the urine smell in a church belfry and hoped that God would purify the land of the unclean infidels; still, he did not continue with a diatribe about European lack of hygiene (which even European travelers decried). The travelers observed and commented—and sometimes criticized their own religious society too: al-Tamjarouti criticized the Turks for their unjust and violent rule in Algiers; over a century later, and after admiring the museum of rarities of Sir Bonier de la Moisson, Ali Agha exclaimed that it was great for him (Moisson) to be under a ruler such as the French emperor who allowed his subject to enjoy himself; had he been in the Ottoman Empire, "il ne jouiroit pas longtemps de ces beautés."[79] Al-Miknasi was critical of what he saw of ecclesiastical hypocrisy and rudeness in Spain—as he was of the tyranny of the Turks.[80]

The one area in which the Muslim travelers were consistently vociferous and condemnatory was religion. But the hostility to the Euro-Christians remained doctrinal and historical (based on their own and their predecessors' experiences), not racial or cultural. Qasim spent much of his time in disputations with Christians (and Jews): inevitably, there was acrimony, disagreement, and difference. The errors of the Christians, and their unwillingness to see the truth that he demonstrated to them did not, however, prevent Qasim from admiring, engaging, and praising numerous aspects of Euro-Christian life, manners, culture, and politics. Three quarters of a century later, al-Ghassani was as bitter and condemnatory of the Christians as Qasim had been. Like Qasim, he knew the Bible well, and like him, prided himself on refuting Christians in disputations. But Spain, with its memories of Islamic glory (a glory that he was certain would never be recovered), could not but provoke in him invective and denunciation. As al-Ghassani looked at mosques and villages and citadels, he saw the possessions and cultural property of his people which had been conquered and de-Islamicized.

Al-Ghassani was the most hostile of all the travellers who wrote about bilad al-nasara. His hostility should always be seen, however, in light of the expulsion of his coreligionists from the Andalus. In the same way that Europeans repeatedly denounced the "Mahometans" because they saw them as having conquered the land of Christ, so did al-Ghassani denounce the Christian "worshippers of the cross" (as he called the Spanish Catholics) for having conquered the land of his fathers. But what made his hostility relentless was that the Christians had driven his coreligionists out and had not even permitted the converts to remain in their lands. As he had earlier in his life traveled on diplomatic missions to the Levant and to Istanbul, al-Ghassani knew that while Muslim/Ottoman armies had conquered Christian lands, they had not expelled the Christian populations. Even European travelers admitted to the presence of large populations of Eastern Christians (whom al-Ghassani recognized to be different from Western Christians) in Istanbul, Jerusalem, Cairo, and other metropolitan areas. While the Muslims had permitted the Christians to remain in their lands, the Christians had not permitted the Muslims to remain in the Andalus. Such a realization underpinned al-Ghassani's imprecations that "God destroy them." The Spanish Christians had, after all, destroyed his ancestors.

But not every traveler was overwhelmed by memories of Christian domination or theological difference. Abdallah bin Aisha was able to forgo difference in favor of deep amity and *mahabba* (love/affection)—a word that Qasim, but never al-Ghassani, had also used. Despite the religious chasm between the Christians and the Muslims, there was for Aisha the possibility, at least, of acceptance of, and possibly deep engagement with, his French associates. There was an immediacy that outweighed past conflicts and present tensions—and led to enduring friendship. Fifteen days after leaving Paris on his way back to Morocco, he wrote a letter to his host, Jean Jourdan, thanking him for his hospitality. Through friendship, "the two of us have become," he wrote, "Aisha Jourdan and Jourdan bin Aisha": the French was Moroccan and the Moroccan French. "I have been in your house," he continued, "and have put your daughters in my lap, while their mother sat with me on the sofa, and we all ate together. The pen will go dry if I continue with my emotions." Aisha's *mahabba* spanned religious and political difference.[81] Aisha clearly regarded the European not as an other, separated both geographically and ontologically, but as somebody who had become integral to his own subjectivity and constitution.

In the same way that the views of European travelers to the Levant were varied and nuanced, as Kenneth Parker and others have shown about English travelers to the Islamic Orient,[82] so were the views of the Arab travelers; and in the same way that there were Turks, Moors, Armenians, Greeks, Jews, and Arabs for the European traveler to contend with, so were there Spaniards and Portuguese, Andalusians of Islamic origin, "heretics" (al-Mawsuli's and al-Ghassani's word for Protestants), Jews, New Christians and Old in the lands of the Christians. The accounts reveal different personalities and different preferences—and therefore, different "Europes." Both al-

Ghassani and al-Ghazzal described Spain—and within three quarters of a century of each other; but the former was much more interested in the religious institutions and practices of the monks and nuns than was the latter. Where al-Ghassani's Spain was ecclesiastical, al-Ghazzal's was a land of fiestas; where the former argued with and criticized the friars, the *farayila*, the latter treated them as part of the staff that welcomed him. Earlier, Ahmad bin Qasim had been so riled at the many inaccuracies about Islam upheld by his French hosts that he frequently argued with them, revealing a firm grasp of the Old and New Testaments in both Arabic and Spanish. Meanwhile, no English or French traveler could dispute knowledgeably with Muslims until after the late 1640s, when translations of the Qur'an were published.

The major differences among the travelers, however, were dictated by the time period in which they traveled. The seventeenth-century visitors belonged to an Islamic society that appeared as powerful and wealthy as the society of Europe. Neither Muslim nor Christian was put on the cultural or historical defensive during his European journey. Qasim admired the tidiness of Amsterdam and the buildings in Paris, but he was not overwhelmed, since Marrakesh boasted the palace of al-Badee', an architectural marvel. He felt so much an equal that he may have viewed his journey, according to Abd al-Majid al-Qaddouri, as an act of theological and intellectual jihad against equal adversaries.[83] In his *Kitab Nasir al-Din*, he did not go into detail about the European landscapes and cities as much as he delved into people's minds, challenging their theological and doctrinal "errors." Paul of Aleppo compared his native city to Moscow—to the advantage of the former, where there were "no fear nor fires, nor any thing of the kind."[84] Al-Mawsuli was stunned by the European wealth that he saw, coming as he was from the easternmost outpost of the Ottoman Empire (and one that had been only recently reconquered); but much as his religious emotions were heightened in Rome, he still viewed himself as the subject of a sultan whose imperial power was reverberating throughout Europe. After he served as translator to the Ottoman ambassador who visited Paris in 1668, he wrote an account that revealed his awe at Ottoman might and splendor. Even in America, he could not but frequently recall his native land. Al-Ghassani admired many of the novelties in Spain, but he credited the country's greatness to its Islamic legacy, about which he wrote with passion and sorrow. These travelers were amazed and startled, but not defeated.

By the turn of the century, however, the travelers saw a different Europe. In 1699, Ibn Aisha reflected the North African wonder at the valuable orna-

ments, the objets d'art, the utensils and clothes that the French imported
from America, India, and Siam. In Spain as in Naples, Malta, and Sicily, the
travelers saw how *al-nasara* had developed institutions for education, health,
industrial production, and social organization unmatched by any in their own
countries. Ali Agha's Tunisian delegation of 1743 was simply overwhelmed—
as the French wanted them to be—not only by the opulence and novelty
they saw but by the advances in technology, science, and art. Despite recog-
nizing the inadmissibility of human representation in Islam, as he noted to
his host, Ali Agha was awestruck at the beautiful paintings in the churches he
visited.[85] Also, so much was new to al-Ghazzal that his account, like al-Ghassani's, is full of arabized Spanish words, ranging from *chair* to *hat, mile* to
coach.[86] Al-Ghazzal admired much of what he saw in Spain: hospitals, gardens, maritime schools, and royal entertainment. He described with fascina-
tion statues that looked like human beings and painted pottery that could not
but have life in it. He marveled at bridges with impressive arches; the numerous water sources; the vegetation; flowers ("their myrtle is not like
ours"); and animals, including those in Carlos III's private zoo—specifically
the lions from *al-Hind* (America), which were smaller than those in North
Africa. It was clear that the "modern" centralized states of Europe had su-
perceded the archaic Islamic polity.[87]

There were wonders among the *nasara* that could not be denied: Ali
Agha was so taken by the "ouvrages mecaniques" on the residence grounds
of Comte d'Evreux that he did not feel the rain drenching him.[88] In Sicily,
al-Miknasi marveled at anatomy lessons and orphanages, dancing dogs and
fossils; but he could not help but add that the earthquake that killed thousands in Messina on April 5, 1782, was God's judgment on that "protectorate
of sin," or that all the attention that the travelers received was actually intended for "our imam and master al-Mansur."[89] Like other travelers, al-Miknasi knew that outright praise for the Europeans could not be easily
tolerated by their rulers. As a result, and every once in a while, travelers re-
sorted to a policy of using the description of Europe to serve in the glorifica-
tion of the ruler. Al-Miknasi, who visited Malta, Sicily, and the kingdom of
Naples and Spain between 1781 and 1793 could not help but deride in ex-
pressions of Islamic superiority the European luxuries he saw; it would have
been dangerous to reveal to Mulay Mohammad and to the tradition-bound
jurists who dominated social and religious life in Morocco his admiration of
European wealth and advancement. For him and for other travelers, the European world was more powerful, affluent, and possibly attractive than their

own—although they did not dare admit to that. They knew that they had to temper exhilaration with denunciation: after a detailed and exuberant description of a pleasurable visit to France in 1845–46, the Moroccan ambassador Muhammad al-Saffar could not but end his account with a statement in which he rather gratuitously denounced the trickery and deceit of the Europeans, adding the Qura'nic verse (*Ruum* 7) that they "know only some appearance of the life of the world, and are heedless of the Hereafter."[90] But it was one single denunciation, written at the end of a book of wonders, praise, and envy.

Curiously, similar disavowal of the greatness of the cultural other had appeared in English seventeenth-century writings. In that century when Islamic might was still at an enviable height, from Aghra to Istanbul, authors such as William Biddulph, Henry Blount, and Paul Rycaut had to insist in their prefaces that much as they had admired the Turks, they still believed that England was superior and better. "For hereby all men may see how God hath blessed our Countrie above others, and be stirred up to thankefulnesse," wrote Biddulph;[91] the purpose for writing about Morocco, John Harrison told Charles I, was to "discerne betwixt a blessed Christian gouernment whereunis God had ordained you, and a cruell-tyrannous Mahometan gouernment."[92] While these writers included criticisms of the Turks and Moors as a precautionary measure, others censored their writings before sending them to press, deleting sections that could be misunderstood as too favorable to the "infidels."[93] Neither rulers nor readers, Muslim nor Christian, could bear too much reality.

Europe was complex and challenging, and the Arab Muslim travelers knew that they had to learn and ask questions, sometimes relying on their mastery of European languages (as was the case for all seventeenth-century travelers) and at other times relying on translators. What they wrote down was a product of measurement, observation, and evaluation—not fantasy. They were learning and correcting old misconceptions. When the Moroccan ambassador to England in 1682–83 was about to leave, he explained that his visit had dispelled his previous misconceptions about the *nasara* of England. During his visit, he had listened to what they had told him about Christianity and had subsequently changed his views. He promised to change the views of his compatriots too upon his return. "[W]e have Beene Towld," he was quoted to have said in his farewell statement, "that the Christians worship a god mad[e] of wood or Stone wch they may throw into the fiarre e see Consumed e this we have believed but I have this day with my Eyes I thank God (of whome he allwayes speakes with a great Deale of Reverence) seene the contrary I doe believe the English Nation the best people."[94]

The travelers recognized the limits of their knowledge about Europeans and tried to learn: sometimes they got their information wrong, as with al-Ghassani's account of the Protestant Reformation, and sometimes accurately, as with his account of England's Glorious Revolution. Al-Miknasi explained to his ruler (twice) that Jews killed Christian children and that, as a result, the Spaniards had expelled them. The ambassadors asked about the new, the different, and the strange, and wrote down everything. After the Messina earthquake, Al-Miknasi reported that some reports had put the number of the dead at 20,000 while others put it at 100,000; some had put the number of cities that had been destroyed at 50, others more. Al-Miknasi wrote down all that he heard, including speculations and conjectures.[95] He admitted that he was in no position to make a judgment; but he was also not willing to invent or impose anything. While European writers all too often indulged in orientalism, Arab writers did not construct a parallel "occidentalism."

The numbers of Arab travelers from the lands of Islam to *bilad al-nasara* were never as high as those of the Europeans to Islam. Still, in the early modern period, numerous ambassadors, emissaries, and merchants; captives and spies; and priests and jurists ventured across seas and mountains into Spain and France, Holland and Italy, England and Russia—and wrote first-hand descriptions of the peoples and customs, the geography and ethnography of the "lands of the Christians." No other people wrote more about the Europeans than did the Arabs.

Notes

All Arabic names and book titles in this work appear as they are transliterated in the online HOLLIS library catalogue of Harvard University. These transliterations are often different in other catalogues since, unfortunately, there is no standardized convention for the transliteration of Arabic among the Library of Congress, the British Library, and the Bibliothèque Nationale.

1. Ahmad bin Qasim (bin al-Hajari), *Nasir al-din 'ala al-qawm al-kafirin,* ed. Muhammad Razzuq (Al-Dar al-Bayda': Kulliyat al-Adab wa-al-Ulum al-Insaniyah, 1987), 53.

2. Anthony Pagden, *Facing Each Other: The World's Perception of Europe and Europe's Perception of the World* (Brookfield, Vt.: Ashgate, 2000). Pagden would have greatly benefited from reading Abd al-Majid al-Qadduri, *Sufara Mahgaribah fi Urubba, 1610–1922* (Rabat: Jamiat Muhammad al-Kamis, 1995) which surveys Moroccan travel history. Bernard Lewis, *Islam and the West* (New York: Oxford University Press, 1993), 15; and *The Muslim Discovery of Europe* (New York: W. W. Norton, 1982), 299. The same opinion was repeated by Norman Cigar: the Arabs were not "interested" in Europe; see Cigar, ed. and trans. *Muhammad al-Qadiri's Nashr al-Mathani: The Chronicles* (Oxford: Oxford University Press, 1981), xv.

3. Khalid Ziyadah, *Tatawwur al-nazrah al-Islamiya ila Urubba* (Beirut: Mahad al-Inma al-Arabi, 1983), 13. I am grateful to Dr. Bekkaoui for this reference.

4. See the study of sixteenth-century Turkish traders in Venice and other parts of Italy: Cemal Kafadar, "A Death in Venice (1575): Anatolian Muslim Merchants Trading in Serenissima," in *Merchant Networks in the Early Modern World,* ed. Sanjay Subrahmanyam (Brookfield, Vt.: Variorum, 1996): 97–125; see also the unit on Ottoman cartography in Jerry Brotton, *Trading Territories: Mapping the Early Modern World* (Ithaca, N.Y.: Cornell University Press, 1998); V. L. Menage, "Three Ottoman Treatises on Europe," in *Iran and Islam*, ed. C. E. Bosworth (Edinburgh: University Press, 1971), 421–33; and Virginia H. Aksan, *An Ottoman Statesman in War and Peace, Ahmed Resmi Efendi, 1700–1783* (Leiden: E. J. Brill, 1995), chapter 2.

5. The term Arab is used in this book to refer to writers whose language of thought and expression was neither Turkish, Aljemda, nor Syriac, but Arabic. All four authors whose works are translated in this book, along with every other author who is mentioned, wrote in Arabic. Arab/Arabic is used not to suggest a national identity but a linguistic commonality.

6. Muhammad bin abi al-Surur, *Sirat al-Ashab wa Nuzhat dhawi al-Albab*, MS 4931, National Library of Tunis.

7. Hussayn Khujah, *Kitab bashair ahl al-iman bi-futuahat Al Uthman*, MS 6554, National Library of Tunis, 412. For a description of the text and a study of Khujah, see Ahmed Abdesselem, *Les Historiens tunisiens* (Paris: C. Klincksieck, 1993), 206–21.

8. Abdallah Guennun, *Rasail Sadiyah: Cartas de Historia de los Saadies* (Tetuan: Instituto Muley el-Hasan, 1954), 188–89.

9. Ahmad bin Ghanem, *Kitabz-ul Izz wal-Rifa*, MS 1407, National Library of Tunis, 4r-6v. See the translation of some selections in David James, "The 'Manual de Artilleria' of Ahmad al-Andalusi with Particular Reference to its illustrations and their Sources," *Bulletin of the School of Oriental and African Studies* 41, no. 3 (1978): 251.

10. Alastair Hamilton, "An Egyptian Traveler in the Republic of Letters: Josephus Barbatus or Abucacnus the Copt," *Journal of the Warburg and Courtauld Institutes* 57 (1994): 123–50.

11. Asad Rustum and Fuad Afram al-Bustani, eds., *Lubnan fi ahd al-Amir Fakhr al-Din al-Ma'ni al-Thani* (Beirut: Manshurat al-Jami'a al-Lubnaninya, 1969), 208–41. I am currently preparing a study and a translation of this account. For the ideological impact of the journey, see Butrus Daw, *Tarikh al-Mawarina al-Dini wa-al-siyasi wa-al-hadari* (Junieh: al-Matba'a al-Bulusiyya, 1977), 4: 225–51.

12. Paul of Aleppo, *The Travels of Macarius: Patriarch of Antioch: written by his attendant archdeacon, Paul of Aleppo, in Arabic*, trans. F. C. Belfour (London: Oriental Translation Committee, 1829–36). An abridged version of this text was published by Lady Laura Ridding, *The Travels of Macarius, Extracts from the Diary* (1936: rep. New York: Arno Press, 1971).

13. British Library, MS Harley 7575, "The Conversion and Baptism of Isuf," 19.

14. Cl. Larquié, "Les esclaves de Madrid à l'époque de la décadence (1650–1700)," *Revue Historique* 224 (1970): 62, n.8.

15. Hussayn Khujah, "Al-Asrar al-kamina bi-ahwal al-kinah kinah," MS 14117, National Library of Tunis.

16. In a letter to Madame de Saint Olon, the wife of the French Ambassador to Morocco, he stated that he was going to "parler de vous à nos Enfans, du bien que vous nous avez fait." *Mercure Galant*, May 1699, 218.

17. *Tenth Report of the Royal Commission of Historcal Manuscripts* (London: Eyre and Spottiswoode, 1885), 456–57.

18. Captain John Braithwaite, *The History of the Revolutions in the Empire of Morocco* (London: J. Darby, 1729), 65, 73.

19. Mahmud bin Said Maqdish, *Nuzhat al-anzar fi ajaib al-tawarikh wa-al-akhbar* (Beirut: Dar al-Gharb al-Islami, 1988), 2:216. The historian Abu al-Qasim al-Zayyani (1734–1833) visited Leghorn where he stayed for four months, then continued by land to Marseilles and Barcelona and then returned to Morocco—where he wrote an account of his travels and the world at large: *Al-Tarjumanah al-kubra fi akhbar al-mamura*, ed. Abd al-Karim al-Filali (Rabat: Wizarat al-Anba 1967), 373 ff. See also G. Salmon, "Un voyageur Marocain à la fin du XVIII siècle," *Archives Marocaines* 2 (1905): 330–40.

20. See Tahar Mansouri, "Les Relations entre Marchands Chretiens et Marchands Musulmans au Maghreb à la fin du Moyen-Age," in *Chretiens et Musulmans à la Renaissance*, comp. Bartolomé Bennassar and Robert Sauzet (Paris: H. Champion, 1998), 411; Samir Ali Khadim, *Al-Sharq al-Islami wa-al gharb al-*

Masihi . . . 1450–1517 (Beirut: Muassasat al-Rihani, 1989). Charles Issawi, "The Decline of Middle Eastern Trade, 1100–1850," in *The Global Opportunity*, ed. Felipe Fernandez-Armesto (Aldershot, England: Variorium, 1995), esp. 141–47. For earlier accounts of Arab-Islamic travel, see R. P. Blake and R. N. Frye, "Notes on the *Risala* of B. Fadlan," *Byzantina Metabyzantina* 1 (1949): 3–37; Abdurrahman A. El-Hajji, "At-Turtushi, the Andalusian Traveler and his Meeting with Pope John XII," *Islamic Quarterly* 11 (1967): 129–36; Houari Touati, *Islam et Voyage au Moyen Âge* (Paris: Seuil, 2001).

21. Devon Quarter Session, 128/99/6.

22. *Chronique Anonyme de la Dynastie Sa'dienne*, ed. Georges S. Colin (Rabat: F. Moncho, 1934), 45.

23. L. P. Harvey, "The Literary Culture of the Moriscos, 1492–1609," MS. D.Phil, d. 2040-1 (Oxford University, 1958), 325. There are many articles on the flight of Moriscos and the routes they took: see Abdeljelil Temimi, "Le passage des Morisques à Marseille, Livourne et Istanbul d'apres de nouveaux documents italiens," *Revue d'Histoire Maghrebine* 55–56 (1989): 303–16. Until the expulsion of 1609, many Moriscos and Moors traveled from Spain to North Africa and vice versa—as one of Francisco de Tàrrega's characters in the play *Los Moriscos de Hornachos* declared; see Jean-Marc Pelorson, "Recherches sur la "Comedia" *Los Moriscos De Hornachos*," *Bulletin Hispanique* 74 (1972): 41; C. B. Boubland, ed., "Los Moriscos de Hornachos" *Modern Philology* 1 (1903–4), scene 3, p. 556. Even after the expulsion, they continued to correspond with the remnant of Moriscos in Spain: Hossein Bouzinelo, "'Plática' en torno de la entrega de la Alcazaba de Salé en el Siglo XVII," in *Al-Qantara* 15 (1994), 69.

24. The Lebanese Maronites Jibrail al-Suhyuni, Nasrallah al-Aqoori, and Yuhanna al-Hasruni studied in Rome at the Maronite College and later traveled to France to assist in the establishment of an Arabic press.

25. For example, on the travels of Ibn Abid al-Fasi to Aden in 1587, see his *Rihlat*, ed. Ibrahim al-Samarrai and Abd Allah Muhammad al-Hibshi (Beirut: Dar al-Gharb al-Islami, 1993). On the journey of Abu Abdallah Muhammad al-Tamjarouti to Istanbul in 1589–91, see his *Kitab al-Nafhah al-Miskiyah fi al-Safarah al-Turkiyah* (Tetuan: n.p., 1960). His name appears as Majruti in Hollis (although the Arabic is al-Tamjarouti). On the journey of Abu Salim al-Ayyashi to Mecca, Medina, and Jerusalem in 1663, see *Ma al-Mawaid* (Fez: n.p., 1899). On the journey of Ibrahim bin abd al-Rahim al-Khiyari to Damascus and Istanbul in 1663, see his *Rihlat al-Khiyari*, ed. Raja Mahmud al-Samarrai (Baghdad: Wizarat al-Thaqafah wa-al-Alam, 1969). On the journey of Muhammad bin Zakour to Algeria in 1682, see his *Nashr*

Azahir al-Bustan (Rabat: al-Matbaah al-Mulkiyah, 1967). These travelers were very careful about documenting their travels, "I used to take notes during my journey," wrote al-Khiyari, "about everything I saw, observed or thought....Despite the difficulty of travel, I scribbled the information whenever I felt inspired." Ibrahim bin Abd al-Rahman al-Khiyari, *Tuhfat al-Udaba wa-salwat al-ghuraba*, ed. Raja' Mahmud al-Samarrai (Baghdad: Wizarat al-Thagafah wa-al-Alam, 1969) and M. Hadj-Sadok, "Le Genre 'rih'la,'" *Bulletin des Études Arabes* 8 (1949): 195–206. See also Abderrahmane El Moudden, "The Ambivalence of *Rihla*: Community Integration and Self-Definition in Moroccan Travel Accounts, 1300–1800," in *Muslim Travelers: Pilgrimge, Migration, and the Religious Imagination*, ed. Dale F. Eickelman and James Piscatori (Berkeley and Los Angeles: University of California Press, 1990), 69–84.

26. Mohammad al-Manooni, "Malamih min tatawwur al-Maghrib al-Arabi fi bidayat al-usuor al-haditha," in *Ashghal al-Mutamar al-Awal li-Tarikh al-Maghrib al-Arabi wa-Hadaratih* (Tunis: al-Jamiah al-Tuniisiyah, 1979), 106n.

27. Mulay Ahmad, quoted in chapter 3 of Mohammad Hajji, *al-Harakah al-fikriyah bi-al-Maghrib* (Rabat: Dar al-Maghrib lil-Tailif, 1976), part 1, 248–50.

28. Abd al-Majid al-Qadduri, *Ibn Abi Mahali al-Faqih al-Tha'ir* (Rabat: Manshurat Ukaz, 1991), 165.

29. See the introduction to Jack D'Amico, *The Moor in English Renaissance Drama* (Tampa: University of South Florida Press, 1991); chapter 1 in my *Turks, Moors and Englishmen in the Age of Discovery* (New York: Columbia University Press, 1999); and Albert Mas, *Les Turcs dans la Littérature espagnole du siècle d'or* (Paris: Centre de recherches hispaniques, 1967). For pictorial representations, see Yvette Cardaillac-Hermosilla, "Images du Maure en Europe à la Renaissance," *Chretiens et Musulmans à l'Epoque de la Renaissance*, ed. Abdeljelil Temimi (Zaghouan: Fondation Temimi, 1997), 79–114.

30. "An Heroick Poem to the King, upon the Arrival of the Morocco and Bantam Embassadors, to his Majesty of Great Britain" (July 1682), 3–4.

31. Ibn al-Sarraj, *Uns al-sari wa-al sarib*, ed. Muhammod al-fasi (fasi: Wizarat al-Dawlah, 1968), 7.

32. Muhammad Tammam, *Tilimsan abra al-usur* (Al-Jazair: Al-Muassasah al-Wataniyah lil-Kitab, 1984), 241.

33. Charles Penz, *Les Emerveillements Parisiens d'un Ambassadeur de Moualy Ismail, (Janvier-Fevrier 1682)*, (Paris: Editions Siboney, n.d.), which was taken from Compte Henri de Castries, *Les Sources inédites . . . Dynastie Filalienne . . . Archives et Bibliothèques de France* (Paris: E. Leroux, 1922), vol. 1; Eugène Plantet, *Mouley Ismael Empereur du Maroc et la Princesse de Conti* (Paris: E. Jamin, 1893/1912); Jean Baptiste Lully, *Atys: tragedi en musique* (Paris: Christophe Ballard, 1682).

34. Castries, *Les Sources inédites . . . Dynastie Filalienne*, 1:656.

35. For the list of gifts, see *La Gazette de France*, February 28, 1682, p. 142.

36. Jean Baptiste de Fiennes, *Une Mission Tunisienne à Paris en 1743* ed. Pierre Grandchamp (Tunis: J. Aloccio, 1931), 11, 21, 41.

37. Muhammad bin al-Tayyib al-Qadiri, *Kitab iltiqat al-durar*, ed. Hashim al-Alawi al-Qasimi (Beirut: Dar al-Afaq al-Jadidah, 1983), 2:135. For the impact of Arabic books on sub-Saharan Africa, see Anouar Majid, *Unveiling Traditions* (Durham, N.C.: Duke University Press, 2000), chapter 3.

38. Quoted in Mulay Bilhemissi, *Al-Jazair min khilal rahalat al-maghariba fi al-'ahd al-Othmani* (Al-Jazair: Al-Sharika al-Wataniya lil-Nashr, 1981), 75–76.

39. Ibid., 59.

40. I am indebted to Dr. Ibrahim Chabbouh, former director of the National Library of Tunis, who passed on this information in a private conference held with him in Amman, Jordan, June 18, 2000.

41. See Wahid Qaddurah, *Bidayat al-tibaah al-Arabiyah fi Istanbul wa-bilad al-Sham* (Tunis: Markaz al-Dirasat wa-al-Buhuth, 1993), 170 ff.

42. Gustavus Fluegel, *Lexicon Bibliographicum et Encyclopaedicum a Mustafa ben Abdallah Katib Jelebi*, 7 vols. (London: R. Bentley, 1835–58). For books circulating in the Maghreb, see 6:648–64. For a brief biography of Khalifa, see the introduction to the Arabic text by Shihab al-Din al-Najafi (Baghdad: Maktabat al-Muthanna, 1972).

43. *Correspondence des Beys de Tunis*, ed. Eugène Plantet (Paris: Ancienne Libraire, 1894), 2:228, 234.

44. For the Maliki injunction (Maliki is the Islamic school of jurisprudence in North Africa, excluding Egypt.), see Jerome Weiner, "Fitna, corsairs and diplomacy" (Ph.D. diss., Columbia University, 1976), p 114. See also the long note in Majid, *Unveiling Traditions*, 183, n. 44.

45. Actually, at a time when early modern Christendom was still deeply apprehensive about *curiositas*—the quality that had led to Adam's primeval sin—it is not possible to find travel curiosity among Europeans: "it is difficult to discover in the [European] literature of the period any whole-hearted and unqualified commendation of travel," notes Samuel Chew in *The Crescent and the Rose* (New York: Oxford University Press, 1937), 29. See also G. K. Hunter, "Elizabethans and Foreigners," in *Shakespeare in His Own Age*, ed. Allardyce Nicoll (Cambridge: Cambridge University Press, 1965), 37–53; Carlo Ginzburg, "High and Low: the Theme of Forbidden Knowledge in the Sixteenth and Seventeenth Centuries," *Past and Present* 73 (1976): 28–41. See Edward Said's reaction to Lewis, as if curiosity toward Europeans was "the only acceptable criterion" of knowledge: "Orientalism: Reconsidered," in *Orien-*

talism: A Reader, ed. A. L. Macfie (New York: New York University Press, 2001), 351.

46. Al-Hasan bin Masood al-Yusi, *Al-Qanun*, ed. Hamid Hamani (Rabat: Matbaat dar Al-Furgan, 1998), ch. 7.

47. *The Letters of John Chamberlain*, ed. Norman Egbert McClure (Philadelphia: American Philosophical Society, 1939), 1:108.

48. State Papers (hereafter, SP), Public Record Office, London, 71/12/165.

49. SP 71/17/118.

50. Ahmad Bucharb [Bu Sharb], "Les Conséquences Socio-Cultuerelles de la Conquête Ibérique du Littoral Marocain," in *Relaciones de la Peninsula Ibérica con el Magreb siglos XIII–XVI*, ed. Mercedes García-Arenal and María J. Viguera (Madrid, 1988), 492–93 in 487–539.

51. Paul Sebag, "Une ville Européene à Tunis au XVIe Siècle" *Cahiers de Tunisie* 9 (1961): 97–108; and Noureddine Saghaier, "Un Faubourg Chretien à Tunis au XVIe Siècle," in Temimi, ed., *Chretiens et Musulmans*, 221–231.

52. Plantet, *Deys d'Alger*, 1:158, note. Algiers had been one of the most attractive cities on the Mediterranean. Half a century earlier, in 1638, even an English captive in Algiers praised its beautiful buildings, noting that its "houses [were] built stairelike one over the other, enjoying a most wholesome ayre and pleasant situation: scarce any house of the City but hath the prospect of the Sea, there are in her many stupendious and sumptious edifices. . . . [there is] a multitude of people, and excessive Riches, in gold, plate, and household furniture her women for beautie give place to none": Francis Knight, *A Relation of Seaven yeares Slaverie vnder the Turkes of Argeire, suffered by an English Captive Merchant* (London: T. Cotes, 1640), 32.

53. Ahmad Bu Sharb, *Dukkalah wa-al-isti'mar al-Burtughali* (Al-Dar al-Bayda: Dar al-Thaqafah, 1984), 438 and 334–401. See also the drawings of Portuguese fortifications in Ahmad bin Ghanem's *Kitab ul-izz*, reproduced in Mohammad Abdallah Annan, "Min Turath al-Adab al-Andalusi al-Moorisci," *Revista del Instituto de Estudios Islámicos en Madrid*, 16 (1971): plate 4.

54. Al-Fasi, *Rihlat Ibn Abid al-Fasi*, 85. For the presidios, see chapter 2 in Henk Driessen, *On the Spanish-Moroccan Frontier* (New York: Berg, 1992).

55. See *Christians and Moors in Spain*, comp. Colin Smith (Warminster: Aris and Phillips, 1992):3: 128–33.

56. See the seminal article by Comte Henri de Castries, "Les Corsaires de Salé," *Revue des Deux Mondes* 13 (1903): 823–52. Castries was writing at the height of French colonialism and may therefore be excused for failing to see the fear of the colonized. No excuse, however, can be made for Bruce Taylor, who repeated, uncritically, Castries's ideas in "The Enemy within and without: An Anatomy of Fear on the Spanish Mediterranean Littoral," *Fear in Early Modern Society*, ed. William G. Na-

phy and Penny Roberts (Manchester: Manchester University Press, 1997), 78–99. See also the chapter by Jean Delumeau, "La menace musulmane," in *La Peur en Occident (XVIe–XVIIIe siècles)* (Paris: Fayard, 1978).

57. Laurent D'Arvieux, *Memoires du chevalier d'Arvieux*, 6 vols. (Paris: C. J. B. Delespine, 1735), 1:22. For studies on European piracy, see Neville Williams, *Captains Outrageous: Seven Centuries of Piracy* (New York: Macmillan, 1962); Kenneth R. Andrews, *Elizabethan Privateering: English Privateering During the Spanish War, 1585–1603* (Cambridge: Cambridge University Press, 1964); Christopher Lloyd, *English Corsairs on the Barbary Coast* (London: Collins, 1981); and Alberto Tenenti, *Piracy and the Decline of Venice, 1580–1615*, trans. Janet and Brian Pullan (Berkeley and Los Angeles: University of California Press, 1967), chapter 2. For the Arab-Islamic reaction to this piracy, see my unit on "Christian Piracy, Muslim Jihad" in the introduction to *Piracy, Slavery, and Redemption: Barbary Captivity Narratives from Early Modern England*, ed. Daniel Vitkus (New York: Columbia University Press, 2001).

58. Al-Tamjarouti, *Al-Nafha al-Miskiyya*, ed. Suleyman al-Sid al-Muhami (Tunis: n.p. 1988), 44. I have only found a copy of this edition in the private library of Dr. Abdeljelil Temimi.

59. Al-Safadi, *Tarikh Lubnan*, 208.

60. Abu Muhammed al-Jilani al-Ishaqi *Amir Maghribi fi Tarabulus 1143 H.*, ed. Abd al-Hadi Tazi (Rabat: Jamiat Muhammad al-Khamis, 1976), 119.

61. N. A., *Histoire Nouvelle du Massacre des Turcs faict en la ville de Marseille en Provence* (Lyon: n.p. 1621). See also *Muqaddimat wa watha'iq fi tarikh al-Maghrib al-arabi al-hadith*, ed. Dalinda al-Arqash, Jamal bin Tahir, and Abd al-Hamid al-Arqash (Manuba: Kulliyat al-Adab, 1995), 295.

62. Henry Koehler, *L'Eglise chretienne du Maroc et la Mission Franciscaine, 1221–1790* (Paris: Bibliothèque missionaire fransiscaine, 1934), 94.

63. SP 71/23/305-306. For an account of the Libyans, see El Mokhtar Bey, *De la Dynastie Husseinite: Le Fondateur Hussein Ben Ali, 1705–1735/40* (Tunis: Serviced, 1993), 557–82.

64. I have used the French translation of Diego de Torres, *Histoire des Cherifs, et des Royavmes de Maroc, de Fez, de Tarvdant, et autres provinces* (Paris: L. Billaine, 1667), passim; see also Richard Hakluyt, *Navigations, Voyages, Traffiques and Discoveries of the English Nation* (Glasgow: James MacLehose and Sons, 1904), 6:43; and André Raymond, *The Great Arab Cities in the Sixteenth to Eighteenth Centuries: An Introduction* (New York: New York University Press, 1984), 44–46, 58. While the arabized term *funduk* derives from the Spanish, as Mohammad bin Abd al-Wahab al-Ghassani shows, there is, paradoxically, no theory of the funduk as a res-

idence for the religious or national other in the history of the European city of the Renaissance. See also Pierre Grandchamp, "Le Fondouk des Francais," in *Etudes D'Histoire Tunisienne, XVIIe–XXe Siècles* (Paris: Presses Universitaires de France, 1966), 39–49, esp. 45, for the design of the funduk. For the Ottoman Empire, see Robert Mantran, "Foreign Merchants and the Minorities in Istanbul during the Sixteenth and Seventeenth Centuries," in *Christians and Jews in the Ottoman Empire*, ed. Benjamin Braude and Bernard Lewis (New York: Holmes and Meier, 1982), 1:127–40; and Suraiya Faroqhi, "The Venetian Presence in the Ottoman Empire," *Journal of European Economic History* (Rome) 15 (1986): 345–85.

65. For a cemetery other than the one in St. George's, see Pierre Soumille, "Le cimetiere Europeen de Bab el Kahdra," *Les Cahiers de Tunisie* 19 (1971): 130–32, esp. 129–36.

66. Henry Boyde, *Several Voyages to Barbary* (London: Olive Payne, 1736), 70–72. See also the map of Meknes, which shows the Christian quarter, the Franciscan hospital, and the Christian cemetery in Magali Morsy, *La Relation de Thomas Pellow* (Paris: Editions Recherche sur les Civilisations, 1983), 75; L. A. Berbrugger, "Charte des hopiteaux chrétiens d'Alger," *Revue Africaine* 8 (1864): 133–44.

67. For Catholic missionaries in Iraq in this period, see Sir Hermann Gollancz, *Chronicle of Events between the Years 1623 and 1733 Relating to the Settlement of the Order of Carmelites in Mesopotamia* (London: Oxford University Press, 1927).

68. Castries, *Les Sources inédites . . . Dynastie Filalienne*, 1:571–72.

69. Koehler, *L'Eglise chretienne*, 123.

70. Muhammad bin Muhammad Wazir al-Sarraj al-Andalusi, *Al-Hulal al- Sundusiyah*, ed. Muhammad al-Habib al-Hilah (Beirut: Dar al-Gharb al-Islami,1985), 3:596.

71. John Weale, *The Journal of John Weale, 1654–56*, ed. J. R. Powell (London: The Naval Miscellany, 1952), 157. See the chapter on "Debasement" in David Spurr, *The Rhetoric of Empire* (Durham, N.C.: Duke University Press, 1993).

72. Paul of Aleppo, *The Travels*, 1:3.

73. See Aldo Scaglione, "The Mediterranean's Three Spiritual Shores: Images of the Self between Christianity and Islam in the Later Middle Ages," in *The Craft of Fiction: Essays in Medieval Poetics*, ed. Leigh A. Araathoon (Rochester, Mich.: Solaris Press, 1984), 453–73.

74. Ahmad bin al-Mahdi al-Ghazzal, *Natijat al-ijtihad fi al-muhadanah wa-al-Jihad*, ed. Ismail al-Arabi (Beirut: Dar al-Gharb al-Islami, 1980), 45.

75. Chloe Chard, *Pleasure and Guilt on the Grand Tour* (Manchester: Manchester University Press, 1999), 9.

76. Stephen Greenblatt, *Marvelous Possessions: The Wonders of the New World* (Chicago: University of Chicago Press, 1991); Gayatri Chakravorty Spivak, "Can the Subaltern Speak?" in *Marxism and the Interpretation of Culture* (Urbana: University of Illinois Press, 1988): 271–313; Edward Said, *Orientalism* (New York: Vintage, 1994).

77. Mary Louise Pratt, *Imperial Eyes: Travel Writing and Transculturation* (London: Routledge, 1992), 2.

78. See the introduction to Pratt, *Imperial Eyes*.

79. Fiennes, *Une Mission*, p. 37.

80. Mohammad Menouni and Mohammad Benaboud, "Rihlat B. Othman al-Miknasi ila al-Quds al-Sharif wa manatiq min Filastin," *al-Manahil* 39 (1990): 43; and Menouni and Benaboud, "A Moroccan Account of Constantinople," in *Les provinces arabes à l'époque ottomane*, ed. Abdeljelil Temimi (Zaghouan: Centre d'etudes et de recherches Ottomans, 1987), 56.

81. See my discussion of this theme in "The Question of Occidentalism in Early Modern Morocco," in *Postcolonial Moves*, ed. Patricia Clare Ingham and Michelle R. Warren (New York: Palgrave, 2002).

82. Kenneth Parker, ed., *Early Modern Tales of Orient* (London: Routledge, 1999). See also Gerald MacLean, "Ottomanism before Orientalism? Bishop King praises Henry Blount, Passenger in the Levant," in *Travel Knowledges*, ed. Jyotsna Singh and Ivo Kamps (New York: St. Martins Press, 2000), 75–97. For an excellent study of the difference between French and English responses to the East, see Lisa Lowe, *Critical Terrains: French and British Orientalisms* (Ithaca, N.Y.: Cornell University Press, 1991).

83. Abd al-Majid al-Qaddouri, "Suwar 'an Oroba min khilal thalath rahalat maghribiyya," *Majalat Kuliyyat al-Adab wal-'Uloom al-Insaniyya* 15 (1989–90): 49.

84. Paul of Aleppo, *The Travels*, 2:396.

85. Fiennes, *Une Mission*, 22.

86. Contrast, however, the indebtedness of Spanish and Portuguese to Arabic in earlier times, in *Glossaire des mots Espagnols et Portugais dérivés de l'Arabe*, 2nd ed., ed. R. Dozy and W. H. Engelmann (Beirut: Librarie du Liban, 1974). See Henri Pérès, *L'Espagne vue par les voyageurs Musulmans de 1610 á 1930* (Paris: Librarie d'Amerique et d'Orient, 1937), 16, for a list of al-Ghassani's "arabized" words.

87. For the superiority of Europe, see the study by Said Binsaid al-Alawi, *Uruba fi miraat al-rihla* (Rabat: Jamiat Muhammad al-Khamis, 1995). I am grateful to Dr. Khalid Bekkaoui for drawing my attention to this study and for providing me with a copy.

88. Fiennes, *Une Mission*, 35–36.

89. Mohammad bin Uthman al-Miknasi, *Siqiliyya fi mudhakarat al-safir bin Uth-man*, ed. Abd al-Hadi al-Tazi (n.p.: n.p., n.d.), 31, 27.

90. Muhammad al-Saffar, *Sudfat al-liqa' ma'a al-jadid: Rihlat al-Saffar ila Faransa (1845–46)*, ed. and trans. Susan Gilson Miller and Khalid bin Saghir (Rabat: Jamiat Muhammad al-Khamis, 1995), 227.

91. William Biddulph, preface to *The Travels of certaine Englishmen into Africa* (London: Th. Haueland, 1609), sig A2.

92. John Harrison, *The Tragicall Life and Death of Mvley Abdala Melek* (Delph: n.p. 1633), a2r.

93. For the issue of self-censorship, see Andrew Hadfield, *Literature, Travel, and Colonial Writing in the English Renaissance, 1545–1625* (Oxford: Clarendon Press, 1998), 4–5.

94. Public Record Office, London, ADM 77/2 no. 10, n.p.

95. Mohammad bin Uthman al-Miknassi, *Al-Badr al-Safir*, MS, al-Khazanah al-Ammah, Rabat, ff. 101-102. I am most grateful to Mr. H. S. for providing me with a microfilm copy of this journey.

The Texts

A NOTE ON TRANSLATION AND SELECTION

THE TRANSLATIONS in the following chapters aim to be as faithful to the original texts as possible. While I have avoided being literal, I have attempted to retain many of the quirks and idiosyncrasies of each author's style. All four of the authors wrote in a mix of classical and colloquial Arabic, using many terms that derived from their own dialects and geographic backgrounds. I have transliterated some of these terms where I felt that they conveyed a uniquely Arabic sense or image—or where they showed the lack of an Arabic equivalent for a European or American novelty. The writers frequently added synonyms and repetitions for emphasis: I have retained these repetitions.

The manuscripts that I was able to consult use neither paragraphs nor reliable punctuation. I have paragraphed the text in the way I thought most appropriate.

With the exception of Ilyas Hanna al-Mawsuli, the writers used the Hijri calendar. I have thus provided the equivalent Christian date.

1

FRANCE AND HOLLAND

Selections from *Kitab Nasir al-Din ala al-Qawm al-Kafirin* (*The Book of the Protector of Religion against the Unbelievers*)

Ahmad bin Qasim [al-Hajari]
1611–1613

A DETAILED BIOGRAPHY of Ahmad bin Qasim appears in the "general intro-duction" to the Arabic text by P. S. Van Koningsveld, A. Al-Samarrai, and G. A. Wiegers. I have relied on that introduction for the information herein, along with some other studies.[1]

What is known about Qasim derives chiefly from an autobiographical account describing his early life in Spain, his escape to Morocco, his jour-ney to France and Holland on a mission from Mulay Zaidan (reg. 1603–27), and possibly a visit to Rome (since he refers at one point to the Magians [*majus*] he had met there). After his return to Morocco, he trav-eled to Tunis and to Egypt and then returned to Tunis.

Qasim wrote a lengthy account of his journey, to which he gave the ti-tle *Rihlat al-Shihab ila liqa' al-ahbab* (*The Journey of the Meteor* [his nickname] *to Meet the Loved Ones*), an account that is now lost. However, during his visit to Egypt, and having told stories about his journey to so many people, he was asked to write a summary, specifically describing his encounter with the Christians. He started writing it in Egypt, and showed it (for approval) to a Maliki jurist who advised him and praised the work. Upon his return to Tunis, he continued adding to it until he finished it on 21 Rabi' al-Thani, 1047 [September 12, 1637]. He showed the text to the mufti of the Jami' al-Turk (the Turks' Mosque), Ahmad al-Hanafi, who also approved of it. Four years later, he added an appendix. The title that he gave to the abridged version is *Kitab Nasir al-Din ala al-Qawm al-Kafirirn*.

At the outset of *Kitab*, Qasim mentioned that the purpose of his writing was to present an account of his intellectual and theological encounters with the Christians of Europe. He was therefore more interested in people and their beliefs than in cities, landscapes, and histories. Actually, in his *Rihla*, he had shown interest in general information and data: he had described, as he mentioned, Andalucia and the Canary Islands, surveying the geography and demography of Al-Andalus before and after the Islamic conquest, and describing the plight of his coreligionists under Spanish rule. In the *Kitab*, he turned to summarize (written evidently from memory) his meetings with Europeans and his disputations with Christians and Jews in France and Holland. Very significant in this context of disputation and dialogue with religious counterparts is Qasim's deep knowledge of the Old and New Testaments, which he had read in both Arabic and Spanish. His disputations with the Christians are based on what he sees as his corrective reading for them of the Bible, for he refutes them not on the basis of the Qur'an, as one might expect, but of the Bible, which, he argues, they have either misunderstood, ignored, or falsified.[2] Having become familiar with Protestants in Holland, and therefore with the Protestant critique of Catholicism, Qasim used the "Protestant" method in refuting his opponents. It was a method that also helped him in his disputations with the Jews when again he showed his detailed knowledge of the Hebrew sources.

During his travels, Qasim often found himself confronted and rebuffed by Christians: the *nasara* were not all friendly or hospitable, and some bluntly told him that he was not welcome among them. Still, despite the sometimes hostile and tense environment, Qasim built warm relationships with them and returned to North Africa with memories of highly stimulating discussions—and of deep friendships.

Born circa 1569–70, in the region of al-Hajar al-Ahmar in Andalucia, Qasim later lived in Seville and Granada. He was lucky enough to grow up with a good command of Arabic at a time when any familiarity with that language was an offense that could lead to burning at the stake. Qasim mastered Spanish, too, and as a New Christian, practiced the full range of Christian ritual while secretly retaining his Islamic faith. His was a time of segregation, when Moriscos (Qasim never used that term but used instead *al-Andalus*/Andalusians) were viewed as outsiders and untrustworthy: when one of Qasim's cousins married an Old Christian, the relatives of the Christian bride were so angry that they threatened to kill both bride and bridegroom, and never visited them at all after their church wedding.

Qasim opened his *Kitab* in 1595. He was in Granada when the Lead Books were discovered—a series of plates on which Arabic writings were inscribed, purporting to be from the time of Jesus, and prophesying the advent of Muhammad. Spanish ecclesiastical authorities were fascinated by this finding (not until a few years later would the books be denounced as a forgery), and employed Qasim to translate them. Qasim described his fears about being discovered with an excellent knowledge of Arabic: he knew that he was too young to claim that he had studied Arabic in the times when the language was not yet proscribed. Although Qasim was re-munerated handsomely for his labors, he felt that he could no longer stay in his country and should flee to "God and the land of Islam."

The escape was dangerous and Qasim described it in detail—how he and a friend sailed to the Spanish presidio of Breijah, and from there made their way to Azammur. As Portuguese Inquisition records show, many of the captives and residents in Iberia tried to escape to Morocco. Qasim was so happy at his success that he described his escape as a passageway through the terrors of Judgment Day, and his arrival among the Muslims as his entry into paradise. Others described their escape from Christian Iberia to the House of Islam as a *hijra*, the same term that had been used to describe the departure of the prophet Muhammad from pagan-dominated Mecca to Yathrib in A.D. 622.

Qasim's account revealed both the details of escape as well as the au-thor's ideological and theological goals. On the one hand, and not unlike European accounts of escape from among the Muslims, the escapee-turned-writer showed himself to be smart, devious and courageous, while his Christian opponents were gullible but vicious. He also showed how pious he was and how he never forgot his religious duties even in the most dangerous situations. And most important, he showed how un-happy he had been in Spain, and how he had been willing to go to any length to return to the Muslim community. In this respect, the escape nar-rative becomes an indictment of Spanish society, with its bigotry and hos-tility toward the Moriscos: Qasim had been born and bred in Spain, but he was still made to feel so much of an outsider that he was willing to risk his life in order to escape to those who were not his compatriots but his coreligionists. The speech by Don Fernando de Valor, El Zaguer, in Diego

Hurtado de Mendoza's *The War of Granada*, describing the plight of the Moriscos and the cruelty of the Spaniards lends support to Qasim's own description of desperateness and fear.[3]

Qasim went to Marrakesh, "a big city, with a large variety of fruit," where he met the legendary Mulay Ahmad al-Mansur on July 4, 1599. He soon got married and had two sons and two daughters. After the death of al-Mansur in 1603, a civil war broke out until Mulay Zaidan succeeded his father to the throne. Impressed with Qasim's excellent command of Arabic and Spanish, Zaidan appointed the émigré/exile as his official translator.

In 1609, Philip III ordered the expulsion of the Moriscos/Andalusians, many of whom were robbed by the sea captains of the Christian ships on which they sailed to North Africa. It was thus decided in Marrakesh that a delegation of those who had been robbed, led by Qasim, would go to France and the Netherlands, to seek restitution. Qasim sailed from Safi to Le Havre, and then continued to Rouen, arriving in Paris sometime in April or May of 1612. He then continued to Bordeaux, St. Jean De Luz, and then back to Paris—at which point this chapter selection below begins.

NOTE: I have relied in my translation on the excellent edition and notes of the Arabic text by P. S. Van Koningsveld, A. Al-Samarrai, and G. A. Weigers (Madrid: Al-Majlis al-Ala lil-Abhath al-Ilmiyah, 1997).

ON OUR RETURN TO THE CITY OF PARIS AND WHAT TRANSPIRED THERE

When I realized that the letters of the sultan [Mulay Zaidan] had been ineffective, and that most of the possessions from one of our ships had been safely unloaded [but had not been returned to us], we decided to go back to Paris and ask the sultan [Louis XIII] to give us back our possessions. The Andalusian judge joined us to Paris.

One day before sunset, I walked to the judge's house to attend to some formalities. The judge said, "Would you like to have dinner with us?"

"I am not permitted to eat some of your foods," I replied.

"We will give you only what you are permitted. We have a visitor from among the nobility of the kingdom. We would like to have you."

It was the evening of the Prophet's birth day—God's prayer and peace be upon him—of the year 1021 [May 13, 1612]. I soon realized that the judge was eager to discuss religious matters before his guest, for the notables among the *ifranj* [French] enjoy discussing recondite matters.[4] So I entered and was given a chair like theirs, with the table between us. The judge's mother-in-law was sitting too, who was in possession of a city called Ultiri [?]. Her son was a judge, and so too her brother [both of whom were at the table] along with the important dignitary. They turned to the guest and said, "This is a Turkish man," for the *ifranj* do not describe a Muslim except as a Turk. They told him the reason that had forced me to come to their country, and other details about me. Meanwhile, the mother-in-law was serving food for me, and for her brother and her son-in-law. The judge began the discussion, I mean the Andalusian [Spanish] judge. He said,

"Do you have a prescribed fast in your religion?

"We have a lunar month each year," I said to him.

"How is your fast?" he said to me.

"We neither eat nor drink from sunrise to sunset," I said to him.

"We too have a prescribed fast every year, longer than yours. It is for forty-nine consecutive days."

"How do you fast?" I said to him, although I knew [the answer].

"We eat moderately at noon for an hour, then refrain from eating until night when, at its beginning, we eat a little, less than at noon," he said.

"What is the purpose and goal of your fast? For in our religion, the purpose of fasting is to deflect the soul from desires and reduce their strengths," I said.

"The same for us," he said to me.

"Rather, you strengthen [your desires] by your fast," I said to him.

"How?" he said to me.

"Hippocrates, Galen, and Avicenna have said, and all physicians concur with them, that if a man wants to preserve his health, he ought to eat at midday more than he eats in the evening. By fasting the way you do, you do not weaken the body but increase its strength; for whoever preserves his health increases his strength."

The judge then started talking in *franji* [French] because he knew, as I mentioned earlier, the Andalusian *ajami* [Spanish] language. They were discussing what to say to me. Then he said, "Know that in the days of the fast, we do not eat [red] meat. On other days, we eat chicken meat, which, no doubt, gives strength, especially capon, which supplies strength."

"Yes," I said, "chicken meat is good and gives strength. And a little can suffice a man. If there is no [red] meat, but there is plenty of food just like what I see here before us, one should eat of every kind in order to get the nutrition that is equal to meat. One should eat as much as one can."

We were in their fast days. So they started talking to each other, hoping to find something to say. But they could not find anything to support their argument. So the judge changed the subject. He said, "What was the reason that your prophet prohibited wine?"

"God almighty prohibited it because the greatest gift He gave to the descendants of Adam is reason," I said to him. "Wine overcomes reason, which is the worst thing that can happen to man."

"Even among us," he said, "it is prohibited that man drink to inebriation."

"It seems to me that it was prohibited in the Gospel," I said, "but you did not notice the reference."

"Where is the reference?" they said.

"In the invocation that our Sayyid Issa [*Sayyidna Issa*], peace be upon him, told you to use, and which begins, "Our father in heaven," until you say, and "Do not let us fall into the temptation" of the soul. Others translate this, "Do not lead us into temptation," and they are the more numerous. The first is to me the accurate one."

"We have this [invocation]," they said.

"Is it permissible to hold temptation in your hand and then pray that God not let you fall by it? For if you add a little wine to what is customary, reason will be overcome, and if reason is overcome, you will fall into temptation, despite asking God not to let you fall."

"We drink moderately so that our reason won't be overcome," he said.

"I believe," I said to them, "that judges, scholars and noblemen like you want to be just and to avoid lying and committing falsehood. Can you swear by your religion that you never overdrink and [thus have never] lost control of your reason?"

They laughed and started talking among each other, and by their laughter, they admitted what they saw in themselves that they have frequently fallen into temptation because of excessive drinking. The mother-in-law took her glass and put a drop of wine in it and poured a lot of water over it, and then said to her son-in-law,

"Ask him: what strength does wine have with so much water?"

"In the case of this glass," I said, "it is evident that it has very little wine. But on many occasions, it is mixed with very little water."

She laughed as if admitting [that I was right]. I said to them, "I read one of your *ajami* books. It said that in a big city—I think in Italy, in the lands of the Christians—people appoint rulers for one whole year. And once the year is over, they appoint others in their positions for another year. They have a rule that they implement: Whoever is to arbitrate among the people will not drink any wine for the whole year. It is clear and obvious that they are forbidden from drinking wine, be it little or much, because of all the harm it can bring to drinkers and to the people whom they govern."

"That is correct," they said, "but drinking [wine] is permitted if one does not overdo it."

The woman then said to her brother-in-law, "Ask him: why did your prophet permit you to marry four women but forbid you to drink wine?" Her words showed that she believed wine to increase sexual potency.

"Wine brings disease and lethargy to its drinker," I said to her, "while water brings health." I then said to them, "I read in the Gospel that an angel from God came to the prophet Zacharias, peace be upon him, and said to him, 'God has accepted your prayer, and your wife, Elizabeth, will have a son with you who will be named John [*Yuhanna*]. And you will have great joy and jubilation. People will rejoice in his birth and he will be great before the Lord, neither drinking wine nor any other intoxicant.' Is this not in your Gospel?"

"Yes," they said," it is so."[5]

I said, "What the angel of God said about the child not drinking wine or any intoxicant—is that to be viewed as a defect or a sign of perfection?"

"It is perfection in him," they said.

"And it is also perfection in our religion," I said to them, "that we do not drink wine or any intoxicants."

So, they started conferring among themselves, and said to me, "We have met many of your coreligionists and have spoken with them, but we have never met anyone who has debated with us the way you have, giving us the kind of answers we heard and saw from you."

So I said, "Know that I am the translator for the Sultan of Marrakesh. Whoever fills that position needs to be well read in both Islamic and Christian sources in order that he be able to respond to and to translate in the presence of the sultan. Had I been in the presence of the learned men of our religion, I would not have felt competent to discuss such matters."

I started to leave to the residence where I was staying. They said, "Don't leave yet. We will send our servants with you [when you leave]. Stay with us and let us continue our discussion."

The woman said, "Why did your prophet permit you to marry four wives, while God, blessed and exalted, only gave to Adam, peace be upon him, one wife only?"

When the judges who were there saw that this question was reasonable, they repeated it adding some more arguments against me. I said to them, "Our mother Eve was more blessed [fertile] than any four women in our time. For she bore many many children, both male and female. Meanwhile, women in our time are either unable to have children because of illness, or are barren and can have no children at all. There are so many ills in women that were not in our mother Eve."

They said, "Our Sayyid Issa, peace be upon him, commanded that a man marry only one wife. But you take four."

I said, "The early prophets, peace be upon them, such as our Sayyid Abraham, and our Sayyid Jacob and others—how do you view them?"

"Very highly, for they are acceptable to God," they said.

I said, "Our religion tells us that they had many wives and concubines. Our Sayyid Solomon, peace be upon him, had seven hunderd wives and three hundred slave women, as the Torah states."[6]

"In that time," they said, "[plurality of wives] was permissible in order to increase the population. But now the world is well populated."

"I read in the Torah," I said, "in the books of history,[7] that some of the early sultans mobilized an army of 800,000 men. There is not a single sultan in the world today who can mobilize such an army except *the* Sultan, the [Ottoman] Grand Signior. This shows that the world used to be well-populated [but is not anymore]."[8]

Then the judge said to me, "And pork. Why are you prohibited from it?"

"Because it is unclean and eats only unclean things," I said. "Even in the gospel it is prohibited."

"No," they said, "it is not prohibited. Where in the gospel do you find such prohibition?"

"I read in the Gospel that there were two crazed men near the tombs, so wicked that no one could go near them. [As Jesus approached them,] they called out: 'What do you want with us, Jesus, son of God? Did you come here to torment us?' At a distance from them, there was a herd of grazing pigs. So the demons [inside the crazed men] called out to him, saying, 'If you take us out from here, send us into that herd of pigs.' So he said, 'Go.' When they went out, they entered into the pigs whereupon the herd jumped off the cliff into the sea and drowned in the water. The shepherds fled."[9] End.[10] "There were two thousand of these pigs," I continued. "The prophets, peace be upon them, would they make people lose their property?"

"No," they said.

"There were around two thousand pigs worth a lot of money. But our Sayyid Issa, peace be upon him, permitted that they should perish and be destroyed. Their owners lost the value of the pigs; had they been [unclean] animals that were not forbidden, our Sayyid Issa, peace be upon him, would not have allowed the crazed spirits to enter into them, and lead them to destruction and annihilation."

The judges considered my words, and reflected on some answers. "Their number was not as many as you mentioned."

"That is what I read," I said.

So the Gospel was brought and they found the number I had mentioned. Actually, this episode was mentioned twice in the Gospel: in chapter fifteen of Mark. It was he who said that they were around two thousand.[11] So they continued in their discussion but could not find anything with which to refute me. It was already midnight, so I left to my residence, and they sent their servants with me. I saw that they had enjoyed my company, and they thanked me. They had not heard from me anything other than what I have related, all of which contradicts their religion.

On another morning, I walked over to the judge. He gave me the forms without charging me any fee. Then the woman with whom I had had the discussion saw me, and making sure that nobody saw her, she gave me a not insignificant amount of gold—from the benevolence of God and for the cause of His religion, and a blessing on the day of the birth of the Prophet [Muhammad], God's prayer and peace upon him.

Hubert mentioned that there is in a city by the name of Saint Denis, six miles from Paris, a large building for monks, where there are treasures and kings' crowns, and other possessions of previous sultans and bishops.[12] Inside, there was a big glass chalice with Arabic inscriptions, the letters carved in the middle. It used to belong to our Sayyid Solomon, son of the prophet of God, David, peace be upon both of them. So I said, "I would like to see it."

We walked until we reached the building. There were visitors there who had come from other countries to see the treasures. We went up to an upper floor where a man came and opened the room of the treasures. He took a gold crown and spoke about it, saying, "This is the crown of sultan so and so." Then he took another crown, and mentioned to whom it had belonged. He continued doing so, taking one crown after another, all of which were decorated with precious stones, diamonds and rare sapphires. Then he took a chalice as long as the arm of a man, with its handle in the middle, and removed a garland on which was inscribed some Arabic writing, similar to Kufic script. I held it in my hand and I read in the inscription two of the names of God on it, "Guide" and "All-sufficing." Had he left it with me, I would have read the whole script. Then he closed the treasure [room]. I marveled at having held in my hand a chalice of our Sayyid Solomon, peace be upon him, and the garland that we had mentioned above which was from the time of Cecilio,[13] scribe to the virtuous Mary, peace be upon her, and some of the books of lead paper from that time, too.

Consider how ancient the Arabic language is, and how sacred it is so that the prophet of God, Solomon, peace be upon him, chose none other than the Arabic letters [to inscribe] the names of God into the chalice at the place where he held it. For those who know Arabic, it is better to speak it than any other language. The prophet [Muhammad], God's prayer and peace upon him, said that he loved it.

Toward the end of my stay in Paris, I was given the sultan's letter with the large seal of the court. It was addressed to all governors in all the courts in the lands of the *ifranj*. It stipulated that whatever is found of what had been looted from the Andalusians should be returned to me. The keeper of the sultan's seal said that in Olonne there were twenty-one sea commanders, each of whom had robbed the Andalusians who had rented their ships. Among them was one who had robbed a ship over which I had [a legal] proxy. So we agreed to leave Paris with him.

ON OUR ARRIVAL IN OLONNE AND THEN IN THE CITY OF BORDEAUX

Having taken the advice that the keeper of the seal had given me, we traveled to his city. We reached his house, which stood on a river outside the city. It was a large building, made of carved stone, with a few cannons. A spacious orchard, some forests, and a large piece of arable land were near it, and a large piece of land for agriculture—all the property of the aforementioned sea commander.

His wife approached to welcome us along with her male and female servants. There was in that house a girl, a relative of theirs, with a large inheritance left to her by her parents.[14] She was twenty-four years old, and very

very beautiful. Many men of the nobility of the land had asked her hand in marriage, but she had not accepted any of them.

They offered food to me and to my companions, but we did not eat of it, saying, "This [food] is not permitted in our religion." Then they brought us what we told them to bring.

The girl came in and asked me to describe to her the beauty standards of women in my country. So I told her what I could. She said, "You are right." For she was somewhat white with a little reddishness, her hair black, and so too her eyebrows and lids, with very black eyes. Among the French, such a woman is not considered beautiful and they say that she is black.

I used to tell my companions stories about what happened to virtuous men who were stationed at the frontiers; I wanted to strengthen their spirits and minds against forbidden women and the temptations of Satan. For Satan used these unveiled *hareem* to incite us to sin, but we were patient [in resistance].[15]

The girl used to preen herself and ask me whether there were women in our country who dressed in silk like she did. Then she said, "I will teach you *ifranji*." And I became her pupil, and she began honoring my companions. Love grew between us so much that I was distraught by it and I said, "Before meeting her, I was at odds with the Christians over money, and engaged in the holy fight for religion. But now I am at odds with myself and Satan." For the soul wants to fulfill a desire, and Satan helps her, but the spirit forbids what is prohibited, and reason adjudicates between them. Some people understand the spirit to be the heart. The soul turns to Satan for help because he is of its nature, the nature of fire, which is heat and dryness. They do not tempt man to do anything other than the deeds of the inhabitants of fire [hell] whereupon the spirit turns to God for help.

After the devil defiantly refused to bow before our Sayyid Adam, peace be upon him, he said, "He [God] created me of fire."[16] Since Satan and the soul are of the nature of fire, they tempt man to follow them. Satan learned that the only power he had over man was to tempt him: man can sometimes resist temptation easily, but at other times man needs to invoke God the exalted. I therefore started taking walks in the garden and invoking God to strengthen me.

So Satan went to the most senior of my companions, and whispered to him to go and talk to me about the girl. I had not told them how distraught I was in order not to expose my weakness to them. For I used to urge them to remain steadfast against women who were forbidden them. So my companion secretively came to advise me, saying, "Sir, I am concerned about the failure I have seen in you."

"Tell me what you have seen," I said to him, "maybe you will help me."

He said, "This girl does not disguise her feelings; rather, she is treating us so well because of her love for you. That is quite obvious. You know the custom in this country that a man stretches forth his hand and fondles the girls. No one here views such action as shameful. She repeatedly stands near you hoping for you to touch her, but you do not respond to her nor make her happy."

I said to myself, "This [temptation] is stronger than Satan's." And I said to him, "My dear friend, we are prohibited in our religion to do anything like that. The text reads: "Do not touch what is not permitted you in money or body." And this woman's body is not permitted me [is not *halal*]."

He said, "I am only asking you to fondle her."

I said, "The author of the *Burda* said: 'Do not think to conquer desire by doing what is not permitted; food increases the desire for gluttony.'"

"What does that mean?" he said.

"What meaning can be gleaned, as far as I have learned [is the following]: do not think that if you give the soul a little of what it desires of the prohibited things it will be satisfied. Rather, its desire will increase, and it will grow strong and overpower you and lead you to more prohibited actions than you had intended. For example, when a man fasts, he can endure his fast until he begins eating, and then his desire takes over, driving him to eat until satiety. It is better and more virtuous to defy and oppose the soul and Satan."

But nothing of what I said could dissuade my friend. Once, as I was standing and talking to the girl, he came from behind me and pushed me at her. When she left, I quarreled with him about his stupid action. Then she [returned and] asked me whether I had a wife in my country.

I said to her, "I do."

She said, "And do you marry more than one wife?"

"It is permissible in our religion," I said to her.

Then she said, "Do you have children?"

"I do," I said. And I said to myself: when she hears this, her love [*mahabba*] will diminish. But it did not at all.

One day, I met her, after she had dressed herself up. She was looking at me but I had no idea what she thought. I walked to the garden. In that country, gardens are not surrounded by walls; rather, the people dig deep trenches around a garden to prevent entry except through the gate. I heard her calling me and as she stood on the other side, I went from the garden to the edge of the trench. There was a little footpath that led down the trench and to the garden. The trench was full of wild trees so that its bottom was only visible in a few places. We spoke with each other, and I realized the state she was in, which she could not hide.

Then some of my companions started talking in the garden and walking in the direction where I was standing. So she left. And God released me [from her] through His benevolence, kindness, protection, and gentle support. I beg God's forgiveness for what I said to, and how I looked at, her. God is merciful and forgiving. He forgives the small sins in order for us to avoid the bigger ones.

A girl from the nobility came from the city of Fontenay to visit an idol near the house where we were staying. After visiting it, she came to the wife of the sea commander and to the girl about whom we have spoken, and they invited her in. After food was served, they invited me and offered me a chair. So I sat down with the wife of the commander to my right, and the girls in front of me, including the one who had come to visit. She was more beautiful and elegant than the one in the house, and her clothes, along with two maids who served her, showed her to be of the nobility. Before inviting me, they had told her about me.

When she sat down, she looked disdainfully at me, and her face showed her hostility. Then she said:

"Are you a Turk?"

"A Muslim, praise be to God," I said to her.

"How come you do not know God?" she said.

"Muslims," I said to her, "know God better than you."

"Better than we?" she said.

"Yes," I said to her.

"What is your proof?" she said to me.

So I looked at her, and saw that she held a book under her arm, as is the custom among the daughters of wealthy *ifranj* merchants and nobility. Each girl carries her book, containing exultation, with five invocations, or *suras*,[17] which it is the religious duty of every adult to memorize. I said to her, "The proof of what you want is in the book you have. With it, I can prove what I said to you."

She took the book and laid it in my hands on the table. "Here is the book."

"Look at the ten divine commandments," I said to her.

So she searched in the book and said, "Here they are."

"Read the first of the ten about the religion of God," I said to her.

So she did and said, "The first commandment of the ten is: 'God almighty said, Do not carve statues, and do not worship them. Worship God alone.'"

After she had read it, I said to her, "Muslims don't carve statues and do not worship them; indeed, with God's help, they desist from making them. Even women who embroider decorations do not portray anything that has a spirit. Similarly, artists who draw and decorate the palaces of kings and mosques never depict anything with a spirit."

"We do not worship the idols themselves," she said, "but what the idols represent."

"I could answer you about representation and the represented," I said to her, "but let us move to another problem to which you have no answer."

"What is it?" she said.

"The divine commandment," I said to her, "in the text. [Did it not say]: Do not make statues and do not worship them?"

"Yes," she said.

"Do you or do you not make idols?" I said to her.

She had to give in to reason and truth. So she looked at the women and said in their language:

"He won. I cannot find anything with which we can answer him."

So I looked at her, and found that she was now happy and relaxed, as if a veil had been removed from her heart. She then started talking with me in a friendly way, the anger and hostility she had felt for Muslims now gone. She said to me, "In what year did your prophet appear? And do you count the years from his birth, as we do from the birth of Issa, peace be upon him?"

"In this year, the history of the people of our religion reaches 1021 after the Hijra [1612], which is the year in which our prophet, God's prayer and peace upon him, left Mecca to proclaim the religion of God the exalted."

"Is your year like ours in the number of its days?" she said.

"You have a solar year," I said to her, "which has 365 days and a quarter day. Our year is lunar and has around 354 days."

"Are your months like ours?" she said.

"Every Arabic month," I said to her, "is one day shorter than the solar month."

"And are your women veiled?" she said.

"Yes," I said to her.

"And how do girls fall in love, and who marries them?" she said.

"A man will not see the girl to whom he gets betrothed until she becomes his wife," I said to her. [I realized] that the purpose of her statement and query about courtship was this: the custom in the lands of the *ifranj* and the Flemish is that whenever a man decides to marry a girl, it is permissible for him to meet with her alone and talk so that they can fall in love [*mahabba*]. If he decides to get engaged to her, and she does too, then discussion of marriage takes place. But if he decides not to, he is not beholden to her for having been with her. A girl may have more than one man visiting her in the aforementioned manner. A Muslim should thank God for the religion of Islam and its purity and grace.

As for what we said to the girl about idols, it is said in the Torah that is in their hands now, I mean the Jews and the Christians, it is said in the second book entitled "Exodus" in the twentieth chapter [20:1–17]: Our Sayyid Moses, peace be upon him, said that God the exalted told him to descend from Mount Tur and to say on behalf of God the exalted to the people of Israel,

I am your God who brought you out of Egypt, from the land of slavery.

Do not take any god but me and do not make statues of things in the heavens or on earth or under the earth, and do not kneel before them because I, your God, am jealous.

Do not commit perjury.

Third, He said, honor your festivals.

Fourth: Obey your parents in order to live longer.

Fifth: Do not kill.

Sixth: Do not commit adultery.

Seventh: Do not steal.

Eighth: Do not lie, and do not bear false witness, and do not slander.

Ninth: Do not covet your friend's house, wife, or wealth.

The Christians took these commandments from the Torah and added a tenth, saying:

Tenth: Love God above everything else, and desire for others what you desire for yourself.[18]

These ten are divine commandments. The three religions are in agreement over them. In our dear Qur'an, they are dispersed throughout [the text]. The Christians, God destroy them [for their idolatry], do not abide by the first commandment, which is the foundation. The prophet, God's prayer and peace upon him, has forbidden images and said, "Image-makers are in hell." And he said, "Angels will not enter a house that has images in it." Thanks be to God who made the religion of Muhammad pure and untarnished by this heinous error.

And it is said in the Torah, in a chapter I cannot remember,[19] that there is no benefit to any man in a pagan idol of gold and silver; for its gold and silver will go to the fire [of hell].

And our Sayyid Issa, peace be upon him, said in the Gospel, "Warn your friend against a heinous deed when you are alone with him; but if he does not desist, warn him in the presence of two [people]; and if he still does not desist, then leave him as you would an idolater or a tithe collector." And the meaning of an idolater is one who worships idols and graven images.

And the prophet said, God's prayer and peace upon him, "An alcoholic is like an idol worshipper."

Sheikh Jalal al-Din al-Sayyuti mentioned in *al-Khasais al-Kubra* that when the prophet, God's prayer and peace upon him, entered noble Mecca in the year of the conquest [A.D. 630] there were 360 idols in the Ka'aba with feet of lead.[20] He would point to each of them with a rod in his hand, without touching it, and say, "Truth has come and Falsehood has been overturned. Falsehood was bound to be discomfited."[21] And the idol would fall on its face or its back.

I wrote in my account of the *Rihla* a unit on idols and stories about them. We will only mention the following:

The jurist Ali bin Mohammad al-Barji al-Andalusi, may God have mercy on his soul, told me in Marrakesh that near the city in which he was living in our time [in a Spanish presidio], there had been a Muslim captive, Ahmad, whose master was so and so—he mentioned his rank as marquis or count. That master owned many regions. It happened that in one of his villages the notables decided to buy an idol. After ordering it from another city, they sent Ahmad to fetch it. So they gave him a donkey. He went and put the idol on the donkey and started on the road. As he did not see any Christians [standing by], he said to the idol: "By God, we will not take you except by tying and dragging you." So he threw it to the ground, tied it to the donkey with a rope, got on [the donkey] and continued on his way.

As he approached the village, the ones who had sent him were waiting for the idol. They saw Ahmad on the donkey with the idol trailing behind him. They ran up and uncovered their heads in respect, while touching gently the idol and weeping for its condition. They seized Ahmad and started deliberating what to do with him. Should they kill him or beat him? They all concurred on taking him before his master and the governor of their village to have him killed. They all walked with him. But by the blessing of Ahmad's jihad with the idol, the master said to them, after they had complained to him about Ahmad, "You deserve the worst punishment for sending a Muslim to bring you an idol. He did what his religion required him to do." Ahmad was spared, and he rejoiced and mocked them as they felt ashamed and humiliated at the dragging of their god.

As for the meaning of what is said in the passage, "Do not make images of representations in the sky nor in the earth," the meaning is: do not make an image of anything that has a spirit, but God knows best. The Magians depict the seven planets each in the shape of a man or an animal. Christians still use those pictures in their books of astrology, depicting Saturn as an old man with a scythe in his hand as he gathers spirits, and Jupiter as a judge, and Mars in the shape of a man with a sword in his hand, and each of the seven with an appropriate picture. As for depictions of the horoscope, they include pictures of a ram for the lamb, a bull for the bull, as also pictures of the twins, the crab, the lion, the scorpion, the goat, and the fish. It is forbidden in Islam [to represent these] because they are pictures of things that have spirits in real life.[22]

As for pictures of stars or of earthly trees or of things that do not have a spirit, it is not forbidden to represent them.

Some monks told me, "You make representations of roses and trees."

I said, "The scriptures do not forbid pictures of inanimates and trees; the prohibition is against making a representation of the living."

Regarding the matter for which we came: having brought the Sultan's letter in order to seize the sea commanders who had robbed the Andalusians and were in Olonne, we did not accomplish anything. I think the keeper of the seal received some [bribe] money from them. I wanted to get away from him, and he asked that we leave him the Sultan's letter, but I refused to do so, and we left for the city of Bordeaux.

On Our Arrival in the City of Bordeaux and of the Debates I Had There

Know that it [Bordeaux] is one of the greatest of the French cities. It stands on the bank of a big river. There are eighty judges in it, two hundred agents, and numberless arbitrators and scribes. Its court governs many regions.

What happened to me in the house of the Andalusian judge with some priests is as follows.

Two priests came to attend to a matter, and they were told that I was a Muslim.

So they came to me and said, "Are you a Muslim?"

"Yes," I said to them.

"Do you believe," they said, "that there is food and drink in paradise to be enjoyed in the same manner as on earth?"

"Yes," I said to them, "actually better than what is on earth."

They laughed. So I said to them, "How can you disprove that?"

"Because food produces waste that is impure, and it is impossible that there are impurities [in paradise]," they said.

"Don't you have," I said to them, "in your books, that when God the exalted created our father Adam, peace be upon him, he allowed him to eat of all the fruit in paradise except of one tree? He said to him: 'Do not eat of it because if you do you will die?'"

"That is so," they said.

"Had Adam not eaten of that tree," I said to them," would he have still been there?"

"Yes, that is so," they said.

"He was thus eating of all the fruit and they were not producing waste [in him]," I said. "Had he stayed there, [his condition] would have remained the same. Only the tree of which he was prohibited to eat produced waste. And so if our father Adam, peace be upon him, and all his descendants of that happy place, returned to eat of the fruit there, nothing impure would come out of them."

"The paradise of our father Adam was on earth. The one to which people will go at the end of time is in heaven," they said.

"Our father Adam, peace be upon him, could not but have been in a heaven[ly paradise]. For nothing on earth can be called paradise because it is confined by the four elements that cause change, as there is between light and darkness. Paradise has no change and no darkness. This proves that our Sayyid Adam, peace be upon him, was in the paradise of heaven." The unbeliever[s] were confounded.[23]

Know that the Christians and the Jews believe what is in the first part of the Torah. It says, "God, exalted and almighty, created Adam, peace be upon him, in the paradise on earth. In that paradise, there were trees watered by a fountain, from which four rivers sprang: the Nile, the Euphrates, the Oxus and the Tigris."[24] These rivers are now well-known and each is in a different country from the other. Their sources and mouths are known. This proves that the text is as evidently wrong as the sun [is evident]. The prophetic *hadiths* report,[25] and God knows best, that the rivers originate in paradise, which means they carry the blessings that God infused in them. The [true] belief is that paradise is in heaven, not on earth, but rivers begin and end in earth. It is said in some of the books of Abd al-Wahab al-Sha'rani,[26] may God make him beneficial, that "our Sayyid Gabriel [the angel], peace be upon him, brought down the waters of paradise and placed them in various locations on earth from which the four rivers sprang. Each was different from the other, and paradise is in heaven." All the commentators on the *Epistle* [of al-Qayrawani] have said[27]: from paradise descended our father Adam, peace be upon him.

Sultan Mulay Zaidan [d. 1628], God rest his soul, ordered me to translate for him a thick *ajami* book that had been given the title of *Badran* by its author. It is named after a great mountain of that name, because geographers consider it the greatest of the known mountains in the world. We have not seen in all the geography books anything like it. The book was in the language of the *ifranj*, and the author was a Frenchman named The Captain [*al-qubtan*]. All the countries of the world are represented in that book, showing the length and breadth of each, and showing in which region each river is, and where it originates and begins. It also shows the cities on its banks, each with its own name, and all the seas, islands, and regions.

All geography books concur that the Nile Sea originates in the Moon Mountain, and is located eighteen degrees from the equator to the south, in the direction of Sudan [the country of the blacks]. The three [other] rivers are not in the African region, which is one quarter of the world. Only the Nile is in this region, but none of the other three. Each of the three is in a country far from the other. As for the Euphrates, it originates near the land of the Georgians and then merges with the River Tigris, which passes through Baghdad. The third [river] is in the lands of the Tatar. And the fourth is in the land of Armenia, according to one who claimed knowledge of the world.

After noticing the error in the Torah, the French captain said, "The information we have in the Torah about the rivers, that they all originate from one location, is clearly incorrect and false. [The Torah] states that these four rivers spring from one source; but the opposite is evident to whoever knows the regions of the world." End.

This proof is evident and apparent to whoever decides to inquire about the four rivers. Where they originate is contradicted by what is said about paradise where our father Adam was, peace be upon him. Whoever observes and verifies what had been unknown to him will find that whoever says the four rivers originate from one spring in paradise on earth is wrong. It is equally wrong to say that our father Adam, peace be upon him, was created on earth by God the exalted and almighty.

As for what the Christians and Jews say about paradise—that there is nothing in it of the blessings of the world in food and drink and others—they have said the truth for themselves because paradise is denied them since they are unbelievers. Paradise is only for the Muslims by the goodness of God and His power, and the intercession of His prophet and messenger, our Sayyid Muhammad, God's prayer and peace upon him.

I had other discussions like the one above in the city of Bordeaux with the judge named Fayrad. I had legal matters to clear with him and he used to give me advice always. He knew the Andalusian *ajami* language, and I owed him a large sum of money that I wanted to pay him back, but he did not accept anything from me, saying, "O, so and so, I am amazed at you being a follower of the religion of the Muslims."

"Why?" I said.

"We have it in our books," he said, "that the Muslims visit Mecca to see their prophet in the middle of an iron ring hanging in the air. The ring is in the air because it is the center of a domed [building] with a magnet stone. It is known that the magnet draws iron and, inside the dome, it draws from all sides equally, which is why the ring stays in the air with your prophet. Muslims believe that to be a miracle of their prophet."

I said to him, "Is it permissible in your religion for someone to lie and insult the religion of another in order to glorify his own religion and magnify it before his own coreligionists?"

"Not at all!" he said.

"The Christians who said that committed a heinous sin [by the standards of] your religion," I said.

"How is that?" he said.

I said, "The prophet, God's prayer and peace upon him, is not in Mecca and is not in an iron ring. He is buried in Medina, and between it and Mecca there are ten [travel] days. The Muslims visit the Ka'aba because it is a blessed house built by our Sayyid Abraham, peace be upon him."

"Did you visit it," he said, "and see the grave of your prophet under the ground?"

"No," I said to him, "but those who have gone there from among us uniformly say so. There is no doubt about this matter."

"There is another matter," he said. "You believe that the inhabitants of paradise eat and drink and enjoy there what they have on earth."

"Even our Sayyid Issa, peace be upon him," I said to him, "did not deny that, saying in the Gospel: "As for the juice of this tree—I mean the juice of the grapevine—I will not drink it again on earth until I drink it with you in the kingdom." Is this [not] in your Gospel?"[28]

"Yes," he said.

"And why do you deny it?" I said. "For the blessings of the world anticipate the blessings of paradise, except that in paradise, they will be perfect. In paradise, there are things which neither human eye has seen nor ear has heard nor heart has conceived. And our Sayyid Issa, peace be upon him, mentioned drinking in paradise and taught about it because he believed that there will be eating and drinking there."

The judge continued to reflect on what to say, but he did not find anything. And he was one of their top scholars.

This is the passage in the Gospel. Matthew said in the eighty-ninth section:[29] "As they were eating, Jesus took some bread, blessed and broke it, and gave it to his disciples, saying, 'Take and eat, this is my body.' And then he took a cup and blessed it, and he gave it to them, saying, 'All of you, drink of it because this is my blood, the new covenant that will be shed for the forgiveness of sins. And I say to you: I will not drink the juice of this vine until that day when I will drink it anew in the kingdom of my father.'" And Mark too said in the forty-sixth section,[30] "Truly I say to you, I will not drink the juice of this vine until that day when we shall drink it anew in the kingdom of God." End.

In the Gospel, they also have [the following]: It is said the Jews came to our Sayyid Issa, peace be upon him, to confront him, and asked him: Luke the evangelist said in the seventy-second section,[31] "The Jews said, 'A woman was married to seven brothers. One after another died. Then she died. On the day of resurrection, whose wife will she be, seeing that seven [men] had married her?' Our Sayyid Issa said to them: 'Mortals marry and get married, but those who die and are resurrected—they do not marry or get married, because they do not die, but become like the honored angels, and they become sons of God and children of the resurrection.'" End.

It is said that Satan, may God curse him, asked our Sayyid Idrees [Enoch], peace be upon him, this question: "Can God almighty put the whole world inside the shell of an egg?" He, peace on him, recognized Satan and repudiated his stubbornness. And so was the reply of our Sayyid Issa, peace be upon him, to the Jews. The Christian polytheists have adopted this answer and ignored the first passage.

Then the judge said to me, "Know that there is an aged sheikh, a judge who lived in your country for years." He then said to me: "I say we go to him," and he insisted on that.

So I said to him, "We will go, God willing."

A few days later, he said to me, "We must go to him."

So I went with him and met him in his house. He was about eighty years old.

After I was introduced to him, he welcomed me, showing his happiness, so I sat down with him. He said to me, "I was in your country for five years, in Constantinople. I asked about your prophet and they vilified him to me."

I said, "Whom did you ask? Muslims know everything about the prophet from the time of his birth—who the women were that suckled him, where he lived, where he traveled, what battles he fought, what sayings, commands, prohibitions and orders he pronounced, what miracles he performed, and who the women were whom he married, until his death. You, however, know nothing about our Sayyid Issa, peace be upon him, where he lived and where he traveled from the time he reached thirteen years of age until thirty-three, when you say he was crucified."

"Our religion," he said, "is the religion of truth because Jesus died to redeem our first sin, committed by our Sayyid Adam, peace be upon him, and the sin of all [humanity] because of the fruit that God the exalted had prohibited but of which Adam ate."

"We have a better salvation than yours from [the sin] we inherited from the fruit," I said. "You say that our Sayyid Issa, peace be upon him, saved everybody; we believe that each is saved by himself."

"How is your salvation?" he said.

"Our father Adam, peace be upon him," I said, "was in paradise but he did not excrete from his body any waste until he ate of the fruit from which he had been prohibited. Then he started excreting what he had never excreted before."

"So?" he said.

"The waste that is excreted by us is a result of what we inherited because of the tree. Know that our religion obligates each adult, male and female, to pray to God five times a day. And one of the requirements of prayer is purification by ablution. For none enters into God's presence except after ablution, which cleanses the body of what was inherited from the aforementioned fruit. It brought about uncleanness in the body, as a result of which man has to wash those unclean parts of the body. He washes his hands because our father Adam, peace be upon him, stretched out his hand to the fruit which God had prohibited; he washes his mouth because he ate of it, and his nose because he smelled the fruit, and his face because he turned toward it. He wipes his head because he walked under the tree, and his ears because he listened with them to what was said about the fruit, and which was contrary to what he had first heard. He washes his feet because he walked with them to the tree. He washes all these parts with clean water because there is nothing better in the world for purification. Only after ablution can man turn to God, having reattained the same state as Adam had before he ate of what had been forbidden him. This purification lasts until man excretes something of what he inherited and thus needs ablution.

This is a salvation better than yours, and you, a judge, can know truth by reason. He who wants to save himself will undertake this action [of ablution] and turn to prayer. He who neither prays nor ablutes will be lacking. Meanwhile, you say that our Sayyid Issa, peace be upon him, saves all humanity."

The judge was amazed and said, "I never heard anybody say anything like this."

We spoke about many other topics, but we wrote down only the above.

I had read about the meaning of ablution, as I had explained it, while I was in the land of the Andalus, before leaving, in a book called, the *Summary of Gabriel*. It stated that semen was found in our father Adam, peace be upon him, after he ate of the tree, and that it comes out from under every hair of the body. That is why all the body must be washed.

After a few days, I met with the nephew of the judge, the same who had told me to visit his uncle. When he saw me he said, "Be careful. My uncle is a distinguished judge. Leave him to his religion and don't convert him to Islam."

I said, "It was you who wanted me to visit him!"

He said: "He wants you to go and visit him again, but I now warn you [against doing that]." I do not remember now whether I did visit him again or not.

I had another conversation in the aforementioned city with a cleric. One day, he said to me, "What do you say about Issa, peace be upon him?"

I said, "He is a prophet, the messenger of God."

He said, "But you do not say that he is truly the son of God?"

"No, we do not," I said.

"Who was his father, then?" he said.

"Whoever was the mother of Eve was his father," I said.

He said, "Explain your words because I do not understand what you have said about our mother Eve."

I said to him, "Know that the creation of humanity is in four ways: the first is the creation by God, blessed and exalted, of our father Adam, peace be upon him, without parents: [the second is the creation] of our mother Eve without a mother; [the third is His creation] of all humankind from two parents; and [the fourth is His creation] of Issa, peace be upon him, from a mother without a father, as He had created our mother Eve without a mother. That is why I said, when you asked me who his father was, I answered, Whoever was the mother of Eve was his father."

I then added, "Do you believe that the power of God can do even more than that or not?"

"Yes," he replied.

He then turned to the Christians who were present and asked them to witness that he was a Christian who believed in all the teachings of their religion and all that was proclaimed from that building in Rome. "I tell you," he added, "the words that this Muslim has said and that we have heard are great words." He then said more in praise [of what I had said] until those Christians who were present said, "It is not acceptable [that you praise him]." But he continued with what he believed was the truth.

One evening, I stood at the door of an apothecary, for in that country, as indeed, in all the lands of Christians, all shops for buying and selling are not closed until after the last meal [of the day]. Some Christians were discussing with me religious matters pertaining to the miracles of our Sayyid Issa, peace be upon him.

I said to them, "A miracle is what defies nature, and is created by God the exalted by means of prophets and holy men."

Then one of the infidel scholars said, "The miracles that appeared at the hands of our Sayyid Issa were done by him."

As soon as those words were said, I saw one of our company leave us quickly. So I asked him later why he had left and where he had gone. He said, "When I heard the Christian say that the miracles which appeared at the hands of our Sayyid Issa, peace be upon him, were done by him without

God, I feared that the high building near which we were standing would collapse on us because of what he had said."

Peter, who wrote one quarter of the Gospel, said in his epistle in the twenty-second chapter: "O sons of Israel, Issa the Nazarene was a truthful witness among you from God with miracles and signs which God performed among you at his hands, as you well know." End. Consider this clear statement, which corroborates our religion and belief and which was said by the one who wrote one quarter of the Gospel—and which is contradictory to [what is upheld by] the Christians of this time.

I also went to the city of Toulouse, which is a big city in France, on the banks of the big river [the Garonne] which passes through it to Bordeaux. Three days [of travel] separate the two cities. I decided to sail by boat to Bordeaux. The night before I traveled, I saw in my sleep a horde of devils surrounding me from all sides. So I started reciting, "Say: He is the One God."[32] I would point at them and the devils would flee from me, but then return and so I would recite the sura again, and they would go away. I was agitated as a result of that vision and said to myself: "In the interpretations [of the Qur'an], the devils are the enemies [of God]." So I got in the boat and decided to recite the [112th] sura of "Say He is the One God" a thousand times that day. I called on God, blessed and exalted, to ward off with the power of that invocation the danger of the enemies.

The boat was full of people, including two monastic priests. One of the passengers in the boat recognized me. As mentioned above, upon going to Rouen, I had seen the need to wear French clothes. He drew the priest's attention to me, so the priest called me and said, "Sit near me." So I did.

He said to me: "Are you a Muslim?"

I said, "A Muslim, praise be to God."

He spoke Italian, which is very close to the *ajami* language of the land of the Andalus.

He said, "I met in Venice some of your coreligionists and I saw them doing something frivolous that has no basis in religion."

I said, "What was it that you saw them doing?"

He said, "If urine or an impurity fell on any of their belongings, they would wash that spot with water. So I asked them why they did that but I did not find that they had an answer."

I said to him, "The reason why they did that is that every Muslim is obligated to pray five times a day to God almighty. Each prayer is at a specific time, both in the day as well as at night. One of the obligations of prayer is that the person who prays be clean in his body and clothes because he is addressing God, his lord. He should be in the best of states. Everything that comes out of man from both orifices is impure because of the tree of whose fruit our father Adam, peace be upon him, ate, having forgotten what God had prohibited. As a result, the body now rejects what comes out of it, which was not the case before; this is what we have inherited.

So, if anything of what the body excretes falls on the clothes or on the body, man removes it with clean water so that he will be pure before his Master, both within and without. In terms of what is without, he should be clean in his body, his clothing, and the place where he worships. In terms of what is inside, he should not think of anything except what he is reciting. This is the origin of and explanation for the obligation to clean every impurity."

He liked the answer very much and told those who were in the boat in their own tongue good things about me. He then queried me on some complex matters, which I have forgotten. After saying good things about me to his companions, and despite my being of a different religion, he could not but continue: "God gave to the Muslims capable minds—in order that their punishment at the end of time be harsher and more severe for not being Christian." He said that in their own tongue, but I understood it.

In truth, I should have told him when I had mentioned that man has to be pure within, I should have said, purity of the heart begins in not worshipping more than one God. The priest had a companion, who was like him in monastic belief, who kept on telling him to discuss with me the trinity of the Godhood, but he replied that it would not be appropriate.

We sailed all the day. At sunset, we left the boat to a house on the bank of the river where I stayed in the upper floor. Outside my room, I repeated, "Say: He is the One God." I sent the priest some bread with sugar and eggs.

He called me and said, "I am fasting these days. What you have sent me contains eggs, which we do not eat during our fast." Then he started telling me about subduing the soul, and how he does not wear cotton, nor touch money nor eat much. He continued praising himself and his religion.

So I said to him, "Neither the devil nor the soul will find a better way to lead you to wickedness than through your superficial act of alms."

He said, "I do not understand. How can alms lead to temptation?"

I said, "You priests visit women and go into seclusion with them. They make you an offering. So you say to your selves, 'Go to so and so because she is a godly woman, and preach to her something about God, and guide her to

Him, and you will receive in return reward and alms.' This is how alms can be the doorway to temptation. For the real goal is for you to sit near her so that love enters your hearts. Then, love will either overpower you and you fall into sin and commit what is forbidden, which is what the devil and the soul desire, or love will so preoccupy you that even when you are praying to God with your tongue, you are thinking about her in your heart. This is my warning to you."

The priest was quiet and neither confirmed nor denied [my words]. In truth it would have been right that he be told "Neither the devil nor the soul will tempt one like you. For the thief only goes to the house that is full of riches. As for you, you associate other deities with the God who is the all-possessing and final judge, and you worship idols. The devil does not have to do anything more than inflate your own sense of pride and importance, and prepare the road that leads to the fires [of hell]."

He then said, "Why is wine prohibited in your religion?"

I answered him: "Because it is an intoxicant which incapacitates the mind, and the mind is the greatest and the highest of what is in man." I added: "When you are fasting, do you abstain from wine?"

"No," he said.

Then one of the devils whom I had seen in my sleep—and it was one of the infidels who traveled on the boat with us—said, "How come you are in our country? Who gave you permission?" He was angry, and showed it in his language.

So I took out the letter of their sultan, which silenced them all until we reached the guest house in which we were to stay for the night. They spoke to the guest master, saying, "This is a Turkish man." For in the land of the *ifranj* and in many other sultanates of the Christians, they call the Muslims *Turk*, as has already been mentioned. "He has come from his country and our sultan has given him permission to attend to his affairs. He merits all due respect from you." And other similar good words.

They were happy to have us on the boat as we sailed down the river. Everything was blessed by the sura of Ikhlas[33]; may God save us from their evil and elevate us in their eyes. Praise be God, lord of the universe.

――――――――――

In the next section, Qasim gives an account of his disputations with the Jews in France and Holland. He prepares himself by reading the Torah in an Arabic translation by a Jewish convert to Islam. As a Morisco, he had also read it in Spanish (which explains why some titles of biblical books are transliterated Spanish words). The disputations focus on practices and legal requirements that Judaism and Islam share with each other, such as ablution and circumcision. Qasim repeatedly tries to show the errors in Jewish practice and teaching, and how the Torah has been altered from the time of Moses. Qasim includes, however, the story of Daniel and Neb-uchednezer (which does not appear in the Qur'an) showing how willing he was to accept the Torah and to recognize Daniel as a prophet of God. He then describes the world's four parts, recalls the history of the battle of Wadi al-Makhazen (August 4, 1578), and refers to various atlases that he has seen, and the fact that the East Indies have large Muslim populations. He mentions proudly how fearful the Christians are of the Ottomans, and then turns to refute the Genesis account about Isaac and Ishmael by telling the story of Hagar from the Qur'anic perspective. He concludes the section with descriptions of his meetings in Paris with an astrologer and with two Turkish women from distinguished families in Istanbul who had been cap-tured while on their way to Mecca. They asked him to help them return home, which he did.

ON THE LAND OF FLANDERS

Know that we traveled toward that land that is farther from our land than the land of the Franks. For man must seek to learn from others as from himself. When I saw and confirmed what the ifranji navy did to Muslims, I said, "We will not travel on their [French] ships but walk to Flanders, because [the Flemish] do not harm the Muslims, but are good to them," as will be shown.

When we reached the city of Amsterdam, I saw the wonder of its magnifi-cent buildings, its cleanliness, and its immense population. Its buildings were nearly similar to those of Paris in France. There was no city in the world with as many ships as it had. It was said that there were in it six thousand ships, both large and small. As for the houses: each was painted and decorated from top to bottom in striking colors. None looked like the other. The streets were paved with cobble stones. I met somebody who had visited the lands of the East, Sicily and Rome and other cities of the world, and he said to me that he had not seen anything like [this city] in beauty and elegance.

Know that this Flanders consists of seventeen islands, all of which used to belong to the sultan of the Andalus [king of Spain]. But then, there appeared among them a learned man named Luther [*Bultari*] and another named Calvin [*Qalbin*]. Each wrote his views on the religion of the Christians— showing the falsification and deviation from the religion of our Sayyid Issa and the Gospel. They also wrote how the pope in Rome misleads the people by [urging them] to worship idols and by interpolating the prohibition of marriage for priests and monks, and many other things. All the population of Flanders joined that religion—I mean the seven islands—and they rebelled against their sultan, and continue in their rebellion until now. The inhabitants of the sultanate of the English are followers of this religion, and many in France [*faranja*] follow it too. Their teachers warned them against the pope and the worshippers of idols; they also told them not to hate the Muslims because they are the sword of God in the world against the idol-worshippers. That is why they side with the Muslims. Of the seventeen islands, seven rose up against the sultan of the land of the Andalus about seventy years ago. He was unable to defeat them and gave up on them. With their ships, they are stronger than all other Christians at sea. Each island is surrounded by the sea from all sides, which is the ocean.

When we visited the city of Leyden, we saw schools for the teaching of science. I also found a man who studied Arabic and taught it to others, and he drew a salary for doing that.[34] I had met him in France and he had taken me to his house. He spoke Arabic with me—he conjugated the verbs and declined the nouns—and he owned many books in Arabic. Among them was the dear Qur'an. As we started talking, he tried to prove his belief in the trinity of godhood—on which they concur with the pope and his followers. He praised his religion and highly glorified our Sayyid Issa.

I said to him, "We concur with you on all the praise and acclamation that you give him [Jesus], except in your saying that he is God or the son of the true God."

He then mentioned the Holy Spirit. I said to him, "Is the Holy Spirit not the Paraclete of the Gospel?"[35]

He said, "Yes, he is."

I said to him: "You know languages and dialects. What does *Paraclete* mean?"

He said, "It is not a Latin but a Greek word. In Arabic it means 'intercessor.'"

I said to him, "This is one of the names of our prophet Muhammad, God's peace and prayer upon him. Is not Paraclete the name of a person?"

"Yes," he said.

"And why do you turn him into a god," I said, "and say that three and one make up one thing?"

Later, a learned and famous man in medicine and scholarship came to see me. He said, "We have a copy of your Qur'an in a Latin translation, and it does not mention miracles by your prophet as we have in the Gospel." And he added: "Do you have a book about the miracles of your prophet?"

I said, "We do. One of the famous books about the prophet's miracles is by Judge Ayyad."[36] And I mentioned something about it. "We have many books about this topic because he, God's peace and prayer upon him, used to perform them in the presence of large multitudes. And when the people saw his virtue, blessings, honesty in word and deed, and his belief in [God's] one-ness, despite him being unlettered, they joined the religion [of Islam]. God, blessed and exalted, always proclaims truth until His religion prevails over all other religions. Most of the inhabited world follows His religion."

The wise man said, "By God, I wish we could read that book [by Ayyad]." Then he added, "There are doubts about these miracles, because many perform miracles through the power of the devil."

I said, "Don't you know how to separate between a prophetic, godly miracle and a satanic deed of fraud?"

He said to me, "Tell me how you would separate them."

I said, "The Prophet never performed a miracle unless it was requested of him. Often some good, both hidden and apparent, would come of it. The hidden good is the certainty it instills in people's hearts, and the confirmation of the truth of what he had told them about God the exalted, and what He commanded them to do or prohibited them from doing. The apparent good is the benefit it brings to people. An example of that is for Him to come to the help of an army of His followers with water or food. For if He does not help, they will all die, as did happen to our Prophet many times, God's prayer and peace upon him. This is an apparent good—as is also the asking for rain or the healing of a sick person. As for the deeds of the devil, they do not bring good except to himself and to none other. Frauds perform deeds without beings asked to, and no real good comes of them—neither apparent nor hidden—and it is they who bring people to see what they are doing. And if one asks those frauds [to do] something other than what they usually perform and which is above the nature of things, they are unable to do it. The fraud performs miracles in order to entertain the onlookers so that they give him some [money] by which he can live. And if someone says to him, 'Teach me what you know and I will pay you money,' he will teach him and the latter will perform the same action."

The wise man then said, "What you have said is correct. This is the truth."

Some scholars there brought to me an Arabic book and said to me, "Can you read this?"

After I read it, I knew it dealt with Sufism. It reported how some godly men did not speak to anyone while inside the mosque. And if one of them had to respond to someone, he would go outside the mosque door and do so. I told him, "I understand the meaning. I can translate it into *ajami*."

They marveled among each other and said to me: "This book was brought from the island of so-and-so from the East Indies. There is a sea of long travel between us and the people there, just short of a year to cross. This is a miracle, for there is a vast distance between your country and that island, and still you can understand what is in the book. This shows that Arabic is the same language in all countries. As for our language, it is different from others; for in the land of the English, there is one language, and the people of France have another language, and in the land of the Andalus, there is another, *ajami* language—and so too in Italy and Germany and Moscovy. Each language is different from the other. But Arabic is the same the world over. Truly," they continued, "it is a blessed language and whoever speaks it always mentions God. That is why some Andalusians used to say, 'There is no Arabic without God, and no *ajami* without the devil.' For the Christians mention the devil repeatedly in their speech. None hates Arabic nor desists from using it except those who do not know its blessing and value. End."

The Arabic book they brought from the eastern islands proved that the inhabitants there were Muslim.

Then we left the city of Leyden to the city of The Hague, where the seat of their prince and their court are located.[37] There I met the prince's representative, whom I had met in Marrakesh. He was very grateful to me for having helped him get out of captivity. The reason he had gone to Marrakesh was that the sultan of the land of the Andalus sent the galleys to the islands, which we had mentioned, and which had revolted against his authority. The islanders attacked and seized the galleys and threw the Christians who were in them into the sea—at least so it was said. The people of Flanders then released all the Muslim captives, who were more than three hundred, and put them in a big ship and sent them as a present to the sultan of Marrakesh—who was the son of Mulay Ahmad, whose name was Abu Faris. It happened about 1014 [1605].[38]

Pedr Marteen was the envoy [who led the captives],[39] whom, by accident,
I met in The Hague, which is his country. This messenger remained in Marrakesh during all the years of confusion and conflict, until Sultan Mulay
Zaidan was established in the kingdom. Zaidan threw him in prison because
he had not brought the gift of captives to him [but had presented it to the rival contender to the throne].[40] After this envoy had spent some time in
prison, I received news about him and I remembered the good his coreligionists had done to the Muslims when they had [freed and] sent them back
[to their countries]. I prepared myself and investigated the matter, then
spoke to the famous scholar mufti, Mohammad Abu Abdallah, who in turn
spoke to the sultan, who released the envoy from prison.

When he saw me in his country, he went to his prince and told him [about
me] and then led me to him. The name of the prince is Maurice [of Nassau].
He came down to meet me, uncovering his head, and took me by the hand
and seated me near him. I visited him four times. One day, after taking my
seat, he said to me, "How many languages do you know?"

I said to him, "Arabic, the language of Spain, and the language of Portugal. We understand the language of the *ifranj*, but we cannot speak it."

He said to me, "We know the language of the *ifranj* and understand the
language of Spain"—which is the language of the people of the land of the
Andalus, as we have said frequently—"but I cannot speak it. So I will speak
to you in *franji* and you will speak to me in the *ajami* language of the people
of the Andalus."

"Yes," I said.

He said to me, "In your opinion, why did the sultan of Spain expel the
Andalusians from his land?"

I said, "Know that the Andalusians were Muslims in the guise of Christians. But sometimes their Islam would become apparent and they would
live by it. When he [the Spanish king] ascertained that about them, he did
not trust them anymore; subsequently, he never sent any of them to war on
his behalf, a war in which a large number of people could perish. He also forbade them to go out to sea lest they escaped to their coreligionists. And the
sea swallows up multitudes of men. Also, and among those [Catholic] Christians, there are large numbers of priests and monks and nuns, and by re-
nouncing marriage, they leave no offspring. Among the Andalusians there
were no priests or monks or nuns; rather they all married and increased by
having children and by neither going to war nor out to sea. This, it appears to
me, was the reason he expelled them. The more time passed, the more their

numbers grew." Then I asked, "Can you understand me?"

He said to me in *ifranji*: "I understood everything you said. What you mentioned is the truth."

Then he said, "If we can reach an agreement with the leaders of the Andalusians, and send them a fleet of large ships that they can board with our soldiers, can we not conquer Spain?"

I said, "The Andalusians cannot agree to that without the permission of the sultans in whose lands they settled after their expulsion."

He said, "If we can reach an agreement with the sultan of Marrakesh and if we communicate with the Grand Master"—I mean the great sultan, the sultan of Islam and religion [Ahmad I]—"we can all join against the sultan of Spain, defeat him, and conquer his land."

I said, "This is a great enterprise if it could be realized. But there is some uncertainty. O that such an agreement could be reached and the [combined armies] conquer the land of the Andalus; may God return it to Islam."

He said to the envoy, "Devise a cipher in [numerical] code, and give him a copy so we can establish correspondence between us." And he gave me a copy.

And then he said to me, "Tell me your wish," which meant, "Ask of me what you want," which is a custom among the kings of the Christians. If they tell a person, "Ask of me what you want," they will give him whatever he asks of them. They only say that on rare occasions, and only to those whom they hold in great favor. So I said to myself, "Christians believe that Muslims are very greedy for worldly possessions—[this is only said] by those who have known a few Muslims, of whom I am one. So that they will know and confirm that what they believe about Muslims is untrue, and that there are Muslims who are not greedy for wealth, we [Qasim and his retinue] will not ask him for any money."

I said to him, " I ask of you one favor."

"What is it you wish?" he said.

"That you tell the ship captain with whom we will sail to look after us well," I said.

"Is that all?" he said.

"Yes," I said.

"Find out," he said, "the ship in which you will sail, and the name of the captain, and the name of the merchant who owns the ship, and bring them to me."

So I told him their names, and he ordered his scribe to write to each of them a letter telling them to look after us well. He then put his seal on them, and everyone was pleased with his letters. The merchant used sugar in many of the meals, and he gave us dates that are unfamiliar to them because they are brought from the lands of the Muslims, for nowhere in the world are they found except in Muslim lands.

I then said to the envoy who had rejoiced at seeing me in his country, "I met two Turkish women in the lands of the *ifranj*, in Paris, and they had converted to the religion of the Christians. They asked me to help them return to the lands of the Muslims. I am now on my way back to Marrakesh, God the exalted willing. So what can I do for them?"

He said, "Write to them to come to my house, and I will arrange that they return to their country."

I wrote to them about the plan, and sent the letter to an Andalusian who delivered it to them. God protected them as they traveled on foot from France to Flanders. Arrangements were made through the prince, who sent them on a trading ship to Istanbul, where they arrived safely. He did all this after I had left the country and so I never saw them. But good brings good. Meanwhile, the captain was delighted to have us on his ship, which is what we had hoped for.

In regard to the city of The Hague, where the prince was: its latitude is 52 degrees in the sixth region of the world. While we were there, the longest day of the year occurred when the sun sets in Cancer. Sunrise and sunset are not as in other countries—I mean Egypt, Morocco, Syria, and the Andalus— for the day there [in Flanders] begins with the sunrise and continues for about nineteen hours; there is very little darkness at night. When the sun sets, redness covers the sky until close to midnight. About an hour and a half later, we would pray the morning prayer.

It will take us too long to describe all that we saw in Flanders. We mentioned something in the *Rihla*, and the story of the six men who came from the land where the day is for six months or close to that with no night, and the opposite during winter time when there is no sun at all.[41]

As for what I had mentioned in this chapter about my answer to the Prince in regard to the reasons that drove the sultan of the Christians [Philip III] to expel the Andalusians from his country, we will mention something here that we did not mention in the copies written before I wrote this summary.

Know that the sultan of the country was known by the name of Philip II—I mean, from among those sultans who were called Philip. I verified this by reading some Muslim books of history that tell about the wars with the sultan of the land who was known as Alfonso, but they did not explain which one it was. For in the lands of the Andalus, there were more than twelve sultans known as Alfonso who are identified by the number in their names: for instance, Alfonso the fourth or the eighth or the tenth. Muslim historians do not mention the number in the name. Before I escaped the country [Spain], this Philip II ordered a census of all the Andalusians, young and old, even those in the wombs of pregnant women: and none knew the secret reason for that. Seventeen years later, another census was carried out just like the first one, as I was told in Marrakesh, and none knew the secret of that either. The general opinion was that the Spaniards wanted to know whether the Andalusian population was increasing or decreasing. As soon as they discovered that they were on the increase, they ordered their expulsion. Sultan Philip III sent a letter in his name to his relative and successor in the city of Valencia ordering him to begin expelling the Andalusians. I translated a copy of that letter to the sultan, Mulay Zaidan, son of the sultan Mulay Ahmad in Marrakesh. The date of the letter, and God knows best, was the beginning of the year 1018 after the Hijra [April 1609].[42] In it he said,

> To the Marquis de Qarasina [viceroy of Valencia], our relative and vicegerent in our sultanate in Valencia, peace.
>
> You know that over the past many years, [we have tried] to guide, confirm and lead the New Christians of the Andalus, the inhabitants of this sultanate and that of Castile, to our glorious religion and faith. But neither the great nor the small [among them] benefited because none of them is a true Christian. Scholars and reverent men have warned us of the danger and evil that would befall us for turning a blind eye [to the presence of those crypto-Muslims], and they have told us that the matter has to be corrected in order to please God and remove His anger against our community. They determined that, without a doubt, it is permitted us to punish them in their persons and possessions, for by continuing in their misdeeds, they were judged and condemned as hypocrites and enemies of the divine and human majesty. It was fully within our power to punish them for the guilt and evil deeds they committed. Despite that, I chose to treat them with patience and leniency, without seeking vengeance. As a result, we ordered the august assembly, which I attended with all the scholars and nobility of that city, to find a way to expel them from our kingdom. In that [meeting], we looked into the matter and confirmed that they

[Moriscos] had sent their emissaries to the Grand Turk in Istanbul and to Mulay Zaidan in Marrakesh asking them for help, and reporting to them that that they had 150,000 Muslim men, just like those in the land of African Morocco. They also communicated with our maritime enemies in the northern region under the pole, who assured them of naval support. Meanwhile, the sultan of Istanbul had reached a peace agreement with the sultan of the Persians, who had fought against him. As for the sultan of Marrakesh, he planned to conquer the land and occupy it.[43] If they all agree with each other, we will find ourselves in [such a dire] situation that cannot be kept undisclosed.

In order for us to do what we have to do to protect our kingdom and keep it safe, we have reached the following conclusion—after I called on God and ordered that He be invoked, trusting in His support and victory for His glory and honor: to expel all the Andalusians who are in the sultanate because they are very near to the coast [where enemy support will arrive]. To do so, we have ordered that the following edict be proclaimed and announced:

First, that all the Andalusian men, women and children in the kingdom and in the regions they inhabit, will, within three days of the announcement of this edict, depart and go to a designated location on the seacoast. From there they will sail out, carrying with them all the possessions and furniture they can take. They will board the ships and the galleys that are available to carry them to the land of Morocco. They will be taken there with no harm to their persons or possessions, and they will be given whatever food they need, as long as they are on board the ships. Whoever wants to take whatever he can carry, let him do so. Whoever disobeys this order will be killed instantly.

Whoever is found three days after the order has been declared outside his city, let whoever finds him rob him of all his possessions and hand him over to the governors. And if he resists, it is permitted to kill him.

No one who hears this declaration is permitted to leave his city to another city. He must join the leaders at the seacoast from where all of them will sail.

Whoever buries any of his possessions that he cannot take with him, or burns any of his crops or trees, will be killed for doing so. We have given our order that his neighbors execute him.

To ensure that the new inhabitants of the country [Spain] will be able to work the sugar presses, plant the rice fields, and irrigate the lands, we have decreed that six Andalusians with their unmarried children should remain in every town of a hundred houses. Each town lord has the authority to select them. They should be old farmers who have a certain familiarity with and leaning toward our religion, and who, it is hoped, will remain in it.

The riflemen and Old Christians will not take anything [of the Muslims' money] and will not go near their wives and children.

None shall hide in his house. Whoever does so will be sent to the galleys for six years or for whatever time appears best to us.

Let them be assured that the sultan just wants to send them out of his lands to the lands of Morocco, and wants no harm to come to them from anyone. He will pay for their maintenance and for their transport on his ships. Once they arrive there, let ten of them return to tell others. The captains of the galleys and ships should abide by this order.

Boys and orphans under four years of age, if they want to stay here, with the approval of their guardians, may do so.

Boys who are the children of Christians will not be expelled; neither will their mothers, even if they are Andalusians. If the father is Andalusian and the mother a Christian, the mother can stay with her children if they are under six. But the father will have to go away.

This order was declared and announced on 22 September 1609 from the birth of our Sayyid Issa, peace be upon him. End.

After the inhabitants of the sultanate of Valencia departed, the expulsion of the inhabitants of the Andalus and of other neighboring regions was ordered. They chartered ships, but while they were near the river of Seville, the sultan sent an order contradicting the first, saying that all boys and girls who are under the age of seven, and who are on board the ships that have been chartered to take them to the land of the Muslims, shall remain here. All the people who were there were expelled. A thousand children were taken from among the inhabitants of al-Hajar al-Ahmar,[44] and so too all the children of those who crossed over to Tangier and Ceuta, as well as the others.

By means of those Muslim sultans whom God has chosen and selected, God the exalted can wrest the right from them [Christians] in this world.

The last chapters in the book mention very little about Europe. Qasim summarizes his disputations and he tells about his subsequent travels in North Africa. He recalls how he helped ransom a priest in Marrakesh who had come from the "Indians": the letters they exchanged together turned into a theological disputation about whether or not Jesus was God, and about the validity of confession as a means of salvation. Qasim also mentions his disputations with an Arab priest in Egypt about eating and drinking in paradise (similar to the disputation he had had earlier), the nondivinity of Jesus, and the trinity. In a later chapter, Qasim describes the (miraculous) cure he was able to effect on people by reading the Qur'an to them. He also writes about the voice that he repeatedly heard that told him to read the Qur'an and to pray—a voice that even a monk who was with him in the palace of Mulay Zaidan heard.

The last of Qasim's chapters is a summary of the book *The True Gospel*, an apocryphal account of the teachings of Mary, the mother of Jesus. It is in the form of a dialogue with the disciples, in which Mary presents to Peter (Pedro) the revelation of the Gospel in eight discussions. The *Kitab* ends with Qasim indicating that he finished writing it in Tunis on 20 Rajab 1051 (October 25, 1641).

NOTES

1. Clelia Sarnelli Cerqua, "Al-Hagari en France," in *Les Practicas Musulmanas de los Morisocs Andaluces (1492–1609)*, ed. Abdeljelil Temimi (Zaghouan: Fondation Temimi, 1989), 161–66; Gerard Wiegers, "A Life between Europe and the Maghrib: The Writings and Travels of Ahmad b. Qasim bin Ahmad ibn al-faqih Qasim ibn al-shaykh al-Hajari al-Andalusi (born c. 977/1569–70)," in *The Middle East and Europe: Encounters and Exchanges*. ed. Geert Jan van Gelder and Ed. de Moor (Amsterdam: Rodopi, 1992), 87–115; J. R. Jones, "Learning Arabic in Renaissance Europe (1505–1624)," Ph.D. diss., London University, 1988, 98–120. See also the biography by Nasir al-Din Saiduni, *Min al-Turath al-Tarikhi w-al-Jughrafi* (Beirut: Dar al-Gharb al-Islami, 1999), 344–49.

2. Qasim knew the New Testament in both a Spanish translation of 1602 and an Arabic Egyptian version with different chapter divisions.

3. Diego Hurtado de Mendoza, *The War in Granada*, trans. Martin Shuttleworth (London: Folio Society, 1982), 1:9. See also the analysis of this speech by Rhona Ziad, "Las Guerras Civiles de Granada: The Idealization of Assimilation," in *Me-*

dieval Christian Perceptions of Islam, ed. John Victor Tolan (New York: Garland, 1996), 313–30.

4. Qasim used the Arabic words *ifranji* for French and *ajami* for Spanish, though he knew the more nationally defined terms *faransi* and *ispani*.

5. Luke 1:13–15.

6. 1 Kings 11:31.

7. 2 Chron. 13:3.

8. Qasim never uses the Christian term, "Old Testament" (as in the translation by P. S. Van Koningsveld et al.). Instead he uses the Qur'anic term "Torah." The reference is probably to 2 Sam. 24:9, in which the Israelites were counted.

9. Matt. 8:28–33.

10. Qasim uses the word *intaha* (end) at the conclusion of citations, particularly when he is quoting from religious documents. This practice was common among Arabic writers.

11. Mark 5:20.

12. Hubert Etienne, a French physician, was sent to the court of Mulay al-Mansur in 1598 as personal doctor and translator. He was a learned Arabist, and after his return to France, taught at the Collège de France. He died in 1614.

13. Cecil, bishop of Granada (d. A.D. 70) was mentioned in the first chapter of Qasim's account (not included here).

14. Qasim uses the term *bint* (girl) to denote virginal/unmarried.

15. The word *hareem* derives from *harama*—that which is prohibited.

16. Qur'an 7:11–12.

17. *Suras* are chapters in the Qur'an.

18. Matt. 22:34–40.

19. Deut. 7:25.

20. Jalal al-Din al-Sayyuti (1445–1505) was an Egyptian jurist who wrote on Qur'anic exegesis, interpretation, jurisprudence, grammar, linguistics, and rhetoric. He is credited with over five hunderd works.

21. Qur'an 17:81.

22. It is strange how ignorant Qasim is of the Arab-Islamic contribution to astronomy. Many of the names of the horoscope derive from Arabic.

23. Qur'an 2:258.

24. Gen. 2:8–14.

25. *Hadiths* are teachings of the prophet Muhammad.

26. Al-Sha'rani was a jurist (d. 1565).

27. The author was Ibn Abi Zayd al-Qayrawani, A.D. 928–996.

28. Matthew 26:29.

29. Matt. 26:26–28.

30. Mark 25:14.

31. Luke 21:28–36.

32. Qur'an 112:1.

33. The Sura of Ikhlas is the chapter on salvation in the Qur'an. It is the same sura mentioned above, sura 112.

34. This was Thomas Erpenius (1584–1624). For Qasim's relation with the Dutch Arabist, see G. A. Wiegers, *A Learned Muslim Acquaintance of Erpenius and Golius* (Leiden: Documentatiebureau Islam-Christendom, 1988).

35. John 16:16.

36. Ayyad b. Musa (A.D. 1083–1149).

37. Maurice of Nassau, (1567–1625).

38. For the return of 135 Muslim captives, both Turkish and Moorish, to Safi and Algiers in April–May 1605, see Henri de Castries, *Les Sources Inédites de L'Histoire du Maroc: Archives et Bbiliothèques des Pays-Bas*, (Paris: Ernest Leroux, 1907), 1:65–67. The name of the representative was Pieter Marteen Coy.

39. Coy was, from July 1605 on, the representative of the States General in Marrakesh. In May 1607, Dutch pirates attacked English vessels; this angered Mulay Zaidan, who proceeded to imprison the Dutch. They were released on July 18, 1607. Coy was recalled on December 13, 1607, to Holland and was not able to regain his post.

40. After the death of Mulay al-Mansur in 1603, civil war broke out in Morocco. The rival to Zaidan, to whom Coy must have gone, was Abu Faris.

41. They were led by the Dutch Willem Barentsz (c. 1550–1597).

42. As Koningsveld et al. indicate, Qasim translated from two texts: the one published on September 11, 1609, and the second on September 22, 1609; *Kitab*, 206–10.

43. See the study of the letters by his scribe, Abu Faris al-Fishtali, in my "The Anglo-Spanish Conflict in Arabic Sources, c. 1588–1596," in *From Silence to Sound*, ed. Mohammad Shaheen (Beirut: Dar al-Gharb al-Islami, 2000), 436–56.

44. Al-Hajar al-Ahmar is the region that Qasim came from.

2

EUROPE AND SOUTH AMERICA

Kitab Siyahat al-Khoury Ilyas bin al-Qissees Hanna al-Mawsuli
(The Book of Travels of the Priest Ilyas, Son of the Cleric
Hanna al-Mawsuli)

Ilyas Hanna al–Mawsuli
(1668–1683)

NOTHING IS KNOWN about the Iraqi writer al-Mawsuli except the very little that appears in his account. He was Ilyas, son of the cleric Hanna al-Mawsuli from the Ammoun al-Kildani family. The name indicates that his family originally came from Musil; but in the text, there is a reference suggesting that he was born in Baghdad. He belonged to the Chaldean Catholic Church, which was uniate with Rome. After the Council of Ephesus in A.D. 431, the Assyrian Church of the East separated itself from the rest of Christendom because it followed Nestorius, who had taught the Monophysite belief that Christ had had one nature. In 1552, after a number of bishops converted to Catholicism, the Church reestablished communion with Rome, and located its see in Baghdad because its followers were primarily from Iraq. It retained its Syriac liturgy and tradition but accepted the authority of the Papacy in Rome.

Al-Mawsuli started his journey in 1668 from Baghdad and ended it in 1683. In 1680, he was in Peru when he wrote the first part of his work. He never stated what the purpose of his travel to Europe was, but there was possibly a clandestine element pertaining to diplomatic activity. Many allusions in the account suggest that he was on a mission to European potentates and ecclesiastics: al-Mawsuli was a "lowly" priest but he had, as he wrote, an official Turkish escort at the beginning of his journey; he offered a sword to the Spanish king, carried letters to European church officials, and interacted with nobility, royalty and the pope. On the galleon that took him to South America, he had his own cabin, which was quite a luxury, and while traveling around Peru, he had a litter, sometimes a coach; always slaves and servants, dogs and rifles. Only rich travelers could afford such amenities and advantages; and from the way he recorded incomes, wages, salaries and monies he either possessed or lent out (at an exorbitant rate), he seemed to have had sufficient means.

What is intriguing is why the Spanish king gave al-Mawsuli a permit to go to America. The story that al-Mawsuli tells is plausible—that he was rewarded for celebrating mass in the king's chapel—but the Spaniards were very jealous of their possessions in the New World and guarded information carefully lest it fall into heretical adversarial hands (those of the English in particular). That a priest who was an Ottoman subject and had worked for the Ottoman administration was not viewed as a threat is perplexing: either he was seen to be too Catholic to pose any danger, or the Spaniards may not have thought of the Ottomans as rivals in America. Al-Mawsuli traveled widely and always noted details and distances, suggesting that he was intent on writing an account of his journey, in Arabic, once he was finished with his *siyahat* (travels).

In his exordium, al-Mawsuli explained that the purpose for writing the account was to show how God had vindicated His church after the secession of the Protestant "heretics": a new world had been discovered whose large populations were Christianized by Catholics and won over to the *sayyid* (master), the pope. The journey was therefore an affirmation of Christian victory, an account of Jesuit, Dominican, Mercedarian, and Franciscan missions in a land that had become the patrimony of Catholicism. As he traveled from one religious site to another, al-Mawsuli showed how the New World had become primarily interconnected by means of its churches, monasteries, missions, convents, and schools which established Catholicism in every corner of the land.

Al-Mawsuli did not reveal much about his background or legacy in the text. Still, it is possible to form an image of this adventurous priest. He was a strong-willed man, handy with guns, which he used both to defend himself against robbers and to hunt. He was, of course, always conscious of himself as coming from the East—both geographically and ecclesiastically. He recalled the Tigris and the coffee of his homeland, proclaimed his pride in celebrating mass in Syriac, and luxuriated in his bushy beard, which fascinated the Indians. He was very alert to financial matters, noting repeat-

edly the incomes of bishops and archbishops, perhaps with some envy. He
did not hesitate to break the law and accept gifts of gold and silver from
mine owners. He knew that as a priest he was immune to searches by customs officers and other officials. The journey to America not only satisfied
his curiosity, but may well have brought him a little fortune. Toward the
end, we read, he was already trading in vermilion and would have lent
100,000 piasters to a Spaniard had he been assured of his ability to pay the
sum back. Like the Jesuits, especially, but also like other members of religious orders and high ecclesiastical officers, al-Mawsuli engaged in trade
and became very much a cleric-merchant.[1]

Comparing al-Mawsuli's accounts with others, a consistent pattern of
visits and stops for travelers appears. Visitors followed set routes, saw the
same "tourist" attractions, listened to and recorded the same stories, and developed the same views of the native populations. An anonymous Spanish
description of Peru that had been written at the beginning of the seventeenth century curiously anticipates many items of information that
al-Mawsuli mentions.[2] Furthermore, al-Mawsuli read extensively about
the Spanish conquest of the Americas and the descriptions of the lands and
peoples; it is not clear when he did that reading, but the ideas that he
found there influenced his views, particularly in regard to the Indians. The
first Arabic text about America repeats the same views of the Indians as
"infidels" and "devil worshippers" as the Spanish sources.[3]

Al-Mawsuli had a good command of Arabic, considering the time and
region in which he lived. Although his writing exhibits numerous idiosyncrasies in grammar, vocabulary, and spelling, his Arabic was competent. As
a Chaldean Christian, he learned both Syriac and Arabic as his mother
tongues; as a priest in the Chaldean Church, he used Syriac in his liturgical
and ecclesiastical duties; Arabic was used for all other facets of his life. That
is why, and because he was writing in Arabic, he did not seem to have
equivalents for many ecclesiastical terms that prevailed in Catholic Europe;
his use of church titles is interchangeable and often undifferentiated. Al-
Mawsuli knew Turkish, too, since that was the language of the Ottoman
administration (and the northern part of Iraq was heavily influenced by
the Turko-Ottoman legacy). There are numerous Turkish words in the text.
Some phrases and terms in his preface are Qura'nic—showing how the
Arabic of the Qur'an had become the practiced Arabic of all the religious
communities within the world of Arabic-speaking Islam.

Although the date of al-Mawsuli's death is not known, the Russian historian Ignatii Krachkovkii maintains that the Iraqi priest died and was buried in Rome in 1693. A year before, he had paid for the printing of an Arabic book of prayer in Rome. The book shows the numerous titles which al-Mawsuli received—including the title of Bishop of Baghdad—from both the Church of Rome and the Court of Spain for the services he rendered.[4]

NOTE: One manuscript of this account is in the Syriac Bishopric in Aleppo. It is in 369 pages: pages 1–100 constitute the journey, followed by 214 pages of translations from European writers on the discovery of America. From page 314 to the end, there is an Arabic translation of the account of the visit of the Turkish ambassador to France. Al-Mawsuli was methodical in his writing, filling twenty-one lines on each page. The inscriptions on the manuscript show that it was first owned by Hanna, son of Diyab al-Maruni in Aleppo, and then passed on to Jibra'il, son of Yusuf Qirmis on December 5, 1817. I am deeply grateful to the Syriac patriarch for giving me permission to examine the manuscript, and to the librarian and staff for their assistance and numerous cups of tea.

This manuscript was edited by Antoine Rabbat in 1906. The editor "modernized" the text by changing terms and titles, and he deleted sections that he thought were unnecessary. A new edition has just been published in Beirut and Amman that reprints the Rabbat edition.[5]

The other manuscript is at the British Library (MS Oriental 3537). This is a later manuscript, purchased by Issa al-Rassam from the "son of the deacon" in 1786. It includes the account of the journey, along with the translated material from Spanish sources, but not the visit of the Ottoman ambassador to Paris.

I have used both manuscripts as well as the published edition. I have traced the place names on the *Rand-McNally World Atlas*, and where I failed to locate the places, I have used the Rabbat entries in French. Some places appear in Willem Blaeu's *Grand Atlas of the Seventeenth Century*, but not in the *Rand-McNally* atlas, suggesting that some mining towns and small hamlets through which al-Mawsuli traveled have faded away. As Guillermo de Zendegui said at the height of colonial pride, "It was the period [seventeenth century] in which cities in what would one day be our Latin America appeared and disappeared on the maps as if by magic, and when only Spain, lady and mistress of the vast territories she had discovered, could add them or remove them according to her whim."[6]

[Let us] invoke the name of God
And confirm His ancient name.

(The British Library manuscript opens with these words, written in Karshuni, Arabic in Syriac script.)

In the Name of the Father, the Son
and the Holy Spirit—One God.

THE EXORDIUM OF THE BOOK. GOD IS THE GUIDE TO TRUTH.

The First Preamble

PRAISE BE TO GOD for creating the world in His wisdom. He made things by His word and command, and made man in His image and likeness. By His grace, He gave him dominion over all the creatures, and forbade him a fruit which if he ate, he would die the death. When this weak creature disobeyed the command of his creator, and ate of what was forbidden, he lost the grace in which he had been clothed and was expelled with his progeny and seed from the paradise of Eden [*Firdaws Aden*] to the regions of misery and pain.

Then the almighty and exalted felt compassion for him and sought to free him: He sent his beloved son, the second person of the Trinity and His eternal word, through a pure unmarried virgin, the noblest of beings, and entered her womb in an unknowable manner. Through her, he assumed a body and became free of sin. He wandered around the world and performed miracles [*ayat*] by healing the sick and raising the dead. He then selected disciples, simple people, fishermen, and he made laws and canons for them, and commanded them to go into the world and preach the Gospel "Going therefore, teach ye all nations; baptizing them in the name of the Father, and of the son, and of the Holy Ghost."[7] He who believed would be saved, and he who did not would be judged. He also said, "And he that shall receive one such little child in my name, receiveth me" [Matt. 18:5]. He promised them that upon his ascension he would send them a comforting spirit that would endow them with wisdom and strength. After his ascension, and sitting at the right hand of the Father, he sent them the Paraclete spirit, which descended on them like tongues of fire. They began to speak in different languages and went throughout the inhabited world, preaching the Gospel. Their miracles witnessed to their preaching.

Some went to the east, while others went to the west; some to the *qibla*,[8] and some to the north so as to fulfill the words of David the Prophet, who said in the twelfth psalm: their "sound hath gone forth into all the earth: and their words unto the ends of the world" [Ps. 18:5]. "They were destitute, afflicted, tormented . . . in sheepskins and goatskins" [Heb. 11:37].[9] Their light shone into the dark regions and by their ministry they purified the inhabited world of idol worship and led [people] out of blindness and tyranny; they chose disciples and successors to whom they imparted the gifts and the grace of the Holy Spirit in order for them to assume leadership after them for generations to follow until the end of the world [*aalameen*].

After the glorious ascension [of Christ], St. Peter the rock was made the head and leader of the holy church, the bride of Christ, and of those who would succeed him. The church continued to spread and expand so that not a single place or region in the four corners of the world was without the preaching of the Gospel and of the orthodox faith in different languages and among all believers. But the cursed one, enemy of truth and virtue, continued busily to unsettle the consciences of believers in order to overpower them and cast them away from the fold of their mother the church. He cast before them his nets and traps, and he planted in the hearts of some the seeds of envy, pride, and rebellion so much so that some groups rejected obedience to the Roman Church and to its leader and head who is the Holy Pope and the pastor of pastors.[10] They chose new leaders, who opposed each other, as a result of which the blessed Almighty set upon them their enemies, to whom they became slaves and servants. The words of the Lord Jesus in his holy Gospel were confirmed through the tongue of Saint Luke the Evangelist in the fifty-second chapter, addressing the Jews, "If you see Abraham and Isaac and Jacob and all the prophets in the kingdom of heaven—the first shall be last and the last first."[11]

When these aforementioned groups separated from the fold of the holy church, the Lord Jesus decided to admit other people in their stead, who were of different races and customs, speaking in foreign languages and tongues, living in valleys and mountains, following the wild ways with no difference between them and beasts. Tortured and misled by Satan, ignorant of the true God, some of them worshipped stones, others worshiped wild animals, while others worshipped trees. Others offered themselves as sacrifices to the cursed Satan, living in the fourth zone, which had been hidden from sight and was unknown. The great saint and teacher of the holy church, St. Augustine, used to think that zone uninhabited by humans.

Our purpose is to show the return of those aforementioned people to the true faith and their admission into the holy church. Many of them, after believing in Christ, are now considered among the saints. This zone, about which we intend to speak, is vast in length and width, and is larger, in length and width, than the other three zones known as Asia, Africa, and Europe. It has been given a new name, *Meriko maslooba*; we shall speak about him [for whom the zone is named] later and describe the process and motivations for the discovery, and enumerate all the facts.[12] We ask God for His forgiveness for anything that is unnecessarily added or excluded, forgotten or ignored because that [quality of forgetfulness] is in every man. Praise be to God always and forever. Amen.

THE BOOK OF THE TRAVELS OF THE PRIEST ILYAS, SON OF THE CLERIC HANNA AL-MAWSULI, FROM THE FAMILY OF AMMOUN AL-KILDANI

(tells) about the land of the West Indies and the reason why the Spaniards conquered that land, and also what he [the traveler] saw with his own eyes during the twelve years he stayed there in the sultanate of *Yenki Dunia* and in the land of Peru.[13] He has also turned to books of history written by reliable teachers for information that he translated from Spanish into Arabic. He himself organized and arranged [the material] in the year 1680 after Christ, in the city of Lima in Peru.

[FROM BAGHDAD TO ITALY]

I say, I, a lowly priest, in the year A.D. 1668, left the city of Baghdad to visit the sepulchre of Christ. I was in the company of the *tubji basha*, known as Mikhail Agha.[14] We traveled a deserted road, and as we were halfway across we were attacked by bedouin robbers. We fought and defeated them. It was Easter Sunday. We were twelve people and they were a hundred, but because of our guns and the power of God we overpowered them. From there we continued our road to Damascus, and from Damascus to honorable Jerusalem [*al-Quds al-Shareef*], where I was blessed by visiting the holy sites.

A few days later, I returned to Damascus and then went to Aleppo, and after a few days I descended to the seaport known as Iskanderun, where I boarded an English ship and sailed to the lands of Europe. We crossed to the island of Cyprus, where I visited the shrine of St. Lazarus and his sisters Miriam and Martha.[15] A few days after leaving the island, we reached the island of Crete, from where we continued to Zanthe, which, along with two other islands near it, called Corfu and Cephalonia, is governed by Venice, which is known in Turkish as *Wanadeek*. It is famous around the world.

From there we sailed on to the port of the aforementioned Venice. We had spent seventy days at sea since leaving Iskanderun and entering this port. We were taken out of the ship and led to the house of purification, known as *nazarite* in Italian.[16] For fear of the plague, the Venetians made us stay there for forty-one days, as is decreed. The nazarite is outside the city, as is the custom in the lands of Christians. Exactly on the forty-first day, the doctor basha came to look us over and see if anyone among us was sick. After that, we were given a pass to leave the nazarite. We left it and entered the aforementioned city, where I stayed for twenty days. I wandered around and visited the churches. The wealth I saw in the church of St. Mark the Evangelist is beyond description.

Soon after, I went to the great city of Rome and stayed there for six months. I visited the holy sites, especially the church of St. Peter the Apostle, which is unique for its beauty in all the inhabited world. Then I left for France, passing through the territory of a prince known as the Grand Duke of Tuscany, who lives in Florence.[17] This prince is very rich in wealth and possessions. From Florence I continued to the seaport known as Leghorn, which is governed by the same prince. After a few days I traveled to Genoa, a seaport, which is governed by a self-ruling prince. This city is rich in wealth and glorious in buildings.

[FRANCE]

From there I traveled by sea to the port of Marseilles in France. After we landed, we walked to the city of Avignon, which is governed by our sayyid, the pope.[18] This city is in France, but France's old sultans had given it and other villages to the Church of St. Peter. From there, we boarded a river boat that was pulled by horses. We reached Lyon, which is one of the greatest cities in France after the city of Paris, the city of the sultan of France.

In Lyon, I met with a saintly man known as Mr. Piquet.[19] This noble man had been a consul in Aleppo and after returning from there, he was ordained priest and then bishop of Baghdad. He died in Persia in the city of Hamadhan. We still talk about his virtues and good deeds. After a few days, I left Lyon and went to Paris, the royal residence of the King of France, where I visited the victorious King Louis, who welcomed me. I then visited his brother the Prince [Duke Philip] of Orléans and presented him with a sword; I also celebrated mass in his palace chapel, after which he showed me great favor. I then visited a prince known as St. Aignan and delivered to him a letter from his uncle, *Patri* [Father] John the Capuchin monk of good memory, who was a *rais* [leader] in Baghdad and later in Aleppo.[20] He showed me great favor because of his uncle's letter.

I resided in that place and started visiting this great city, which is unrivaled in all the world in its beauty, the justice of its laws, and the love of its inhabitants for strangers. I cannot but praise and applaud a particular deed of charity and benevolence: a number of women—seventeen in all—from noble families, some virgins and some widows, have become ascetes, leaving all their money in holy communion, which in the French language is known as *sharitee* [charity], I mean the Sisters of Love.[21] This community of charity was established a long time ago, and many widows leave their possessions to it. All the money donated to this community is kept safely with the people of profit [bankers], and every year, it earns two million piasters, I mean, twenty *karra* [a karra is a unit of 100,000] of money. Every week, these blessed women assemble together to distribute the money among the poor and the needy; they also make offerings to churches and monasteries, to the sick and to strangers, and to the missionaries who preach Christ in eastern lands. From this charity, they also give money to poor girls so that they can get married. I found many things worth praising and describing in this great city.

While I was there, a messenger arrived from Sultan Mohammad [Mehemed IV], sultan of the Turks [1648–1687], to meet Sultan Louis al-Mansur [Louis XIV, 1638–1715].[22] This messenger is known in Turkish and Persian as *eelji*. I visited him many times to translate for him into Turkish. He then asked me to stay in Paris and not to leave. So I stayed there for eight months.

Afterward, I left for Spain, crossing on the way a great city, Orléans, and from there to a city called Bozance[?], and then to Poitiers, and from there to a city known as Bordeaux, which is on a big river. The aforementioned Sultan Louis had cut up the mountains and united the seas together so that

ships could now sail easily in this river [Gironde] and from the Ocean to En-
tre-deux-mers. From there, I traveled to Spain, crossing countless cities and
villages, and, after twelve days, I reached a river that lies at the border between France and Spain. There is a fort called St. Jean de Luz, which belongs to France.

[SPAIN, ITALY, AND PORTUGAL]

We crossed the river and reached a Spanish fort known as Fuenterrabia near
the small town of Irun. From there I continued to San Sebastian, which is a
port on the west sea, and from there I traveled by land to Madrid, the royal
residence of the Spanish sultan, and crossed to a city called Burgos, where I
found an Augustinian monastery. The altar inside the chapel contained the
cross of Jesus, which is known in Spanish as Cristo de Burgos. It has produced many miracles. I also found in a convent the tomb of the King Sis the
Armenian[?], which was called Onasi Taka [?]. The writing on the tomb was
in Armenian. As I continued, I crossed innumerable villages and cities until I
reached Madrid, the royal residence of the sultan. A queen was regent, the
wife of King Philip IV, for the king had died [in 1665] and had left a [four-
year old] child, named Carlos II.[23] I presented the queen with the letters of
the pope, Clement IX, so she ordered that I be given 1,000 piasters by the
governor of Sicily and 1,000 piasters by the governor of Naples.[24]

I took from her the order for the aforementioned money and left Madrid
to Italy. I entered the city of Aragon, and reached a city called Saragossa,
where Spanish kings are crowned and where they swear to preserve and govern by the ancient laws. I met there a brother of the king, called Don Juan de
Austria, a natural brother of the king, who received me courteously. Then I
went down toward the sea and to the city called Barcelona in Catalonia,
which is a port on the Eastern Sea. I sailed from there with the ships of the
sultan of Spain and after two days reached the port of Cadaqués, where coral
is harvested. We stayed there for twenty-five days because of rough storms in
the Gulfe du Lion; the crossing from there is very dangerous.

After the aforementioned time, on Sunday, we celebrated mass and later
that day we set sail. After a day and a night, we reached the port of Toulon in
France from where I continued to Rome. I met with my nephew, the deacon
Yunan [Jonah], who had finished his training and was intent on returning
home from Rome after the holy see had provided him with books and other

necessaries. I took him with me as we continued to Naples and presented the order of the sultana to her minister who governed there, who is known as Virreyes. He read it and answered, "Go to Sicily and get your 1,000 piasters." So I did and went to a city known as Palermo and to another governing minister of the sultana also known as Virreyes. I presented him with the order for 1,000 piasters, which he promised to fulfill. Two months later, he said that he could not give me the money. I then sent my nephew, deacon Yunan, back to Aleppo. When I realized that I had no hope of getting the 1,000 piasters from this hard-hearted man, despite all the difficulties of my journey, I returned to Naples to get my other 1,000 piasters from the first minister as he had promised me. But he too said, "Since the governor of Sicily did not give you the money, neither would I. I don't have any money."

Having lost hope, I returned to Spain in order to consult with the queen. So I went to Rome and from there to the port of Leghorn, and sailed to the aforementioned city of Barcelona. From there I continued to Saragossa, where I saw the above-mentioned brother of the sultan to whom I described my difficulties and losses because I had spent four hundred piasters in sailing to and fro. He felt sorry for me. I had as a companion a Catholic from Aleppo, who served me and whose name was Yusuf al-Fattal. Then I returned to Madrid and presented myself to the queen, who grew angry because her order had not been obeyed. After that, I left Madrid for the land of Portugal. At that time, the king [Affonso VI] had been exiled to the island of Isola Terceira, where he was kept a prisoner. The Portuguese had imprisoned him because of his imbecility and impotence: after being married to a woman for three years, it was determined that he had not consummated the marriage with his wife, and the pope agreed to their separation. As for this unhappy woman,[25] she was French and her first husband had been King Don Affonso [VI] but this, her second husband, was Don Pedro [her brother-in-law]. Although he had replaced Don Affonso, he was not called king but prince because his brother was still alive.[26] After he married her, they had a daughter. I went to this prince and conferred with him.

I stayed in this country for seven months and visited all its churches and monasteries. The inhabitants were good people, generous and devoutly Catholic. There are also New Christians from among the Jews who had converted to Christianity: they are known to everyone and they do not marry with Old Christians. Some of them are truly deniers of the religion of Christ. When they are discovered, the Inquisition condemns them to be burned.

The city of Lisbon is a seaport from where many ships sail to the East Indies and the lands of Guam, which are under Portuguese rule.

After staying seven months there, I returned to the aforementioned city of Madrid and lived in the house of the Duke de Ubro. He and his friends were very hospitable, and a lady by the name of Marquise de Losobles asked the sultan for permission to let me celebrate mass for him. I had a Catholic deacon whom I had taught to assist me in mass. So I went to the sultan's chapel and celebrated mass before him and his mother. After that, the queen ordered the sultan's attendant to acquire for me anything I requested. I asked for time to think, and I conferred with some friends who told me to ask for a permit and an irrevocable order to visit the West Indies. I did not really like that idea but I submitted to God, relying on His power, and requested the permit. For no stranger can cross to the West Indies if he does not have a permit from the sultan.[27] At that time, the papal nuncio in Madrid was Cardinal Mariscotti, a holy man who helped me with his advice and warned me about the monks of India because they were wicked.[28]

I received the permit from the queen, and some of my friends were happy for the blessing she bestowed on me.[29] The prince in whose house I was staying provided me with all I needed for travel; he also gave me letters of introduction to his friends. The permit from the queen was addressed to the minister as well as to the archbishops, bishops, and governors in all the lands of India and commanded them to offer me assistance. Relying on God and His mother the Virgin Mary, I left Madrid for Cadiz, which is a port on the ocean sea. After traveling twelve days by land, I arrived and saw the India ships ready for departure. In this commercial port assemble the cabinet members [of the Casa de Contratación] who oversee the affairs of the sultanate.[30] I presented them with the queen's permit, which they recorded, and they then gave me a pass.

On February 12, 1675 after Christ, I presented my permit along with the letters to the general of the galleon [*capitana*, admiral's brig], Don Nicholas de Cordova.[31] He liked me and welcomed me very courteously and asked me to choose any cabin on his ship. I had my belongings taken into the cabin and closed the door. I took with me from Cadiz a Catholic deacon who was born in St. Etienne because I had not been able to find anyone from my own country or denomination. I regretted very much having sent my nephew Yunan to the East. But regret could not change anything. Some of my friends warned me that once we reached India, the Catholic would "rebel and leave" me. Which is exactly what happened upon my arrival.

[THE ATLANTIC CROSSING]

On the aforementioned day, we set sail. There were sixteen galleons. They bid farewell to the port by firing their cannons, blowing their horns, and flying their flags and banners, with some of the travelers expressing joy while others were sorrowful for leaving their families. This convoy of ships leaves once every three years to the land of the Indies that is named Peru and is 1,500 leagues in the interior of Yenki Dunia. They bring from there the sultan's wealth at the same time that merchants load the galleys with all kinds of merchandise that they sell in that land. They do not permit any foreigner who is not a Spaniard to accompany them, be he a merchant or a priest, unless he has the sultan's approval, as we mentioned earlier. These are laws and canons [*Recopilación de Leyes de Indias*] that were set in the days of Charles V, a king of Spain and Hungary, under whose reign the Indies were conquered. These galleys return with gold and silver booty worth twenty or twenty-five million [piasters] with each million being worth ten *karrat*.

Three days after we left Cadiz, there was heavy turbulence at sea that lasted three hours. Traveling with us was a nobleman called Don Nicholas Anivante, agent to the king. He was so frightened that he died that very night. So the crewmen tied his feet with jars filled with water and cast him into the sea so he would sink and not float, and be eaten by fish. As they were casting him, they fired three cannon shots for him. The aforementioned was going to be the prelate of the *diwan* [council] of Quito. After eight days we approached islands called the Canaries, which are under Spanish rule. We sailed on, the wind toying with us, and halfway we met an English ship loaded with a cargo of black slaves. They were seven hundred in number and had been brought from Brazil, which is under Portuguese rule, to be sold in some of the islands of the Indies.

On the forty-fourth day [after leaving Cadiz], we saw one of the lands of the Indies. As we drew near, the ship captain started examining the water. When he and his crew saw that its color was different, they realized where they were because a big river from the land terminates in that region. The river [Orinoco] is forty leagues wide, and is so powerful and deep that it cuts into the sea for forty leagues. Its water mixes with the sea water so that there is no other river like it in the world. From there we saw a land called Caracas, and then passed near an island that belongs to Spain called Margarita, where twenty years before, we were told, divers dove for big and colorful pearls. One day, before they went diving, they vowed that the first pearl they found would be offered to the church of the Virgin. When they came up with a very valuable pearl, they regretted their vow and said, "Tomorrow's pearl will be offered to the Virgin." They said the same on the following day, and on the third day, too. On the fourth day, the divers went to sea as was their habit to look for pearls, but found nothing at all. Until today, they have not been able to find pearls in that part of the sea.

[Venezuela]

We return to our narrative. From there we sailed to a port called Cumana that belongs to Spain. From this port, people can walk by land into all of the sultanate of Peru, but what prevents them from so doing is their fear of the guerillas [*jalaliyya*], the high mountains, rivers, forests, and ferocious animals. For these reasons, they travel by sea. We anchored in that port and partook of the gifts and fruit that the governor sent us. Two days later, we sailed from that commercial port and passed by an island called Curaçao that belongs to the Hollanders. The governor of this island also sent us a boat full of fruit and alcoholic drink, and fired seven cannon shots from the fort. We returned the greeting with seven shots. From there we continued to an island called Tortuga, an uninhabited island full of turtles more than two arms in length and width. Seamen capture many of these turtles and then salt them for provisions. In this island, we found a small French ship, for this was the time of war between Spain and France.[32] Our convoy consisted of seventeen galleons. When the French saw that we had encircled them, they fled inland, leaving their ship unprotected. Our ships took theirs and found it full of salted turtles. As for the men who fled and left their ship behind, they had another ship on the other side of the island, around nine miles away. They went to that ship and two months later they filled a ship with men and cannons and took revenge on their enemies.

[Colombia and Panama]

We sailed from there to a city called Cartagena.[33] The journey had been pleasant because after fifty-five days we reached the aforementioned city where galleons anchor. We arrived on a holy day, the Thursday of Holy Easter. On the following day, Good Friday, we went on land to rest and were met with the processions that are held for Christ's passion. There are very rich people and a royal court in this city, along with churches, priests, monasteries, monks, and nuns. The people in this city are all Catholics and welcome strangers. They are pure Spaniards. The governor had been our friend and companion on the ship and upon arrival, he prepared for me a great and generous welcome. We remained in this city for forty days until postmen brought letters from Lima, which is the seat of the sultan's minister and of the rich traders of Peru. We then sailed from this commercial port to another called Portobelo, where much buying and selling takes place when the Peru merchants return from the South Sea [Pacific].

We waited for them for two months until they came bringing with them twenty five *lakks* of gold and silver.[34] For the next forty days, there was buying and selling between the Spaniards and the Indians, and among the Spanish merchants themselves. During that time, the aforementioned French ship appeared, and in one evening, the French freebooters silently came aboard the Spanish ships and seized the money that was there, a sum of 200,000 piasters. In the morning, when the news broke, the [Spanish] ships of war went after them, but could not find them. What was lost was lost. The aforementioned freebooters sailed away blowing their horns and beating their cymbals.

In this commercial port named Portobelo, there is a kind of insect that is smaller than the flea and known in the Indian tongue as *niguas*. If a person ignores this insect, it enters his body and after four or five days grows as big as a chick pea. The person then realizes the need to remove it which people do with a needle but without puncturing the insect. They then lay it on a flame of fire where it pops like a firecracker. If, while removing it, it is punctured and falls dead on a man's flesh and pops, it causes inflammation leading to death. There is also in that city the big [vampire] bat that comes at night to a sleeping man. It bites him and then begins sucking his blood and spitting it, while fanning him with its wings so he continues to sleep. It goes on sucking and spitting the blood until the person awakens, half-conscious as a result of the loss of blood. During the forty days that traders sold their merchandise,[35] we suffered from excessive heat and rain. When the sultan's treasury was brought to the city, the general told me to go and view it. I saw an incalculable amount of gold and silver.

After that, I wanted to sail to Santa Fé [de Bogota] where emerald is mined. From Cartagena it is possible to sail the river [Magdalena] up to the aforementioned region of mines. But the general of the galleons advised me against going, saying, "There are poisonous snakes in that region that kill people. The distance is also quite far. I advise you, for the love of God, not to go and get lost and die in that region."

So I heeded his advice and decided against going. Forty days later, we left Cartagena and sailed with the galleons. After twenty days, we reached the port of San Philippe de Portobelo. We anchored, awaiting the Peru ships that sail from the South Sea, which is known as Mar Sureno. They sail to the commercial port of Panama, a very pleasant place, where there is a military governor, along with a bishop, monasteries, monks, and nuns. From there to Portobelo, there are eighteen leagues of mountains and forests separating the North from the South Sea. The roads in this region are difficult; we will describe them later.

They loaded the king's treasury and the traders' merchandise on mules to Portobelo. The distance is three days, and the charge for the rental of a mule is thirty piasters. The trading period is for forty days, during which the galleon merchandise is traded. The king's treasury consisted of 25,000,000 *qurush*/piasters and each million is ten *karrat*, and each *karra* is a [hundred] thousand piasters. The money in this treasury is not all taken to Spain: part of it is used for paying the salaries of employees and soldiers guarding the islands and the forts in the regions of India that belong to the sultanate of Peru. Another part is used for paying the galleons and soldiers that serve the king. This anchorage lies in a very hot region and is infested with disease, but no major outbreak occurred that year. Still, around a thousand people died of both groups, and the rest fell sick. I too fell sick, but God healed me through the queen of saints, the Virgin Mary, and Saint Elias the Living [Mar Ilyas al-Hayy].[36] Meanwhile, the Spanish traders sold their merchandise to the Peruvian traders in return for gold and silver. The Peruvian traders went back while the galleons were loaded with gold, silver, and some merchandise such as taffeta wool (known as vicuña), and cocoa, which smells and tastes like coffee but is denser. They sail from this commercial port to Cartagena and from there continue to the island of Havana, which is a well-fortified island we will describe later.

I, the lowly, decided to accompany those traders to Peru and rented three mules for ninety piasters. But the governor did not want me to go alone because of the mountains where there is a kind of weed that is similar to thin reed. When a traveling white man steps on it, it shoots up from the earth, like an arrow, and cuts him—from which he cannot be cured and later dies. But it does not cut nor harm the Indians and the slaves. When the governor told me about it, I told him that I did not believe what he said until I saw it with my own eyes. So he sent his servant with me, a red man, to show me that weed. When we reached the spot where that weed grows, the servant came up to my horse and hid behind it. Suddenly, ten arm lengths away from the path, I saw this weed shoot up and come to strike me. Immediately, the red [Indian] came out and shouted, "Down you dog." As soon as he shouted, the weed fell to the ground. I saw all that with my own eyes. On this mountain, I saw tree branches of equal length but with no leaves. Each branch had three walnuts resembling cotton. If a walnut is opened, one can see a snow-white pigeon with its fully-grown wings, feet, wine-colored beak and black eyes. They call it the flower of the Holy Spirit. Many of the Spanish governors tried to grow it in Spain but failed.[37]

After leaving Portobelo, we came to a small river [Chagres] filled with rocks and very little water. We walked in it for three hours and then climbed to the mountain top to spend the night. The name of the inn was Port Cavron.[38] On the next day we continued traveling and stayed at another inn called Jaquery. From that inn we descended to the city named New Panama, because a year before, the Old Panama had burned down.[39] When I reached the city, I saw that all its buildings were made of wood. A day later, I stayed with the bishop of this city, whom I found to be a very saintly man and with whom I established such deep friendship that we became like brothers, I giving him my ring and he giving me his. The name of this honorable bishop was Don Antonio de Lyons. He gave me the small cane he used to carry in his hand.

I stayed in that city for a month and then boarded a ship and sailed the South Sea, which is known as the Blue Sea, heading for Peru. Opposite the commercial port of Panama was a small inhabited island known as Taboga, three leagues away from the aforementioned port. I met in the ship a good man known as Captain Francesco from the city of Trujillo. When we reached the island, and it was already two hours into the night, the captain invited me to join him on land because the governor of the island was his brother-in-law. So I agreed and went with him on a small raft made of five logs of wood. As we were drawing away from the ship toward land, the raft overturned in the darkness of the night and I fell in the water. I beat about and clung, with the cane that the bishop had given me, to the raft. And so, the Lord and his mother, the Virgin Mary, helped all three of us reach land safely. We stayed there for three days until our ship was loaded with drinking water. We then sailed, keeping land close to our north. As we were sailing we came across a place called *gorgone* [Isla Gorgona], which means "sea current." If a ship is caught in it, it can only get out with great difficulty and only after a stormy wind blows it out. Otherwise, all on board will starve to death.

[Ecuador]

Sailing in this sea is dangerous because of the rough waves. It is known as the sea of breaking waves because whoever sails into it will be lost, and whoever comes out of it is newborn. Had it not been for God's protection that helped us against its dangerous waves, we would have been trapped in it for a month.[40] But the Redeemer, exalted and praised be His name, made things easier until we reached the anchorage of Santa Elena, which means Saint Helen. We anchored there. I was in the company of three noble men, each of whom was going to be governor in a different place. After we reached land and stayed for five days, for fear of the dangers of the sea, we decided to take the land route, fully aware how exhausting the long paths are.

In that anchorage, I was told about an Indian man who was 150 years old. I decided to see him and found him in good shape and ancient of days. He started talking about old times and mentioned that one league away from the anchorage there is a big cave where giants are buried. He also told me that his father had told him that when the Spanish ships arrived and took possession of the land, the Indians thought that the ships were sea whales, and the sails were wings because that was the first time they had seen ships. When they saw the horses and their riders, they thought horse and rider were united together. When I heard about what had happened in the land, and about the buried giants, I decided to see with my own eyes.

I took with me twelve Indians, fully armed, and we headed to the cave about which the Indian had spoken. When we reached it, we lit our candles, afraid that we might get lost inside the cave. We entered with the candles in our hands, and at every ten steps we stationed a man with a light in his hand in order for us not to lose our direction. I led them with my sword drawn until I reached a spot covered with bones. I examined the bones and found them thick, while the skulls were very large. I pulled a tooth out of one of the skulls—a molar that was big and heavy, weighing a hundred *miskals*.[41] I also examined the leg bones and found that one measured five handspans. A painter in one of these regions estimated that the height of the body was twenty-five handspans. We then left the cave, amazed at what we had seen. I took with me the aforementioned molar.

We returned to the anchorage and rented horses and left with the Indians toward Guayaquil. It is an anchorage on the Blue Sea, four days away through forests, trees, and some small rivers. There is a dragon-like animal called caiman, just like an alligator. Its mouth is five handspans long, and its body is five arm lengths. If it encounters a human being, it will devour him, but it will not eat a dead person. It comes out of the river and scouts around; if it finds a living man or beast, it will devour them and run on its legs and arms, which are like the arms of lions. If a horse or an animal comes to drink from the river, it creeps up and attacks it, pulling it by its nose into the water, where it kills it. Other caimans then gather around and cut the animal in pieces and eat it. When dogs want to drink water, they first bark near the river bank whereupon the animal hears them and comes out to devour them. The dogs then flee, running toward another spot where they drink because they know that the caiman is where they had barked. This is how dogs outwit the caiman.

The Indians use two tricks to capture this animal. The first involves a reed of half an arm length. They sharpen both ends of it and tie a strong rope to its middle. They heat and harden it so that it becomes as piercing as a sword and as solid as lead. Then one of the Indians goes and sits near the river bank. When the animal comes out and sees the Indian, it attacks him, opening its mouth to devour him, whereupon the Indian thrusts the reed into its mouth, and keeps holding it. When the caiman snaps its mouth shut, the reed penetrates the two sides of its mouth; the more it bites, the more the reed penetrates into its flesh. The Indians then pull the caiman out from the river and try to turn it on its back to prevent it from walking. They then cut it up into pieces. The second trick by which they capture it involves one of the Indians going down into the river with a rope. He swims underwater until he reaches the caiman as it is floating on the water surface. He throws the rope on its back, and as he rubs the belly of the animal from underneath, he ties the rope around it. The Indian then quickly swims away from it, for this animal cannot devour anything underwater. When the Indian gets out of the river, the men gather together and pull the tied animal out of the water and kill it.

With my own eyes, I saw them capture two of them after a boy who had been with us on the raft was devoured by one of these animals. The boy was the servant of the village priest. The priest was very saddened and ordered the Indians to gather together and capture this animal. They captured two and opened up their bellies and found pieces of the aforementioned boy's body, which the priest took away and buried. There are many of these animals and on some occasions they come out of the river and lie on its bank with their mouths open to the wind. A small bird flies into the mouth and begins to peck the food residue from between the animal's teeth. When it has its fill, it flies away; the animal likes to have its teeth cleaned.

After four days, we arrived in the aforementioned Guayaquil. The city is inhabited by Indians and Spaniards who hosted us generously, especially the Dominican monks. After staying there for ten days, we left toward a village called Baba, which is inhabited by both Indians and Spaniards. It is a hot region, with orchards of trees like mulberry bearing a fruit called cocoa of which chocolate [*jikolata*] is made. This fruit is just like a watermelon that clings to the trunk of a tree. When it ripens it turns yellow whereupon they harvest it, opening up its inside from where they take the fruit—seeds rougher than peanuts—which they dry and then roast and crush. Cocoa resembles coffee in color, taste, and smell but is so dense that it turns into something like dough. They add to it some sugar, as much as is necessary, along with cinnamon and pure ambergris. They knead it into a dough which they cut up into discoid shapes and then dry in the shade. They then boil the chocolate and drink it like coffee. This fruit is used in all the lands of the Christians; they harvest it here and sell it.

We left that village toward Quito. We walked past another village called Poticas de San Antonio, where there is a kind of cane forty arm lengths in height and thicker than the clog in a weaver's loom. An arm length separates one knot from another. The canes are tied together and used for roofing houses. Some of those canes are full of white and sweet water, of which I drank. I then told the muleteer to cut up six knots full of water and load them on a mule. There are various kinds of wild animals on this road, like big and small monkeys in many shapes and colors. There are also birds like parrots that can talk, and another bird called *pacamaya* that resembles a big rooster but has marvelously colored plumes. We passed through a village called Quanlyo, and after four leagues, we entered a village called Ambato. We saw snow-covered mountains, from one of which volcanic fire erupts.[42] Some time ago, fire exploded from this mountain, like great thunder, and dust and soot so filled the air that neither sky nor sun was seen for two hours. After that, the clouds descended, burning all the grass on the face of the earth, polluting the rivers, and weakening the animals and infesting them with the plague.

We then continued to a village called Nisht, and from there reached another village called Latacunga, where there was a convent for Carmelite nuns. It had been built by a virtuous man, the bishop of Quito, who spent 225,000 piasters on its building. His name is Don Alonzo Bellamonte Nigra. Four Dominican monks came to welcome me in this village, having been sent by their abbot. They took me to Quito and lodged me in their monastery because their abbot had heard that I carried with me the letter of his confirmation from their general in Rome.

I rested at the monastery for two hours. When the governor of the city learned about my arrival and my stay at the monastery, he left his residence and came to see me, angrily chiding me for staying there. I said to him, "You know, my dear man, how the monks came out to meet me and brought me to their monastery. Inform the abbot and I will go to your residence."

The abbot would not let me go, so they agreed that I would spend the day and take lunch with the governor, and at night return to the abbot and stay in my cell with my servant. This good governor had traveled with me from Spain on the same ship. Whenever I was offered delicacies on the ship, I used to honor him with some. So we became true friends.

The city where the bishop lives is rich and full of churches and monasteries. The aforementioned bishop was very wealthy but also very stingy. The drinking water in the village is so foul that many people develop an enlarged gland under their throats. Both Indians and Spaniards live in this city where I spent two months. As for the aforementioned tooth, which I had extracted from the giant bones in the Santa Elena cave, it was borrowed by a man who had a daughter in the convent and who wanted to show it to her. Out of friendship, I handed him the tooth and when he showed it to the nuns, they juggled it from one hand to another until it was lost and I could not find it. The bishop declared a ban on them until they gave it back, but nothing happened.

There was in that convent a nun who had had a bleeding illness for eight years. When the bishop hosted me, he asked me about the benefit of the juice of the aforementioned canes. So I said, "I read in some books and understood that cane juice can help those who suffer from bleeding." So he asked me to give the nun some of that juice—which I did. She drank it for seven days and was cured of her ailment. In this city, I also saw people make broadcloth just like that manufactured in London.[43] They told us about a mountain there [Pichincha] that had spewed thunderous fire a few years earlier [1660]. The force of the fire discharged burning stones to a distance of forty leagues from the mountain.

They also mentioned that a few years earlier, while an Indian was tilling a field, he found a buried icon of the Virgin Mary. It was a marvel to see, and he took it to his house and hid in a trunk. On the following day, when he went to till the field, he found it there. Again, he took it home. On the third day, when he went to till, he again found it there. He repeated his action many times but could not keep it in his house. When the bishop of the city learned about it, he went in a procession to welcome it and bore it reverently to a place near the city where he built a magnificent church for it. The church is known as the Church of the Virgin Mary of Quinche, after the name of the village. People visit it from all regions, and whenever the plague infests the city, the people take the icon in a religious procession to the city of Quito where it is kept in dignity and respect for nine days. It is through this intercessor that the plague departs the city. The icon is then returned in a religious procession to its church in the aforementioned village.

The people also informed us that outside the city there is a twenty-four-league road that leads to a river that descends from the mountains. When the river floods, it brings sand mixed with gold. Many people know when the river floods and go to pan for gold and separate it from sand. The gold is quite special. So I decided to see with my own eyes, but people advised me against taking that road because of its great difficulty. So I desisted although I bought some of that gold in Quito. After staying two months in the city, I left toward a village named Otavalo, above which is a planetary thread known in the *ifranji* [French] language as *linea* [equator]. The villagers there have no skin color and have bloated stomachs. They told us that sometimes birds fall dead from the sky. There is no shade except under a tree, and the sun is relentless. They also reported that twenty-five leagues away from Quito, there are infidel Indians to whom priests go and preach about Christ. From that region, the priests brought the seeds of the cinnamon tree. But no people know better how to grow and care for it than the Indians (the cinnamon that comes from the East Indies burns [the palate])—and the Indians do not want the Spaniards to know about it for fear that they would take their land. They also reported to us that there is nutmeg that the Indians collect and which is green and as big as an olive. They send it to Caracas, where it is sold to the English and the Hollanders, but not to the Spaniards. There was much rain and lightning in this village.

I returned to Quito and then left to the aforementioned village of Latacunga and then to the aforementioned Ambato which is ten leagues from Quito. I continued to Riobamba, which is a city of beautiful buildings, elegant churches, and wealthy nobles. I stayed at the Dominican monastery, where I was received with great joy and welcome. I celebrated mass there. The rite of the mass among this monastic order is similar to ours, so the monks were happy to participate in my celebration. After staying there for eight days, I left to a city called Cuenca, which we reached after seven days.

The road was mountainous and covered with snow. The mountains are known as the Paramo Mountains because of the excessive cold there.[44] A river descends from the mountains where the infidel Indians live. They reported that a few years earlier, the Indians built five small flat-bottomed boats and came down until they reached the road, which the Spanish traders used. While the traders were passing through with their merchandise, the aforementioned Indians attacked them, whereupon the traders fled for fear of death, leaving their possessions behind. The Indians opened the merchandise, took what they wanted, and left gold discs in return. The owners then returned and took the gold.

Upon reaching this city of Cuenca, I fell sick and stayed in bed under physicians' care for ten days. The healer of the sick, the Virgin Mary, gave me back my strength. The governor of that city was my friend because we had traveled together on the ship from Spain. He wanted to celebrate my recovery, a celebration they call in Spain the "feast of the bull." The people fence in a plaza with wooden boards and they lay tables on top of other tables in the shape of a ladder. The people gather and sit on these tables, renting each for the duration of the show. Afterward, a wild bull that had been locked up is led into the plaza. Upon its sudden release, it runs around frightened, unable to find an exit. Then, a horseman moves up against it with a lance in his hand, and taunts the bull. When the bull attacks him, he runs back and then kills the bull. Sometimes the bull kills the horse and its rider with the force of its horns. This celebration is held annually in all the sultanates and posessions of Spain.

[PERU]

I left there to the village of Loja. The road was difficult because rain fell day and night for three days. We reached it and I rested for a day and a night because of the cold and the heavy rains. On the following day, I left for the mountains, where there are gold mines, to a village called Sullana. For three days, we followed a very difficult path between the mountains. I reached the aforementioned village, which is on top of the mountain and surrounded by the gold mines. I observed all the ways used to extract gold from ore. First, they crush the ore by means of a water mill. Then they rinse the crushed ore and sift out the gold. They then melt it and pour it into discs. I bought four hundred miskals of that gold because not all the mills were operating. After ten days, I wanted to continue my journey, but the priest of that village pointed me to another road, saying, "There is another and a better road than the one you took. But it is devoid of people and villages. You need to take provisions with you for five days."

I heeded his advice, and carried with me what I needed, and I took two companions—I mean muleteers—an Indian and a *mestizo*, which means "of mixed blood," the mother being Indian and the father Spanish.

We followed a rough road for a day and a night. Satan wanted to tempt that mestizo muleteer because he had planned to kill me. But God the exalted exposed his plan at the hands of my servant. So I took his weapons from him and remained wary until we reached three contiguous villages, the first called Basilica, the second Jonjonama, and the third Wakanama. When the villagers who were Indians saw me, they wondered at me, saying, "How did you travel through these rough paths? Either you are a prophet or a saint." Their priests are also Indian like them, but the Indians of these regions do not have beards, only a few hairs in their chins. Because I had a full beard, they marveled at me, saying that I had great courage for having traveled that path.

On the following day, we left to a village called Amotapé. That night, as I was sleeping in my tent, the companions of the aforementioned two [muleteers] plotted to kill me. I had an Indian boy with me who knew Spanish. At night, he had woken up and heard them plotting. Shaking with fear, he ran and woke me up, and reported what he had heard. By God's grace, a mule broke loose that night and fled into the mountains. The two companions of the aforementioned mestizo ran after it all night and returned with it at sunrise. At that point, I took away their weapons from them because I had no weapons myself. And fearing their treachery, I took the sword in my hand and called the mestizo and said, "Kneel down and confess to me how Satan tempted you to such a deed. Tell me the truth." So he confessed, asking me for forgiveness. After five days, we reached the aforementioned village. Just before entering the village, however, the two traitors ran away, leaving their mules behind, whereupon the village priest came to welcome me. I told him about all that had happened to me. He said, "God has saved you, because it was in that same path that my brother was murdered."

Near this village runs a river called Colan which has a lot of fish, just like the Tigris. That day I crossed it to a village of Indians called Colan. I stayed at the priest's house and it happened that it was the evening of the feast of St. James, the brother of the Lord [July 25, 1676]. The priest invited me to celebrate mass on the following day and promised that all the offerings would be given to me. So I celebrated mass on the next day and all the Indians attended—all four thousand of them. After mass was over, I sat on the chair and prepared a miracle, I mean the blessed bread. People came up to me, kissing my hand, taking the blessing, and putting an offering in the tray. When everything was finished, I counted 280 piasters of offerings.

Two days later, I wrote to the governor of Piura to send me a litter, which is *litera* in Spanish. This governor and his family had traveled with me on the ship from Spain. As soon as he received my letter, he sent the litter, for in that region, travelers on horseback get very tired as a result of heat and sand. We crossed to an anchorage on the bank of the river Paita, which is two leagues away from Colan. From there we traveled at night fourteen leagues to a city called Piura. I stayed at the house of the governor, who received me with great hospitality. The inhabitants of this city are both Spaniards and rich Indians. It has beautifully decorated churches.

I was told that fifteen years earlier, there was an Indian nobleman known as *cacique*.[45] He was rich and had only one daughter. One day, after he had left for another city, the aforementioned daughter saw a Franciscan monk in shabby clothes. So she said to him, "Why are you dressed in these unworthy clothes?"

He answered, "Because of my extreme poverty and need."

She said, "If you can keep a secret, I will give you what will enrich you."

He said, "Yes, I can."

The girl promised him that when night fell, she would meet him at a specific place from where she would take him to her father's cave, which was outside the city. She took the monk to the cave, after blindfolding him and leading him like a sightless man. When they reached the cave, she gave him as many gold discs as he could carry, then led him back to the city and removed the blindfold and sent him away. After her father returned from his journey, he went to the cave. There he saw footprints and realized that none other than his daughter had divulged his secret. He gave her poison, of which she died, and soon after, he died too. Until today, people are still searching for the cave, but have not found it.

After staying there ten days, I left to a village called Illimo. We followed a deserted waterless path, covered with sand, like the earth of Egypt. All the inhabitants of this village were Indians, but their priest was Spanish. Some of the Indians were true Christians, but others were Christians out of fear. On the following day, I went to a city belonging to the Indians called Lambayeque, a big city inhabited by rich Indians and some Spaniards. The bishop's assistant invited me to his house and asked me to celebrate mass on

Sunday, and to preach to the Indians in Spanish. I celebrated mass on Sunday, and preached to thirty-five priests and about three thousand souls from the common people. They were greatly enlightened by my preaching and marveled at me because of my beard and my different vestments. All welcomed me and came up to me for blessing especially because I gave them rosaries and crosses from Jerusalem. Five days later, I left to a city called Sana, a big city of Indians and Spaniards. Near this city, a big river runs. Because of the excessive heat, I used to travel at night, sitting in the *litera*, I mean the litter.

One night, the muleteer became sleepy and the mules wandered off into a forest. The forest was huge, into which one could enter but not exit. When I realized what had happened, I told my servant to stop there lest we get lost and die as had happened to others before us. In the morning, I told the Indian muleteer to start a big fire with thick smoke. Meanwhile our fellow travelers had preceded us to the house. When we were late, they realized that we had lost our way and so they sent some people to search for us. I told the muleteer to climb a high tree and hang a white flag, I mean a banner. On the next day, around noon, the searchers found us after seeing the banner. They were angry with the muleteer for having lost his way.

The trees in that forest are cotton trees, and have no owners. The cotton is rough, and is as big as pomegranate. It has small strong seeds but the cotton thread is long like wool. Whenever the Indians are in need, they go and collect as much cotton as they want and weave clothes and other necessaries for the women. Two days later, we reached the aforementioned city inhabited by Spaniards and Indians. The governor is called "general." We stayed there for four days, generously honored by the governor and the assistant bishop. Then I left to a city called Trujillo. We spent ten days on a rough road with little water and food. I had taken provisions of food and drink and had a horse and a mule with me. Whenever it was cool, I used to ride on them until I got tired, whereupon I would go back to the litter.

I got to that aforementioned city, which is a big city where the bishop had died and left his seat vacant. There were Dominican and Franciscan monks in the city, along with the Jesuits of Saint Ignatius.[46] There were also priests and about two thousand monks. The Franciscan monks invited me to celebrate mass with them. It was the feast day of St. Francis, which always falls on the fourth of October [1676]. I was pleased to do so in a church that was full of people. They rejoiced in my celebration because I had the vestments that our sayyid the pope had given me, with his seal and insignia on them.

People came to be blessed by them. After staying for ten days in this city, I left for the city of Cajamarca, which is at the mountaintop and had once been inhabited by the king of the Indians known as Inca. We shall speak about this great king [later].

I stayed there for three days and I was shown all that had happened to that king and how the Spaniards had killed him. On the fourth day, I left this city for Lima, where the minister of the sultan who governs the country lives. I descended the mountain toward the aforementioned city and after four days reached a river called Sana. This is a high river without a bridge that people cross with great fear. The Indians had invented something for crossing the river called *balsa*, which means raft. They collect dry pumpkins and tie them together into a raft; then they cover them with wood and on the wood they lay weeds and tree branches. Then, they load luggage and transport people across. The animals cross the river swimming. We crossed the river in fear, reciting prayers and devotions to God and His mother the Virgin Mary. We then continued until we reached farms of sugar cane, wheat, and Egypt corn, and factories for the manufacture of broadcloth. Two poor men who were accompanying me were one-handed: one, a soldier had lost his hand in fighting the Indians; the other man had been bitten by a snake, as a result of which his hand had been amputated.

After eight days, we reached the aforementioned city of Lima and I stayed at the house of the inquisitor, I mean, the head of the council of religion because he had been my friend since Spain. I had lent him the sum of 1,400 piasters in Portobelo, so he gave me forty piasters interest on every hundred, just as the traders do in this country. After resting from the trip, I went to visit the minister and I presented to him the sultan's letter and other letters I had brought with me from Spain. This minister was an honorable man whose name was Don Baltazar de la Condada de Castilla, Marquis de Marañon. He was a Spanish dignitary. He embraced me with great joy and promised to help me in all my needs. I then went to meet his wife, who received me with great welcome. This honorable minister had been married for fourteen years but had not had a child. We shall tell his story later.

I then went to visit the chief friar, who is called "archdeacon" along with the other friars who were assembled in church for prayer. The archbishop of this city had died and his seat was still vacant.[47] This bishopric enjoys an annual income of 50,000 piasters and is served by 120 priests who were all awaiting the new archbishop, who was on his way from Spain. After staying ın this city for twenty days, I fell seriously sick and was confined to my bed, where I was treated by the minister's doctors. The Lord cured me after twenty days through the intercession of the mother of mercy, the Virgin Mary. I went to see the minister again who embraced me with happiness, dignity, and hospitality. During my sickness, he used to send his servant with excellent sweets and inquired about me twice a day. Once, a miner approached him saying that he could extract silver from ore without adding mercury [quicksilver]. When the idea was tried, it failed, and everyone realized that the whole thing was a hoax. I was a witness and saw everything with my own eyes.

Before the Spaniards took possession of this land, none knew the true God. Some [Indians] worshiped idols while others worshiped the sun, moon, and stars. They did not have an alphabet nor did they know how to read or write. When they wanted to petition their sultan, they traced pictures on a handkerchief describing their complaint. During the conquest [*fat-h*]of this land,[48] there were two sibling sultans, one known as Atahualpa and the other Hascarinca.[49] They were at war with each other, fighting with bows and arrows, spears, and slingshots. They did not have livestock, I mean, like horses, mules, donkeys, bulls, cows, goats, or chicken. The only animal there looked like a camel but was the size of a donkey with a hump in its chest. They ate its meat, and used it as a beast of burden despite it not being able to travel far. It could only travel four leagues a day and no more, and when it became tired, it slept and spat on its owners. When an Indian died, the Indians built him a tomb two arm lengths high, and three arm lengths in width and placed inside it the tools of his trade and some corn wine.

Violent earthquakes occur in this city. The minister promised to help me as long as I was in India, and he wrote demanding of all the cities and villages under his authority that they offer me welcome. There are numerous monasteries and churches in Lima, the foremost being the big church [cathedral] that is the seat of the archbishop; there are other churches for priests, four monasteries for the monks of Saint Francis and four for St. Dominic, three monasteries for the monks of St. Augustine, three Jesuit monasteries, three Mercedarian monasteries, four convents each housing a thousand nuns [?], four convents for the poor such as the orphans and widows, and two monasteries of St. John that attend to the sick, I mean, the strangers and the poor. There was also a hospital, meaning a large *maristan* named after the sultan,[50] St. Andrew, because he endowed it. They invited me to celebrate mass in the all churches and monasteries, and always welcomed me heartily.

I stayed in this city for a year in the house of the aforementioned head of the council of religion known as Don Juan Bautista de la Cantera, which means John the Baptist from the city of Cantera. This honorable man was a priest and did not allow me to spend anything on food and drink. The city is very expensive and a chicken costs one and a half piasters. After I recovered from my sickness, all the monks, known as the *capildo*, which means the chapter, came to see me. They led me in a religious procession to the church where the archbishop and priests preside, and after we entered the church, and in order to honor me, they offered me a seat near the archdeacon's seat, which is near the archbishop's seat. They asked me to celebrate mass, so I sent for my vestments and I celebrated mass for them in Chaldean, which means the eastern Syriac, in which they were very pleased. The next day, they held a council and sent me a thousand piasters; similarly, after celebrating mass, the rest of the churches and monasteries of monks and nuns sent me presents. I had a coach with four mules and a black slave for a servant.

After a year, I asked for permission from the minister to go to the mountains of silver. He approved my request and wrote me letters of introduction to all the governors of the regions and to the bishops of the villages under his authority. He asked them to offer me generous welcome and sent one of his soldiers ahead of me on the road to prepare food and drink, and to arrange for me to stay at every village governor's house. I Left Lima with this man in my company to a city called Huancavelica and then walked for two days on a good road. On the third day, we climbed the mountain of snow. The wind became extremely cold, as a result of which our health immediately deteriorated, and we started throwing up because we had left a very hot region and too quickly gone to a cold one.[51] When we reached the top of the mountain, we walked from a place called Puna de Briakaka, which means the "sugar bitter cold," and after two leagues, I met the abbot of the Franciscan monks, who is called the "provincial." He asked me about the road we had taken, so I told him what had happened to us after which he left us and took another road. That day we reached a river called Boni with a bridge on it extending from one bank to another. The bridge was made of hemp rope and tied to trees. We crossed it with great difficulty as others took the horses and went down with them into the river. After ten days, we reached the aforementioned small town of Huancavelica where I stayed at the Jesuit monastery. In this region, the wind changes thrice every day, and rain always falls in the afternoon. The soil is not fertile because of the constant wind change and because of the mountain, which has mercury in it and overlooks the city.

I went with the city governor to view the mine. I saw the mine and all its glory. I saw the laborers digging for ore and carrying it from below the earth to the surface. To show me how they extracted mercury from ore, they took me to a house that had rows of holes in its floor, all very near to each other, in each of which was a small copper jug. The jugs, just like stone urns, had one opening at the top, and a closed one at the bottom. They place the mercury ore on the jugs in the way that the potter lays his pottery in a row. The house has a very high ceiling full of holes to let the smoke out. They place wood on the stones and start a fire that heats the mercury ore to such a degree that the mercury escapes down into the jugs. When the mercury handlers see that, they extinguish the fire and leave the mercury for a day and a night until it cools. They remove the stones and cinder and throw them away, then pour the mercury from the jugs. Meanwhile, there is a royal agent who oversees this whole process and pays the miners fifty-two piasters for each quintal (and the quintal of this country [weighs as much as] six sultan[ic coins]). The royal agent then sells the quintal to the silver miners for ninety piasters so that silver can be extracted from ore. We will speak about that [later], too.

I celebrated mass for them on an altar inside the mine, and I blessed them and their mines. The mine investors offered me a present of fifty quintals of mercury and told me to wait a month until they extracted the mercury from the rock, after which they would give me its value in money. But because of changing winds, I was afraid to stay and so I left an agent there to receive the mercury as soon as it was extracted. But there is an order from the king prohibiting mine owners from selling mercury and anybody from buying it. If anybody transgresses, his possessions will be confiscated and he will be executed.

There is in this city a kind of yellow-colored water that is stored in containers for eight days in the open. It then solidifies and turns into stone from which the inhabitants build their houses. I saw it with my own eyes. If they put a piece of wood in that water and leave it for forty days, the part in the water turns to flint, while the other part above the water remains as it was. A Jesuit gave me a cross made of that material as a present.

After ten days, I left this city accompanied by fourteen men who stayed with me until we reached the outer limits of the city from where they returned. I followed the road leading to a city called Guamanca. There were different kinds of trees on this road, most of them known as *teca*, with leaves as thick as two hand palms and without branches. The leaves are thorny and each leaf grows a fruit at its edge. It is known by the Indians as *tonos*. The fruit is as big as a chicken egg but harder, and its inside tastes as sweet as mulberry. It is a coolant and a laxative. The fruit is covered with soft thorns so one should not handle it until after cleaning it of the thorns. The wilderness and the mountains are full of the fruit.

After four days, we arrived at the aforementioned city and stayed at the Jesuit monastery because the head [of the Jesuit order] was a virtuous man who had written the monks telling them to accommodate me. The city had a very wealthy bishop because he had formerly been the head of the council of religion. His name was Don Christopholo del Castillo. After staying in the monastery for that night, two priests came to welcome me on behalf of the bishop. Early the next morning I went to visit him. He came down to welcome me, and asked me about myself, and then invited me to his house for lunch—an invitation I accepted. After eating, he gave me a gold chain worth two hundred piasters. When the city dignitaries heard about how the blessed bishop had honored me, they all came to visit me. Four days later, I went out with two Jesuit monks to return their visit as is the custom in that land. The bishop then sent me four priests to take me to the houses of those who had visited me because the Jesuits had written the names of each one of my visitors. There are in this city very rich churches and monasteries. After I had visited them and rested for eight days, the bishop ordained that a comedy [play] be presented, which means a reenactment of the saintly [life of the] Roman man of God who is known in the *ifranji* language as St. Alexis and in Arabic as Mar Risha. This comedy offers a representation of what this saint did in giving his ring to his bride, breaking through the wall, and then wandering the earth.[52] We attended this representation and enjoyed it. The people of this city honored me very much because the minister was my very good friend. I stayed in the city for twenty days and was very happy.

From there, I left to a city called Cusco. The governor of the city, the Jesuit provincial, and others walked out to bid me farewell. We traveled for half a league, after which we parted and they returned to the city. I continued on my journey and after two days, we reached a river called Apurimac. Less than one arm length in width and twenty in length, a bridge made of tree branches stretched across the river. We crossed it carefully and with great fear while the Indians took the luggage off the mules and carried it on their backs one after another. They then took the gear off the mules and led them on the bridge. If the foot of a mule was caught between the wooden planks of the bridge, they untied the planks, whereupon the mule fell into the water, and swam to the other side. It took great effort to cross the bridge because it shook and swayed like a crib whenever anyone stepped on it.

When we reached the other side, we thanked the redeemer for our safety. The Indians knew how to swim, and if they fell, they came out alive.

From there we continued our journey and saw various kinds of animals, such as wild horses and stallions, cows, antelopes, mules, donkeys, and many others. They graze in these mountains without owners. There was also another animal [called vicuña, which is like a deer but with no horns].[53] It is a very friendly animal and whenever it sees people or beasts crossing through, it descends from the mountains to observe them. Their numbers are high. I had with me a rifle and hunting dogs, so I killed one of these animals, but their meat is only eaten by the Indians. Their wool is as soft as silk from which caps, that is *shabaqat*,[54] are made; the wool is similar to taffeta but has the honey color of deer. In the stomach of this animal, between its kidneys, there is the bezoar stone which is taken out and sold for a high price because of its efficacy against poisons.

Three days later, we reached a sugar cane plantation in a region called Jabantai. The plantation belongs to the Jesuits, who produce annually 30,000 *khandakary* [5,000 quintals] of sugar. The laborers who till the ground are all black slaves; they also work in the production of sugar. From there we continued to the aforementioned city and reached it after three days. This city used to be the seat of the sultan of the Indians known as Atahualpa, brother of the aforementioned sultan Hascarinca. When we drew near and the Jesuit monks heard about us, they came out and welcomed me to their monastery. The monastery had once been the aforementioned sultan's palace; with its orchard, it fills up half the city. The convent of the nuns is inside the palace, too. We found there stone blocks that the ancient Indians had carved without using iron tools. The carved decorations were very beautiful. The dwellings of the city consisted of four thousand Spanish houses and three thousand Indian houses. There was a revered bishop and many orders of monks; there were also schools for the children of the Spaniards and a school built by the Jesuits for the children of the Indians.[55]

A mile before the city, two priests came out to meet me on behalf of the bishop, the governor, and the aforementioned Jesuits. They led me into the city. The bishop had planned for me to stay with him, but the Jesuits would not hear of it. The governor, too, had wanted me to stay at his house, but I declined the offer of both the bishop and the governor who was my friend and who had accompanied me from Spain. Upon reaching Lima, the aforementioned governor got married to a girl who brought him [a dowry of] 150,000 piasters in cash: it is the custom in the lands of the Christians for the bride to give money to the bridegroom in accordance with her status. On the following day, the bishop of the city came to see me, accompanied by all the dignitaries and abbots. Four days later, I went with two Jesuit monks in my coach and returned their visit.

Then they asked me to celebrate mass in the big church in the presence of the bishop, the priests, the dignitaries, and the common people. So I did, using the eastern Syriac language. The communities of the monasteries and the churches repeatedly came to ask me to celebrate mass for them. I had two deacons helping me with my mass. I was viewed with dignity and reverence and received presents from the convents and from other places. The council of priests in the big church sent me a worthy gift and so too the bishop who sent me a gift of the same value. Other notables and abbots came to visit me too, and four days later, I accompanied two Jesuit monks in a coach to return the visits. [Then they asked me to celebrate mass in the big church in the presence of the bishop, the priests, dignitaries, and the common people. So I did, using the eastern Syriac language.][56] The nuns in the convents also sent me a worthy present.

Some of the friends had offered me a coach to take me to the outskirts of the city to view the buildings of the ancient Indians. Among what I saw were Indian graves: during their days of infidelity, the Indians buried their dead above ground, and constructed a very high tomb, two arm lengths in height, one and a half in width and three in length. These tombs were separated from each other, each lying in a different location.

During my stay, a violent earthquake struck two leagues out of the city. There was a mountain standing above a running river that, as a result of the earthquake, collapsed into the middle of the river and blocked the water course. Water flooded the ground and destroyed the farms of three villages. At the same moment and hour that the mountain collapsed, an earthquake struck in the aforementioned city of Lima and people fled the city in fear because many houses and some churches collapsed. During my stay, a decree from the Spanish sultan ordered the removal of my friend the minister from office. I stayed five months in this aforementioned city of Cusco because of the winter season and the impassability of the rivers.

After the aforementioned period, I left the city to another, called Paucartambo, which we reached in six days—each night of which I slept in a different village. When I entered the city, people came out with the Dominican monks and the city governor to welcome me and they led me into the city and to the house of the governor where I stayed. He was under the authority

of the minister my friend. This city serves as a buffer, meaning a border between the infidel Indians and the Spaniards. Sometimes, the infidels descend onto the roads and seize as many Spanish men, women, and children
as they can and carry them into their regions, where they enslave them; and
when they have a feast or banquet, they slaughter one of the Spaniards,
roast, and eat him. Those Indians have a kind of weed, which when it is
chewed, turns them into drunks and imbues them with courage and
strength, just like wine. This weed is called coca. They do not have wheat or
barley, only Egypt corn, which they turn into an alcoholic drink on which
they get inebriated. Those Indians are numerous in number and ferociously
strong; the Spaniards are unable to fight them because the Indians inhabit
high mountains and have an intelligent and able prince who rules over them.

Three days later, I left this city to the silver mine known as Condoroma,
which we reached in two days. Because of the intense cold and wind, I could
not stay for more than three days, after which I traveled to another mine
known as Cailoma, a day's journey near a village where silver is mined. There
we observed how they mined for silver—how they crushed ore into sand and
added water, turning everything into clay. After that, they poured mercury
into the mix, and stirred it all day for ten or twelve days as the mercury collected the silver and adhered to it. After the aforementioned days, they
washed it in a large trough covered with cowhides, where the water took the
sand away as the silver sank to the bottom. I watched all this with my own
eyes.

From there I left to a village called Lampa, which I reached in two days. I
saw the Indians there building a new church. Their priest was Spanish, and
had been there for thirty years. He is very wealthy and has spent 200,000 piasters on building the church. I stayed there that night, and left on the following day to another mine called Puno. The owner of the mine was a very
rich man called (the late) Don José Selsido, which means Joseph of the city
of Seville. The silver tithes he gave to the king equaled 2,700,000 piasters. It
was reported that his daily income from this mine was 6,000 piasters [worth
of silver].

Some of his enemies envied him and started maligning him and accusing
him of plotting, with some people, to become the sultan of the city. They reported him to the minister, who came over to the mountain known as the
Puna Mine, and seized the aforementioned man and took him to Lima.
There he hanged a few of this man's associates, and seized their money; he
also confiscated the mine for the sultan and took charge of the silver ore,

which had been dug out from the mine and which weighed 10,000 quintals. The minister put Don José in jail and condemned him to death. So this maligned man said to the minister, "Take my case before the sultan in Spain. If he orders my execution, do so, and if he orders my release, free me. I will pay all that I had agreed on paying [during my interrogation]. Here I am, locked up in your jail [unable to leave]."

The minister and the council ignored him and confirmed his death sentence because of their greed. Meanwhile, all the monks, nuns, orphans, widows, and the poor of the villages and the adjacent regions were appealing to God for his safety because he used to give annually 80,000 piasters in charity. But the hard-hearted minister ordered him strangled in the middle of the night. After killing him, they brought in the [silver] masters to melt the ore and extract the silver. As soon as they put the ore in the fire, a miracle of God happened whereby the silver turned into cinder. This was a great and wondrous deed for both lookers and hearers. As for the mine from which they dug out the silver ore, it was flooded and they had to shut it down—which was a second miracle.

Fifteen days later, the minister who had viciously murdered Don José saw the ghost of the unjustly murdered man standing in the doorway as he entered his bedroom. As soon as he saw it, he grew terrified and started shaking. When his wife asked him what the matter was, he told her what he had seen and collapsed in bed. Six days later he died. This was viewed by both lookers and hearers as a third miracle. A few days later, the judge, who had condemned him to death, became paralyzed in both his arms and legs. This was a fourth miracle. For the murdered man was charitable and kind, as we have already mentioned, and his alms countless. He was like a father to orphans and widows, kind to the poor and the needy, always making donations to monasteries. He also used to help poor girls get married [by providing them with dowry].[57] All his life, he performed good deeds; even during Passion Week, he sent 70,000 piasters with his brother to the aforementioned city of Cusco for distribution among the churches and the poor.

While he was alive, and shortly before he was murdered, a poor man with many children who had been with him on a ship from Spain went to him and told him about his poverty and his big family. When Don José realized that he had been his fellow passenger, he felt kindly toward him and called his financial manager and gave him the keys to the safe, and said to him, "Lead this needy man to the safe and leave him there to take as many bars of silver as he wants."

When the man found himself in the safe, he took twelve bars, each of which was worth 1,300 piasters, and departed, thanking the benefactor for his generosity. The rich man asked his manager, "How many bars did that needy man take?"

He answered, "Twelve."

So he turned to the needy man and said, "Poor man, why did you not take more than twelve?" The man thanked him for his generosity and left. Many similar deeds of incredible charity are told about him.

Don José had a brother who went into hiding after the murder. When a new minister came to govern in that region, he presented the case of his unjustly murdered brother to the sultan. The sultan and his court were very disturbed because Don José had had a lucky star and had helped the poor and the needy, and had contributed to the sultan's treasury. The sultan ordered that the minister give the brother who had gone into hiding 50,000 piasters from the sultan's treasury, and grant him permission to reopen his brother's mine.

As for me, I did not meet the murdered man while he was alive, but I became very friendly with his brother, Don Caspar de Selsido. He labored hard with a hundred men to empty the water out of the mine. One day, he said to me, "Dear friend, why are you in such a hurry to return to Spain? Wait for a year until the mine is cleared, and I will give you of the silver that God provides."

But I could not stay because of my friend, the dismissed minister, who was intent on returning to Spain. That was the reason.

After we left this mine, we went to a city called Chucaito, where the governor was the nephew of the sultan's counselor and had traveled with us from Spain. He is Don Andres de Bernaya from Viscaya. Four days later, we reached the city and saw the sultan's silver-melting operation. There were craftsmen and supervisors sent by the sultan to collect the silver that is mined from the areas around that city. They bring the silver, melt and pour it into bars and stamp it with the sultan's seal. If any man takes away silver dust that has not been melted, it is seized and deposited in the sultan's treasury.

On one side of this city there is a lake, Titicaca, sixty leagues in circumference. I was told that the Indians threw into the lake a gold chain that had belonged to the aforementioned Inca sultan when the Spaniards killed him. The chain was so heavy that four thousand men were needed to carry it. When the sultan organized contests, the chain was laid on the ground around the city after which the nobles of the sultan came in and played, and who ever fell on the chain or outside it was laughed at. The Spaniards do not know in which side of the lake it was thrown. In those days, the Indians did not have money, but traded by barter.

In the lake, there is an island, two leagues in size, that used to be inhabited by infidel Indians who worshipped a mountain standing in front of them called the Red Mountain. None could cross over to them because they had weapons such as spears, arrows, and slingshots. They used to foray into the mainland, capture Spaniards, and seize male mules, which they slaughtered and ate. My friend, the aforementioned minister, ordered the governors of the villages in those regions to a meeting. Four thousand men came together and built forty rafts, which they loaded with bags of sand and some horses. They then took their weapons in their hands and crossed the lake on the rafts. As they were approaching the island, the Indians prepared to fight them and began shooting arrows at them while the Spaniards fired bullets at them. The Spaniards threw the sandbags on the island shore so that horses would avoid the deep mud. When they landed, they got on their horses and attacked the Indians and defeated them, killing a large number of them, and capturing the rest—three hundred Indians, excluding the women and children. Six hundred Indians died in the fighting. They took the Indians away from the island to the city of Cusco, where the minister asked the bishop there to instruct them in Christian doctrine, baptize them, and then disperse them around the country.

I stayed there for eight days, after which I left to a village called Pomata, two days away. There was an Augustinian monastery there with an icon of our Lady the Virgin Mary known as Copacabana; people came to see it from all regions because it performed great miracles. I went and visited the glorious queen and received her blessing. I then left to a village called Barnicillia but was followed by four robbers who wanted to take my horses and mules. But the Virgin blinded their eyes and God did not allow them to fulfil their goal. The governor of that city was my friend and his name was Don Elias, just like mine. He came out to welcome me, accompanied by some priests and commoners, and he took me to his house. On the following day, the priest of the Indians came and said, "In this governor's jail, there are seven Indians who are held for minor deeds." So I went down to the jail with a paper, on which their names had been written. I called the jailer and told him to open the door, which he did. I called them out, one after another outside the jail, and freed them. When the governor heard what happened, he said,

"What you did is acceptable. You have honored us by coming here."

Half a league near this village, there is a high mountain that has a mine producing glass-like marble. From this marble, the governor wanted to build a pigeon roost with a small dome. He decided to put marble blocks in crates and send them to the sultan of Spain, but he died before he could finish his work.

[BOLIVIA]

Eight days later, I left the aforementioned city to another called Sicasica. The governor there was one of the children of my friend to whom I had lent 2,000 piasters in Lima. So he came out to welcome me. Near the road, there was a lake of half a league where we hunted a variety of game until evening. Then we entered the aforementioned city with great festiveness and went to the governor's house, where all the monks and common people came to see me. The inhabitants of this city are both Indians and Spaniards.

They mentioned a priest in that city who had died four years earlier. This miserable man had been an anchorite for twenty-two years and had dishonestly gathered a large fortune. Before he died, he confessed to the priest and wrote his will, saying that he had buried under his bed two large casks, one filled with silver and the other with gold. He wrote in his will, which he signed before the judge, that the money was a bequest to his brother and sister. I knew his brother, who was a priest called Don José, which means Yusuf, and his sister, Dona Ignes. After he died, they took his body away, and closed and sealed the house door. After they buried him, the officers and government officials went to dig out the aforementioned money—and found two casks full of blood, without a single dinar. All who were present marveled at this miracle because the justice of God had been manifested. When the archbishop of the city learned about the matter, he ordered the holes to be covered because they represented a bad example [of a priest]. But the incident became a lesson to all people.

Eight days later, I left to Oruru on a very difficult and rocky road. Five days later, we reached the outskirts of the city and the Jesuit monks came out to welcome us and to lead us to stay with them. The governor was called Don Alonzo del Coral, a stingy man who ate nothing but the worst food. Three leagues outside the city was a very rich silver mine from which silver is extracted without mercury—which is against the law in all mines. But there is no better silver than this, so I went to the aforementioned mine and bought silver dust for five hundred piasters.

Eight days later, I left to the city of Potosi and, for the first part of the journey, I stayed in an Indian village. Instructions had been given to provide me with mules from one village to another and I was charged the same rental fees as the sultan. So I called the sheikh of the Indians and after I had paid him, I told him to fetch me the beasts, insisting that he do so one hour after midnight. But the time went past, the sun rose and the day broke, and he still had not fetched me the beasts. I sent for him and they brought him to me, drunk. I spoke to him in Spanish and he replied in Indian. I ordered him tied to a house post and whipped. On the first blow, he begged to be untied and spoke in Spanish saying that the beasts are tied at his house. So I asked him why he did not speak to me in Spanish until only after he had tasted the lash. He answered, "We Indians do not cooperate with the Spaniards if they do not whip us."

I left there and reached a place of hot sulfate-smelling water. Those who are sick come from various regions to bathe, after which they are cured of their sicknesses. The name of that place is Tinquipaya. Six days later we reached the aforementioned city of Potosi and the governor came out about a mile with ten of his associates to welcome me. This governor is a relative of the wife of the minister who had mentioned me in his letters. I stayed at the Jesuit monastery, where some people came to see me, after which I returned their visits.

One day, I went to the money mint where piasters, half piasters, and quarters are made. There were forty slaves working there and twelve Spaniards. We saw the piasters piled like a hill on one side, the half piasters on another, and half quarters on another. They were stepping on them the way they walk on dirt. Near this city is the mining mountain that is known all around the world. It has such rich deposits that for the last 140 years an incalculable revenue has been generated from all four of its pits.[58] They have encircled it and descended into its bottom to locate the silver. They have built wooden posts to hold up the mountain from each side so that it will not fall: from the outside it looks solid, but it is hollow inside.[59] Nearly seven hundred Indians labor inside in the digging of ore for people who have bought shares from the sultan. Each miner owns specific Indians who work in his [part of the] mine by order of the sultan who decreed that every Indian village should provide men for the mines. The law is to take one of every five men, and if the village governors refuse to send these men, the minister dismisses them. When the Indians arrive in Potosi, the governor distributes them to the miners.[60]

There are thirty-seven mills in this city where silver ore is crushed night and day, except on Sundays and feast days. After crushing the ore into fine sand, [the laborers] take fifty quintals and mix them with water, as we have mentioned earlier. They then add the necessary amount of mercury, stir the mix many times with ladles, and add more mercury if needed, until it is ready. If the ore is cold, they mix it with copper to make it hot, and if hot, they mix it with lead to make it cold. The way they find out whether it is hot or cold is by putting some of the ore on pieces of pottery and washing it until the clay falls off. When the silver and mercury remain, the craft master touches them with his finger; if they disintegrate, they are hot; and if they are solid, they are cold. If they are heated for the right time, they come out flat and shiny. They then are put in a trough with running water over them, whereupon the silver and mercury sink to the bottom, while the sand is swept out. When [the laborers] finish washing all that pile, they turn the water off, empty the water out of the trough, and scoop out the silver and mercury at the bottom. They pour them into canvas bags and hang them up. There are containers under the bags that are covered with cowhides, into which the mercury drips while the pure silver remains in the bags like sugar cubes. The wheels of all the tools used in extracting the silver are run by water mills.

I had a friend who owned a mine. He told me about his father, who had had a mine in this mountain that had produced very little silver. So he ordered the Indian laborers to close it and cover its entrance with the rock deposits they had dug out. They did as they were told, and opened up another mine. Thirty-seven years later, my aforementioned friend returned to that mine and found that the deposits that had been useless had changed over the days and ripened like a fruit. So they dug them out and extracted the silver. The mine gave each [investor] thirty [khandakary?] because this silver mountain is under the star known as Mercury, which transmutes silver.

I saw in this city four very rich men who oversaw the minting of money. Every Friday one of them worked in the mint and earned 200,000 piasters a week because they bought the silver from the miners and produced the piasters. They bought the silver at the rate of twelve and one-half piasters for each miskal, but after it was turned into money, it became worth sixteen piasters. Every year these miners paid a tithe to the sultan of two and a half million piasters. Outside this city is a lake that, it was reported, flooded a few years before and destroyed many houses, but the people were unharmed. I stayed in this city for forty-five days.

From there I went to a city named Jocaz, known in the Indian language as Chuquisaca. On the way, we stopped at thermal baths that spring from the ground, which the Spaniards call Los Bagnos Calientes, where I spent the night. On the following day, I reached the aforementioned city, whereupon the Jesuits came out to welcome me and led me to their monastery. In the city, there is a council of the sultan and the magistrates of the region, but all are under the jurisdiction of the Lima minister. There is also an archbishop whose annual income is 120,000 piasters. He had been previously the bishop of the aforementioned Acumanca and he had given us a present in his bishopric. After that, the sultan bestowed on him this diocese. So on the next day, I went to see him and he hosted me with great generosity. Meanwhile, the head of the council is a priest and was my friend and so he too hosted me because he was the minister's friend. His name was Don Bartalomeus de Paveda. He sent an emissary to visit me. Two priests also came to visit me, sent by the archbishop. Eight days later, two Jesuit monks accompanied me as I returned the visits to all the priests, monks, and common people who had come to see me.

Twelve days later, the archbishop asked me to celebrate mass in the big church on the Feast of the Apostles. I had with me the vestments that Pope Clement IX had bestowed on me.[61] Later, the head of the sultan's council invited me to celebrate mass in the council church, which was inside his palace, and he gave me a more valuable present than the archbishop's. The abbots of the monasteries then started inviting me to celebrate mass in their churches and in convents. One of my friends who had sailed with me from Spain, Don Juan Gonzales, was a member of the council. While I was there, an order came from the sultan for this good man to go to Lima and to take over responsibility from the dismissed minister who was also my friend.

One of the Jesuit monks had a sick sister, so he asked me to visit her and treat her with whatever medicine I knew. I visited and treated her with whatever was appropriate for her ailment, giving her a concoction of frog powder. Through God's power, she recovered. There was another nun in the convent who was sick, so the archbishop sent me permission to visit the convent and treat her, for without his permission none can enter through the convent door. I went and treated her. Through God's wisdom and care, she recovered. As a result, a great commotion arose in the city because the people wanted me to stay with them, telling me that they would pay me five hundred piasters a year. But I told them it was not possible.

In the monastery, there was a Jesuit monk who was the deputy over the province of Tucuman, where his order had many monasteries. The bishop of that city was my friend and companion from Spain. So the monk asked me to go to that province, which is five hundred leagues away from the city of Chuquisaca. People travel by rafts on which they install sails in order to be pushed by the wind. He promised me a thousand mules if I agreed and went with him, for cattle in that part of the world are very valuable, but are worthless when running wild in the mountains.[62] I declined because of the length of the journey and because there were fearsome infidel Indians in those mountains who frightened me. The province is vast, vaster than the other three, and richer in its mines of gold, silver, and precious stones. But the population is small. There is a place called Santa Fe [Argentina] from where emerald is mined. The bishopric owns five hundred leagues and near the city is the commercial port of Buenos Aires which is on the ocean near the land of Brazil, governed by the Portuguese.[63] In Buenos Aires, people grow a herb called Yerba del Paraguay [yerba maté tea] which the native born people boil in water and drink hot with sugar. If a man drinks one cup, it does him good; if he wants to vomit, he drinks more and then he throws up all the rottenness inside him. This drink is as popular among people in that country as coffee is among ours.

To the right [east] of this city of Chuquisaca there is another called Mizque, which is inhabited by Indians and Spaniards, with a governor and a bishop. The [Spaniards] descend from it for about five hundred leagues toward the sea and reach a place called Chile, Calchaquí, and Valdivia. There is in Chile a bishop, a sultan's court, and a governor called "General." They are in constant warfare with the infidel Indians who had not known anything about warfare before they came in contact with the Spaniards; nor had the Indians known anything about horse riding. Now, like the [bedouin] Arabs, they ride their horses with lances in their hands, fight the Spaniards, and if they capture one, roast and eat his flesh. As for the skull, they remove the brain and turn it into a cup from which they drink the wine of their land. These Indians are very rebellious and hard-hearted and have been hereditary enemies of the Spaniards from the times of their grandfathers and fathers. Some of them fled the regions during the times of conquest [fat-h] after their sultans had been killed, and settled in high and forbidding mountains.

Forty-five days later, I left this city accompanied by the judge, Don Juan, who was to replace my friend, the dismissed minister, in Lima. I returned to the aforementioned Potosi. While in Chuquisaca, I had with me an icon of the face of Jesus that I had brought with me from Rome, which I gave as a present to a Jesuit monk. When I reached Potosi and opened my trunk, I found it there. I and my servants became perplexed at this miracle. Then the abbot of the monks of the Mercedarians, which means the order of Mary the Giver, asked me for it; I gave to him, hoping that it would return to me again. But it did not.

Let us go back and talk about the minister in Lima, my friend, who was dismissed for no reason. An order came from the sultan to the archbishop in Lima to take over and govern in the minister's place until another governor or minister arrived. This dismissed minister had used his influence to get the diocese of Lima for the archbishop. When the minister was dismissed, the archbishop turned against him.

The reason for his dismissal is that the merchants from India [South America] had maligned him to the sultan. When their petitions reached the sultan, they were seized by the natural [illegitimate] brother of the sultan, which means not from his mother. After the father died [King Philip IV], there was this natural son whose name was Don Juan de Austria, and there was the real son of the sultan, Don Carlos the Second, who inherited the sultanate from his father and who now reigns. Because he was a minor, his mother was appointed as regent until her son reached the age of fourteen, which is the age at which he could succeed to the throne, as the laws of kingship dictate. When the sultan [Philip IV] died, the sultana despised the natural son and did not want him to go near her son, fearing that he might poison him and become himself the sultan. So she ordered him sent into exile to another country. When her son the sultan became fourteen, he acceded to the throne and was crowned king. He then called his natural brother back. When he saw that he was intelligent and courageous, he appointed him his deputy in kingship and gave him power to govern.

Let us now go back and talk about the dismissed minister. After the complaints had reached Spain from India, the aforementioned sultan's brother learned about them. He was a great enemy of the minister because the minister's brother was of the family of the queen. And the queen, as we have stated, was the enemy of the sultan's brother. It is because of this enmity that he ordered the dismissal.

[PERU]

As for me, I left Potosi in the company of that man who was going to replace the minister and, after a month, we reached a city called Arequipa near the

Blue Sea. The night before we went into the city, the mules got lost, so we
spent the night in great anxiety because I had a load of silver dust on the
mules. In the morning, we thanked God after we found them because that
region is full of robbers. On the following day, we entered the aforementioned city, where I met the aforementioned bishop, who had been in
Panama and who had given me his walking cane, which had saved me from
drowning in Taboga. He welcomed and hosted me like a brother. While staying there, I was told about an Indian who owned a very rich mine that the
Spaniards had not discovered. He used to go with his son to the mine at
night, and cut out some silver ore, then carry it to his house, where he and
his son purified it with fire. When they told me that he had given 40,000 piasters for a mass, I sent for him and said, "Tell me why did you not tell the
sultan about the mine so he could bestow the governorship of this city on
you, your children, and your grandchildren?"

He answered, "I saw how other Indians who revealed what they knew to
the Spaniards died under torture. This is the reason." I believed him in regard to the injustice which the Spaniards inflict on the Indians.

The judge and I stayed in that city for ten days until we found a ship
ready to sail. We sailed for eight days until we reached Lima's harbor, called
El Callao, two leagues away from the city. My silver dust would have been
confiscated for the sultan had it been with anybody else, but my luggage was
not searched.[64] We entered Lima in the coach of my friend, the head of the
council of religion. He then went to stay in a different place from where I
stayed. Eight days later, he started issuing announcements, which he posted
on the city walls and corners, alerting any man who had a complaint or a petition against this minister [Don Balthazar] to come forward within a period
of three months. After the aforementioned three months, he was going to
close the complaint book and none would be able to present any further
complaints.

Meanwhile, the archbishop who was to sit in judgment opposed the judge
who came to be in charge and confined him to his house, saying, "You should
first send the minister to a place of exile two hundred leagues away, after
which you can receive the people's complaints."

The minister was brought and told about the exile order; he obeyed because the laws of Spain stipulate that whenever a basha or a minister is dismissed, he is to go two leagues away in exile. But having, as we have
mentioned, Don Juan, the sultan's brother, as an enemy, this minister was ex-

iled [to a place] two hundred leagues away. He obeyed the sultan's order and left to the appointed place, known as Paita, a hot region where drinking water is brought from two leagues away. His wife and servants remained two leagues out of Lima because of poor health. I accompanied the minister with some friends and bade him farewell at the port of Callao. He had great faith in, and love for, the Virgin and said, "Even if they force me to drink poison, it will not harm me because of our Lord and his mother the pure and saintly Mary." Then his ship sailed and we returned to the city.

I went to the archbishop and addressed him, saying, "How can you exile this unfortunate man to such a faraway place, and he being in poor health? The physicians say that whoever goes to that hot region will die. Our Sayyid Christ commanded us to perform acts of mercy, to visit and help the sick, not to reject and exile them to a distant place where they might die."

He answered, "I am angry with his wife because she cursed me. That is why I wanted to avenge myself by exiling her husband to that place."

While bidding me farewell, the minister had asked me to look after his house and wife, fearing that his enemies would poison her. For a year and two months, I stayed in his house to look after her.

Let us return to the judge who came to replace this dismissed minister. One of the deputies was the head of the council of religion and was sharing the house with him. Every night, the lady [the minister's wife] would send me to the judge where we wrote down in a notebook the names of all the people of the city, both those who supported the minister and those who opposed him. We placed the mark of the cross near the names of the supporters. Whenever anybody came to visit the judge, his name was checked and if there was a cross near his name, he was treated as a friend of the minister, while the adversary was applauded for his enmity to the minister. The supporters left the judge happy in the secret [that he supported the minister] and the adversaries also left happy because they believed the judge an enemy of the minister.

The archbishop informed the judge not to proceed with his case until he gave him permission. So the case remained inactive for seven months. Then he gave him permission to act within three months. During Passion Week, the judge sped up the investigation of the case for fear that the archbishop would send for and seize the evidence. In that week, he recorded everything in registers and sealed them. Then he ordered announcements to be posted on street walls declaring that the dismissed minister was innocent, that no proof had been found in regard to any of the accusations and suits, which had reached 40,000 piasters. When the archbishop heard the news, he tore his clothes in fury and said that everyone had betrayed the sultan. Thereupon, the minister returned from his exile to the city of Lima. All the city nobility and dignitaries went out to welcome him and accompanied him to the village where his wife was. There was great joy among the Spanish dignitaries and the Indians for his safe return.

This minister had been married for sixteen years, but had not had a child. After his return, and after knowing his wife, the power of God and the intercession of the Virgin Mary to whom he always turned bestowed on him a son after nine months whom he named Fernando de la Coeva, Conde de Castilla, and Marquis de Marañon. When people saw this miracle, they said that God was with the righteous and will never disappoint them. A year later, his wife gave birth to a girl. So they rejoiced after all the difficulties and calamities. None of the complaints that had been made against him were upheld because he was a man who walked in the fear of God and obeyed the laws of God. Despite the archbishop's enmity, and despite the bribes that the archbishop gave to people to bear false witness against the minister, the justice of God prevailed.

Let us go back and talk about the sultan's brother, who had been the main reason for the minister's dismissal. Forty days after the judgment on the minister, he was given poison and died.

During the minister's exile, the archbishop sent for me, saying, "Why are you so attached to this man? Leave him and I will give you residence here and help you in all your affairs."

I said to him, "I cannot leave my old friend and reject the friendship of such a good man just because he has been dismissed. God commanded us to help the helpless and to raise the fallen; a man who is truly honorable [his parents' son], proud of his family roots and the honor of his forefathers, will not desert his friend as soon as the latter is dismissed. Rather, he will help that friend, and try to alleviate his suffering and share with him. I still bear affection to you and am in your service; and in the same way I am your friend, I am his, too."

He said, "Do what you want!"

After two months, the archbishop sent one of the soldiers in his service for me. As soon as I reached the city, I went to my friend the head of the council of religion and told him [about the summons]. He said to me, "Go to him and tell him all that is on your mind."

So I went to him and spoke with him. He said to me, "Why do you not get out of the country?"

I said to him, "If I decide to go back to my country, nothing can stop me. But now I do not intend to leave here."

He said, "Your permit and the license that was given you are for four years. They are expired."

I replied, "That is correct. But I do not want to go and leave the minister. You can do what you want."

"Why do you love that man," he asked, "and defend him? You do not love me as you do him?"

"Yes," I replied, "in our country and traditions, we defend and help the man who is fallen, thereby fulfilling God's commandments of loving the neighbor as the self. As for me, I love the minister, love you, and love my neighbor."

He rose from his chair and embraced me, saying, "May God bless you. You are the son of noble parents. Your blood and deeds are witness to that."

Meanwhile, the head of the council of religion had sent four men from among the city's nobility to the archbishop's palace to await me outside. They feared that if the archbishop intended me harm, they would charge in with their weapons and intimidate him. When I came out into the archbishop's courtyard, they rejoiced upon seeing me, and I returned to my friend, the head of the council of religion, and told him what had transpired. He was very happy. From there, I went to the minister's wife and told her the same. She said, "May God have mercy on the souls of the parents who brought you forth. May your honor be magnified."

In those days, I withdrew to a village half a league outside the city, called Madalena [del Mar], because my friend owned a beautiful house there with an orchard. I stayed there for five months, awaiting Spanish ships. In that period, I started writing the account of my travels. When the ships arrived, there was a new minister on board. I had been in that land for six years because of my dismissed friend, who had promised to attend to all my affairs after resuming his ministerial office. When I saw that a new minister had arrived, I gave up hope. As soon as the Spanish ships anchored in Portobelo, the archbishop in Lima, who was then governor over all the lands of Peru, ordered that the Lima traders load the treasure on the sultan's ships, which were in that sea, and sail to Portobelo and prepare for the season. The laws of the country stated that when the galleons arrived from Spain to Portobelo, the silver ships would sail to Panama. In Panama, the silver would be transported to Portobelo on a thousand mules for a whole month and over a distance of eighteen leagues. In the middle of the path there was a small river [Chagres], which they crossed with flat-bottomed boats called *kitaws* [*chatas* or flat-bottomed boats] to Portobelo. The season continued for a period of forty days and no more. In that period, they did all their buying and selling.

Let us return to what we were saying. I left with the dismissed minister, who was accompanied by dignitaries and noblemen bidding him farewell. There were traders with us who were on their way to take part in the season. It was a big day, with the firing of cannons and the lighting of fires, Sunday, September 21, 1681. We left the port called Callao, heading toward the port of Panama. Five days later we reached a port called Paita, where we bought all the provisions we needed. A chicken there was worth one piaster and a half, while a goat was sold for five piasters. Two days later, we sailed on and reached a place in the sea called Amortajado, which means "the embalmed" because the sea there is shallow and the water forces the ships to capsize. But God saved us through His interceding mother the Virgin Mary. A heavy fog rose, and the wind died while the waves of the sea, called *corrientes* [currents], kept pushing us toward land and rock, which we saw were drawing very near. We became very frightened and started praying, with the priest blessing and giving unction because we were close to death, while imploring God and His mother the Virgin Mary. After we finished praying and imploring, a wind blew on us from the mountain, like a bellows, and pushed our ship into the sea, saving us from that evil and great danger. The ships that were following us were far away because the wind was dead and the sea calm. When they saw us being blown toward them by the wind, they were amazed. The wind continued with us until the evening of the following day, when we entered the harbor of Santa Elena, which means Saint Helen, where we stayed for eleven days awaiting the fleet from Guayaquil. This fleet of ships, known as the gold fleet, was carrying twelve million bullion of gold. When our ship arrived, the general ordered us to leave that port to Panama, which we reached safely, forty-two days after leaving Lima. We found two ships with Spanish soldiers who came from Yenki Dunia searching for sea pirates, meaning the guerillas in the South Sea.[65]

My friend the dismissed minister suggested that I go to Yenki Dunia because he was embarrassed for not having done what he had promised me. He offered to give me all that I needed and to provide me with letters of introduction to the minister of the New World, who was his relative.

[TOWARD MEXICO]

With God's help and His great blessing, we begin documenting and recording my journey to the lands and sultanate of Yenki Dunia. In the month of January 1682, we boarded a big ship called a *quptan* [*capitano*/Admiral's brig] and sailed for three leagues until we reached the island of the aforementioned Taboga. We stayed there for three days, and we filled up on water and bought vegetables, fruit, and other provisions. Then we sailed to a port called Realejo, and after five days we reached an uninhabited island called Montuosa. There the wind died on us and we stayed for twelve days, unable to move. Nearby was another island known as Isla de los Ladrones, which means Island of Thieves. It was reported that a ship that was sailing to Yenki Dunia met with contrary winds that cast it on that sandy island. The wind died, so after two days the seamen started preparing some food in the ship's kitchen, which had been destroyed by the strong wind they had met at sea. They fetched some sand from the island and poured it into a pit. All of a sudden, the wind started blowing and so they left the island. On the following day, the cook prepared food for them as usual. As he stirred the fire, he found the sand as hard as stone. He took it out and found it a disc of gold. When the seamen saw that, they decided to turn back to the island, but they could not locate it because they had not marked it on their maps. In the books of the ancients, the island was known as Isla de Salamon which means Solomon's Island. They said that when Solomon built the house [of God], he brought gold from this island. The Spaniards now have no other purpose, passion, or goal but to find this island.

We return to what we were saying. After the aforementioned time, God helped us with a good wind and in three days we reached the port of Golfo Dulce, which means the Sweet Gulf because there is a river of sweet water that runs into the sea and mixes with it. We anchored there and the sailors went to fill up on water. I went with them because of the immense heat and washed in the cool water of the river to soften my skin. The river is one arm length only in depth and I saw that gold was mixed with its sand. So I pointed that out to the ship commander, who was born in that region. He was amazed and perplexed. In all these regions and rivers there is gold but, because of the presence of infidel Indians in the mountain tops, the Spaniards do not dare come for the gold. The Indians there are many.

As we were anchored, the sea grew turbulent, as a result of which the rope of the anchor broke twice.

After staying there for three days, we left and in six days reached a port called La Caldera, which means Cooking Cauldron. So we anchored there. I asked the soldiers on board the ship to gather some sea shells. They brought nine shells, which we opened, one after another, to eat what was inside. I opened one and found a pearl as big as a chickpea. So I said to the general, "What kind of stupidity and laziness is this? How come there are pearls here and you do not collect them?"

He answered, "Again, because of our fear of the infidel Indians."

[Costa Rica]

We stayed in the port for one day. The wind was weak and the rain that fell was hot. Five days later, we reached a mountain called Papagayo [Golfo de Papagayo] whereupon the wind blew violently and broke our mast into three pieces. We gave up hope and despaired because of the turbulence at sea. Our hearts fell, but through the power of the Lord, the wind and the sea quieted down.

[Nicaragua]

Six days later, we reached the aforementioned port of Realejo and disembarked. We spent a day and a night there. The general wrote a letter to the bishop of the city of León, which was nine leagues away, and he informed him of my arrival. When the bishop heard the news, he became very happy because, during my stay in Paris, we had become friends. He had had a legal suit against the priests in Paris, and he too was a priest, a Mercedarian. When he won the suit and went to Madrid, the king bestowed this bishopric on him. On the next day, I left for León. As I drew near, I saw the bishop coming to receive me two leagues outside the city. We embraced and then he took me to his house, where I stayed for eight days. There I met a man whom I had befriended and known in Lima. This good man gave me a strong mule as a present, and so did the bishop.

Eight days later, we left for a village two leagues away known as Silwaja and from there we continued to another village known in the Spanish language as Nuestra Señora del Vejo [El Viejo], which means the village of *sittna* [Our Lady] of the *sheikh*. This Virgin has performed many miracles, especially to sea travelers. While in the midst of the waves of the sea, with the mast broken, as I had mentioned earlier, I had vowed on my life that if I reached her church I would celebrate mass in her honor for nine days. I stayed in that village for nineteen days and fulfilled my vow. I was waiting for a skiff, which is known as a *canoe*, to cross the strait, which was forty-three leagues. The bishop had advised me not to cross the strait because it was very dangerous and many ships had sunk there. But I relied on the help of the Virgin Mary, whom I viewed as the daughter of my country, and I got into the skiff.

[EL SALVADOR]

In twenty hours, we crossed that strait and reached the other side, a village of four Indian houses called Amapala. I met there a Spaniard from Yenki Dunia on his way to Peru. He told me that in order to cross the strait, he had sold his horse, saddle, and reins to an Indian for two and one-half piasters. From there we traveled forty leagues in eight days and reached an Indian village called Amushayo. We continued from there for eight leagues and reached a village called San Miguel and from there eight leagues to a village called Rozwakin, and then six leagues to the village of Jiquilisco and then six leagues to a river called Lempa. We continued for seven leagues and reached a village called Istepeque and then seven more and to a village called Cojutepeque and then two more leagues to San Martin and from there to San Salvador. Indigo is grown in this vicinity and it resembles the husks and desert plants used in horse feed. Farm owners plant the indigo seed as they do wheat. In some years, it grows taller than a man and thus its price in Yenki Dunia falls. After the harvest, they collect the weeds in a big trough and leave them there to ferment. There are water wheels in the trough that push the water into another trough. After three days, the workers skim the buttery froth into balls and dry it in the sun. In our country, this is called "squeezed indigo," and the lower layers are turned into "lower indigo."

[GUATEMALA]

Five leagues from there we reached a village called Jalapa, and then after seven more, we reached the village of Apopa, and went eight more to Santa Ana. We traveled six leagues to Texia, which is inhabited by mulattos, I mean, [the offspring of] a white father and a black mother. The mulattos are reddish white but not slaves. We continued eight leagues to the village of Kilyatoko, ten leagues to Esclavos and then we traveled five leagues to a vil-

lage called Jalapa, and from there seven leagues to the village of Apopa, and
then twelve leagues to the village of Pitaia,[66] and then six leagues to Santiago,
I mean, Saint James. From there I continued to the city of Guatemala where
I was heartily welcomed at a Dominican monastery. The head of the sultan's
council in the country, which is called in Spanish *audiencia*, is known as *pres-*
idente, which means the head of the council.[67] There is also a very wealthy
bishop in this city called Don Juan de Ortega, whom I visited and who returned my visit. On the second Sunday in Lent, I went and celebrated mass
in the church without the permission of the bishop but in the presence of the
priest, his confessor. So he went and told him about the vestments I had
from the pope, which made him very happy. He ordered two of his deacons
to help me during mass. I stayed in the city for thirty-four days, well-treated
and entertained. I celebrated mass at numerous churches and in the convents of nuns, too. In all honesty, they offered me wonderful presents. All
this happened during Lent of A.D. 1680 [1682].

After the aforementioned thirty-four days, I left the city with two of the
council *chiaoses* and four deacons from the bishop,[68] all of whom stayed with
me until we were one mile out of the city. Then we bid farewell to each other
and they returned to the city while I continued for three leagues to the village of Chimaltenango and then six leagues to a village called Patzun. Seven
leagues later, we reached the village of Tolo and then it was twelve leagues to
San Antonio Suchitepequez. The governor of this fort was from the city of
Seville, and the Indians had petitioned to the Guatemala council for his dismissal. So I interceded for him and wrote to the head of the council whose
name was Don Juan Miguel de Ahorto, a very good Christian who cared for
the clergy. When I visited him, he fell on his knees and kissed my hand. In
this fort there is cocoa, which they turn into chocolate. There are large numbers of cocoa trees which belong to very rich Indians. Four thousand piasters
are set aside so that if a quarrel breaks out with the governor or the village
priest, the money can be used for litigation and correspondence.

[MEXICO]

I left this village to another called Nabo, which was five leagues away. From
there I continued for six leagues to Santa Maria de Belén and then to the village of San Cristobal, and then for six leagues to the village of San Francesco
Alto. From there it was five leagues to the village of Cholantes, and then five
leagues to San Ramon, two leagues to Jacaltenango, two leagues to the vil-

lage of Viento, ten leagues to the village [and river] of Cuchumatanes, three leagues to San Martin, three leagues to the village of Picatan, five leagues to the village of San Antonio Breskin, two leagues to the village of La Freray-eeta, seven leagues to the village of Isquintenango, three leagues to the village of Pinole, five leagues to the village of Teopisca, six leagues to Ciuidad Real, two leagues to Bilacana, six leagues to the village of Estaba, five leagues to Chiapa, and two leagues to the Spanish Chiapas.

I arrived in this city and stayed at the house of the governor. In this city, there is a bishop called Don Alonzo Birrau who had quarreled with the *provincial*, I mean the abbot of the Dominican monastery, who had actually excommunicated his city. When I saw the hatred and enmity between them, I was deeply hurt and I spoke with both of them, trying my best to reconcile them. Two days later, it was the feast of the birth of the Virgin [September 8] and the holy sacrament was placed on the altar as the bishop celebrated mass. After he was finished, I went up with the provincial and the governor and stood with them in front of the bishop and kneeled down saying, "Thus said Jesus, My peace I leave with you.[69] He commanded us to live in peace and harmony and here, in the presence of Jesus who is looking at us from the sacred altar, we need to leave all evil thoughts and hatred, and change them to love and meekness and to do as he commanded: bless others and not curse them."[70]

The bishop stood up and raised his hand and blessed them as he smiled, saying, "Blessed be the name of the Lord: a priest from the city of Baghdad has come to reconcile us."

He then removed the ban on the city and we went to the bishop's house, where we had lunch. After we finished, the bishop stood up and gave me a chain of gold worth two hundred piasters while the aforementioned governor gave me a young mule and the provincial also gave me a present. Meanwhile the priests, monks, and commoners would not leave me for a minute, and kept on asking me about my country, which they call the Old World. I stayed there for sixteen days.

I left for the village of Tuxtla, which was two leagues away, and then went four leagues to the village of Ocozocoautla, seven leagues to the village of Kikibilla, and four leagues to the village of Tapanatepec. This village is the border between the government of Mexico—that is, Yenki Dunia—and the government of Guatemala because the government of the latter is separate. I continued from there for six leagues to the village of Zanatepec, six more to the village of Ixtepec, nine leagues to the village of Tehuantepec, six leagues

to the village of Aqatenepec, and then six leagues to the city of Jalaba. In this
city there was a governor called Don Juan Betiya whose uncle was the secretary of the Council of the Indies and my very good friend. When he heard of
my arrival he went two leagues out of the city to meet me with all honor and
hospitality and led me to his house.

Near this city was a mountain where guerillas sometimes robbed travelers. So the governor sent two soldiers with me to help me across the mountain path, which we crossed safely with God's help. After four leagues, we
reached the village called Tixia, and after twelve leagues the village of San ·
Juan della Costa [Evengelista]. From there it was five leagues to the village
of Nejapa, ten to the village of San Miguel, three to San Lux, and six to Oaxaca. In this city there was a nobleman from Spain. He had a brother who
served my friend, the dismissed minister, and who had given me a letter to
his brother in Oaxaca. As I approached the city, I sent him the letter as a result of which he came outside the city to welcome me with joy and led me to
a house he had prepared for me.

The bishop of this city had died and the seat of the diocese was vacant.
There was a cleric there, I mean the provincial, who, while sailing from India
to Spain, was taken captive to Algiers. With God's help, he was liberated and
became the provincial in this city. I became very friendly with him and he
hosted me generously. His name was Don Dionisio. The city has beautiful
buildings and churches, especially the Dominican monastery; and numerous
monasteries, convents, and hospitals; the big church, which is extremely ma-
jestic; and other churches. I had with me eight hundred piasters, which I left
with my aforementioned friend whose name was Don Francisco de Castro. I
asked him to buy some vermilion because in the areas around this city it is
found clinging to some trees. Its leaves are thick, as we mentioned before,
and thus it adheres like worms to the leaves and resembles smallpox. When
it is ripe, they take it out and put it in a hot oven where it dries, after which it
is sold.

Fifteen days later, I left the city for the aforementioned Mexico which is
the residence of the sultan's minister. Four leagues later, we reached a village
called Ayeeta, and after six leagues Tatoka; then it was nine leagues to
Cuicatlan, five leagues to Uanatepetepec, five leagues to Cus, two more to
San Anton, five more to San Sebastian, four more to the village of Tehuacan,
seven more to the village of Anajotepec, seven more to Tepeaca and then to
the city of La Peubla de los Angeles, which means City of the Angels' People.
I arrived in this city and stayed with a friend. It is a big city, with grand

palaces and buildings, and noble churches such as the big church which is very rich in gold, silver, and holy relics. A bishop lives in this city whose name is Don Emmanuel de Santa Cruz, a scholar and a man who fears God. His annual income is 80,000 piasters. There are also monasteries and seven convents belonging to all orders.

Two days later, I left for Mexico, which is twenty-four leagues away. I arrived there and stayed with one of the friends for whom I had brought a letter from Guatemala and who welcomed me heartily. A day later, I fell sick and stayed ten days in bed. I had also brought a letter to the city magistrate from his relative, the minister my friend who was in Peru. So he kept on sending me his physicians and after the aforementioned ten days, I recovered with God's help. I went and visited the minister and his wife who welcomed me with smiling faces. The minister invited me to stay at his palace but I thanked him in appreciation of his offer. I did not stay at his palace, but rented a house for an annual 360 piasters, and bought a coach with four mules for 650 piasters.

I then started visiting the nobility, the archbishop of the city, and the other notables. The archbishop gave me permission to celebrate mass wherever I liked. Every evening I used to go to the minister and spend two hours chatting with him and then return home. The whole region is low and near the city, there is a lake that springs from the ground. A few years earlier, it rained so hard that the city was flooded and many houses collapsed. Whenever a house collapsed, they built another because houses did not have solid foundations. And what can I say about the churches in this city, the glory of their construction and their indescribable and immense wealth? There are three Franciscan monasteries in the city, two Dominican, two Jesuit, three Augustinian, two Mercedarians, two hospitals for the sick, seventeen convents, a Carmelite monastery, and a big church—along with many other churches outside the city.

Half a league away there is a church named after the Virgin Mary which they call Guadeloupe. I was told that a few days after the Spaniards had conquered this land an Indian by the name of Juan Diego was walking outside the city when a virtuous woman of great beauty appeared to him and said, "Go to the archbishop of the city and tell him to build me a house on this spot."[72] The aforementioned Indian was frightened of the light of her face, and hastened to obey her. He told the archbishop [Bishop Zumárraga] about the matter, but after the archbishop saw the Indian in shabby and poor clothes he ordered him thrown out. The unfortunate man went back to

where that virtuous lady had spoken to him, whereupon she appeared to him
again in the same aforementioned place. She repeated what she had told him
about going to the archbishop and she reminded him of her request. He
obeyed her and went again to the archbishop and conveyed to him all that
she had told him. Again, the archbishop humiliated him and ordered him
out. Saddened, the Indian returned to that place whereupon she appeared to
him for the third time, saying, "Why have you not done anything of what I
have told you to do?"

He replied, "Madame, I have done what you have asked me to do and
have gone twice to the archbishop and have conveyed to him all that you
have told me. But he expelled me and did not believe me."

She said, "Go to him for the third time, and tell him about all that I have
commanded you. Take with you this rose and give it to the archbishop and he
will believe you."

She then gave him a rose, which was not in season. The Indian took the
rose and hid it inside his cloak and went to the archbishop's house. When the
servants saw and recognized him, they drove him away. So he said to them,
"For God's sake, let me speak to the archbishop because I have a present for
him from the Spanish Lady."

When they informed the archbishop, he ordered him to be brought in. So
he stood before him and said, "My sayyid, the madame has thrice sent me to
you asking you to build her house in a specific spot. Here, she has sent you
this rose so you may believe me and trust that it was she who sent me to you."

When the Indian brought the rose out of his cloak, the archbishop was
amazed because it was not the season for such roses. He also became more
amazed when he saw the face of the Virgin stamped on the cloak, which was
like a thick shawl. At that point, the archbishop fell on his knees before the
Indian and asked him for forgiveness. Then the priests seized the rose from
that Indian and the archbishop took the aforementioned cloak on which the
face of the Virgin had appeared, and they all went in a procession accompanied by the ringing of bells and placed the cloak on the high altar in great
festivity. Then they went out to the designated spot and the archbishop ordered the building of a church in that spot where the Virgin had appeared to
the Indian and he called it the Church of the Virgin Mary de Guadeloupe.
The aforementioned Indian, Juan Diego, continued his life in the service of
the Virgin in that church and became one of the blessed.

This church is half a league out of the city of Mexico, as we have mentioned, and it is very rich in gold and silver and gilded ecclesiastical vest-

ments. The steps to the high altar are nine and are made of silver, and the columns on the altar are of silver, too. The people have built something like a bridge extending from the center of the city to the church entrance, and it is two arm lengths high because in summer, when it rains, the ground turns into a lake. So they walk on this boardwalk because in this city, the rainy season begins from the first of September, contrary to the weather patterns in our country.

I rested in this city for six months until ships arrived from Spain bringing letters and news to the merchants from their associates. A fraud arrived on one of the ships and claimed that he was there on behalf of the sultan to apprehend the guilty and to take charge of the sultan's treasury. This wicked man threw fear in the hearts of many guilty people. When the minister heard about him, he wrote to the governor of the port to examine the orders that the man had; but the man refused to present them. The minister then realized that the man was a fraud and so he sent his soldiers to arrest him, which they did. The minister then ordered his imprisonment. We shall talk about him later.

In those same days, some pirate ships attacked the port of Vera Cruz: they were all heretics, gathered from all peoples and denominations.[73] They arrived at night, and landed a league away from the port, and then like thieves entered the city because the port had no wall. They went to the house of the governor and seized him and then forced all the people, men and women, into the big church and locked them up, placing guards at the doors. For three days, they robbed and looted the monasteries, churches, and private residences. They then brought the people out of the church and made them carry all the loot as they led them to where the ships were anchored, half a league away. Then they hauled all the money, men, and slaves onto the ships and sailed to an island about a league away. They put the captives down and told them either to ransom themselves or be killed. They demanded 150,000 piasters. They sent two men to the aforementioned puebla to collect the ransom. Ten days later, the men returned with the 150,000 piasters whereupon the pirates released the Spaniards but kept the black slaves and all the loot from the city, which was worth eight million [piasters]. The number of these guerilla pirates was six hundred and the Spaniards with their slaves were over four thousand.

The leader of the pirates was a heretic who had a Spanish partner and friend named Laurnesilio. They quarreled over the division of the loot and Laurensilio killed the heretic leader and took his place. In that city, I had a load of vermilion worth one thousand piasters, which I had bought from Oaxaca, and which was taken along with the other loot. While the pirates were on the island, ships from Spain arrived. As they were entering the port, the minister informed the general about the situation, asking him to fight the pirates and destroy them before anchoring in the port. The general raised his flag to gather around him all the ship captains. He wanted them to join him in council and assume responsibility with him lest he alone take the blame; for his ships were stacked with merchandise and he was afraid that they could sink or burn during the fighting. As soon as the general and the captains drew away from the port and met in council, Laurnesilio started taunting them, and sailed in front of them without fear, taking with him more than two thousand slaves, black and red. All that occurred in A.D. 1683.

We Speak about China

One hundred years before that date, during the time of Philip IV, Sultan of Spain, some ships sailed from Yenki Dunia toward China. En route, they saw an island, of which they took possession and named it Philippines after the name of the aforementioned king.[74] The Spaniards settled there and in later years, many ships sailed to that island carrying priests and monks who converted the inhabitants from infidelity to the religion of Christ. Every year, a ship full of Chinese merchandise arrives in Yenki Dunia from this island, taking eight months to complete the crossing. But it takes three months to return. Also, every year a ship sails to that island from Surat; it belongs to two Armenian traders of Julfa who live on that island.[75] They take the money from the ship and lend it to the Spaniards for a year. Once the year is over, the Surat ship arrives, and the Armenians take from the Spaniards the money that they had lent them, and then lend them another sum in expectation of the next payment. No permission is given to any other ship to sail there except the ship of the Julfites. I thought of traveling in that ship to the island [Philippines] and from there taking the ship of those Armenian Julfites to Surat and from Surat back to my country. But then I had an altercation with the man who was going to govern in that island because he asked me to lend him 10,000 piasters. I consulted the minister, who warned me, saying, "Be careful. He has already borrowed 200,000 piasters." So I decided not to travel there, but to return to Spain.

It was reported that fifty years ago, when missionaries used to go from that island to the interior of China to convert people from infidelity to the faith of Christ, Satan, who is the enemy of goodness and mercy, put it in the heart of the sultan of China to kill all the monks who preached there. He killed them and ordered ships and soldiers to sail against the island of Philippines. He launched about five hundred small and big ships, with many soldiers, and sent them to the aforementioned island. When the inhabitants of the island saw this large army intent on fighting them, they were afraid because they were few in number and unprepared. They had no choice but to hide in the church, where they started praying and imploring God. They then carried the holy sacrament in a procession to fight the enemy. With the power and justice of God, which never turns away from those who seek Him, the sea rose against those ships and scattered them, destroying and eradicating them, along with all of that mighty army. Only thirteen ships were spared. When the sultan of China heard the news about the destruction of his fleet, he became so sad and distraught that he died soon after. He instructed his eldest son who was to succeed him to raise another army with well-fortified ships and sail against that island. After his son raised the army and got the ships ready, the same fate befell them as had befallen the first campaign, and all were lost. The same fate befell this sultan, too, who died in frustration and despair. His younger brother succeeded him to the sultanate and he too decided to raise an army and a fleet, but his mother warned him against attacking that island lest he meet with the same fate that his father and brother had met. She advised him to befriend the monks and to allow them to come into the country to preach and not to oppose them in any way.[76] Now, every three years, monks from Spain arrive there, and sail to China to evangelize with no restrictions. I had a friend in that island who was a sea captain for seventeen years; when he came to Mexico, he stayed with me as my guest and told me about the wonders and miracles that have taken place in the Philippines. This man is honest in his accounts and so are the reports by the Jesuit monks and others all of which have confirmed the stories about those disasters.

Fifty years ago, the Spaniards also discovered an island near the Philippines which they conquered. Its inhabitants were Indians and worshippers of idols. When the Spaniards took possession of it, they converted all the people to Christianity and baptized them, and named the island after the sultana who is the wife of Sultan Philip IV and mother of the present Sultan Carlos II. The name of the queen was Marie-Ann of Austria, who was the sister of the Emperor Leopold, and the island was named Isla de Mariannes.

While I, the lowly, was in Mexico, a ship came from the Philippines bringing Dominican monks with a number of petitions to our sayyid the pope. These monks traveled with me to Spain on the same ship and showed me the petitions so I would help them present them to our sayyid the pope. They told me about the conflict between the judges of the Philippines and the archbishop of that city. The archbishop of the aforementioned city quarreled with the Jesuit monks because they were refusing to pay tithes. For that reason they turned the judges of the city against him and had him seized at night, put on a ship, and sent into exile to a place thirty leagues away. The archbishop was a Dominican monk and he died in exile, just like St. John Chrysostom.[77] When these two monks reached Rome and presented their petitions, including the petition about this matter to our sayyid the pope, and when the pope heard of that ugly insolence he wrote to reprimand the Sultan of Spain for what the judges had done to that archbishop. When the sultan and the council learned about the matter, the former wrote to the Philippines ordering the removal of those judges from their posts. They were subsequently sent into exile, where they died excommunicated.

Let us talk now about our return. When the ships prepared to return to Spain, I left the city of Mexico to go to the port of Vera Cruz, which is eighty leagues away. I asked the general of the fleet to take me to Spain. He asked for a fare of 1,000 piasters, including food and drink. On those ships, the rental fare is 1,000 piasters for a room, which is two arm lengths in length, one and a third in width, and one and a half in height. When he asked for that sum, I found it hard to pay it, but I did so against my will. Eight days later, the captains of the ships met in council and discussed whether the season was appropriate for them to leave India for Spain. They cast dice and determined that they should not leave before three months. So they fitted a small ship and loaded it with letters and news about the country, and then sent it ahead of them to Spain. When I saw that small ship, I became confused about my decision: the port was hot, the water was unhealthy and the air was sickly. So I boarded that small ship which they were sending ahead to Spain and sailed to the island of Havana, which is the port for the galleons of Peru and the ships of Yenki Dunia, called *al-flota*. In the port of Vera Cruz, a friend of mine suggested that I buy two bags of dried onions and two boxes of apples as presents—which I did.

We left with the help of God, and after twenty days, reached the aforementioned island of Havana, happy and contented. The governor of this island was the brother of the general who took me to Peru. I offered him the onions and the apples as a present. He was surprised and asked, "How did you know that we needed onions and apples on this island? When the islanders try to grow onions here, they come out looking like mice tails; and if they leave them to ripen, they crack and dry up."

I stayed on this island for four and one-half months until the ships from Yenki Dunia arrived. The air on this island is pleasant, the water good, and its people friendly. When I was about to leave the island for Spain, the general came with a present of nine boxes of sugar and jars of marmalade in return for the onions and the apples. I had paid a fare of 350 piasters to the ship that came from Caracas. With God's help we sailed and reached Caicos Island, where the sea grew rough and the wind strong. The turbulence lasted eleven days and the ships were scattered on the face of the sea. In tears and lamentation, prayers and processions, we remained aboard the ship, vowing charities to churches and saints. Twenty-one days later, God made things easier, and the sea grew calm and our ships, which had been scattered, came together again. At night lanterns were lit so that ships would not be lost or separated from each other, or draw too near and crash into each other and break. A good wind blew and so we returned to our route to Cadiz.

Twelve days later, at dawn, we saw land. The wind continued with us until at noon we entered safely the port of Cadiz. The ships of war belonging to the Sultan of France were anchored outside the port with the ships of war belonging to the Sultan of Spain across from them. As we sailed between these ships of war we saluted them by firing our cannons, to which both the French and Spanish ships returned our greeting.[78] Cannon shooting continued from both sides until smoke became as thick as fog. We entered the harbor and anchored. On the following day, friends from the city came in small boats and took us on land. My trunks were taken but not opened or searched as was the custom, by order of the head of the council, known as *presidente*. Ten days later, I went to Seville to retrieve 2,000 piasters from a sea captain who had borrowed them from me to buy a ship mast.[79] After he had reached Cadiz, his ship was confiscated because he owed the Seville church 30,000 piasters. I went and petitioned the *presidente*, who said that before anything else is paid, these 2,000 piasters will be paid, because had it not been for that money, the ship would not have arrived. When I retrieved my money, I returned to Cadiz.

I paid my fare on a Dutch ship to Rome. I had with me two Armenian servants, and I had brought with me from India four birds that are called in the *ifranji* language *papaquay* [parrots] and can talk like a man. I had also brought with me a silver, wonderfully crafted lantern worth 1,400 piasters which I presented to our sayyid the pope and to the Holy See. When the cardinals saw it, they became very happy. My sayyid, Pope Innocent XI, of blessed memory bestowed on me other duties for which I was not suited.[80]

Praise be to God forever.

Amen

NOTES

1. See the unit on cleric-merchants in Peru in Luis Martín, *The Kingdom of the Sun* (New York: Scribner's, 1974), 118–23.

2. N.a. *Descripcion del Virreinato del Peru, Cronica inedita de comienzos del Siglo XVII* (Rosario, Argentina: Universidad Nacional del Litora, 1958).

3. See the discussion of this topic in appendix B of my *Turks, Moors and Englishmen in the Age of Discovery* (New York: Columbia University Press, 1999).

4. I. Karchkovskii. *Tarikh al-Adab al-Jughrafi al-Arabi*, trans. Salah al-Din Uthman Hashim (Cairo: Lajnat al-Talif wa-al-Tarjamah, 1963), 2:701–6.

5. Antoine Rabbat al-Yasu'i [the Jesuit], *Rihlat Awal Sharqi ila America* (Beirut: Catholic Press, 1906); Nuri al-Jarrah, *Al-Dhahab w-al-Asifa, Rihlat Ilyas al-Mawsuli ila America* (Beirut: al-Muassasat al-Arabiya lil-Dirasat w-al-Nashr, 2001).

6. Guillermo de Zendegui, "Portobelo," *Americas* 22 (1970): 21.

7. Matt. 28:19. All quotations are from the Douay Bible, 1609, and are hereafter cited within brackets in the text.

8. The *qibla* is the direction of prayer in Islam—Mecca. The *qibla* is south of Musil. Al-Mawsuli uses the term again when he is in America, again to mean south.

9. Verses 37–38 read, "They were stoned, they were cut asunder, they were tempted, they were put to death by the sword, they wandered about in sheepskins, in goatskins, being in want, distressed, afflicted: Of whom the world was not worthy; wandering in deserts, in mountains, and in dens, and in caved [*sic*] of the earth."

10. Al-Mawsuli adopts the polemic that the Catholic Church instituted against Protestants. Later in the text, he will castigate them as heretics.

11. Only the last part of the quotation is from Matthew 19:30, "And many that are first, shall be last: and the last shall be first."

12. Meriko Maslooba refers to the Italian explorer Amerigo Vespucci (1451–1512): "Among the discoverers was a man whose name was Meriko from Italy, from the city of Florence. He was a sailor on the ship, with knowledge and intelligence. He drew that land and its Indians on a paper and presented it to the Sultan of Spain after which that land was called *Merika*," f. 103 in the BL ms.

13. *Yenki Dunia* is Turkish for "New World," specifically indicating Mexico.

14. Mikhail Condoleo was born in Crete, lived in Damascus, and traveled throughout the Ottoman Empire as an inspector. He was mentioned in Jesuit missionary letters as early as 1646. The title "tubji basha" refers to an artillery commander.

15. One of the legends about St. Lazarus (John 11:1–44) is that he was put with his sisters in a leaking boat in Jaffa and was conducted miraculously to Cyprus. He then became the bishop of Larnaka (Kition) and served for thirty years.

16. Al-Mawsuli derives the term *lazaretto* from the hospital of St. Mary of Nazareth, outside of Venice.

17. This is Duke Ferdinand II (1621–1690). The princes of Tuscany had representatives in Aleppo and other parts of the Ottoman Empire—which may explain al-Mawsuli's mention of the duke.

18. Bought by Pope Clement VI in 1348, Avignon became the residence of the popes from 1309–1377 (the Babylonian Captivity).

19. Born in 1626, François Piquet became consul of France and Holland in Aleppo in 1652. He returned to France in 1662 and was later chosen by Louis XIV as ambassador to Persia. He died in Hamadhan in 1685.

20. This is Jean Baptiste de St. Aignan, missionary to Aleppo and Musil.

21. The order of the Sisters of Charity was founded by Vincent de Paul (1580–1660) with Louise de Marillac in France. Vincent de Paul was canonized in 1737.

22. Suleiman Agha, ambassador for Mehemed IV, reached Toulon on August 4, 1669, and from there proceeded to Paris, where he met Louis XIV. Throughout the text, and with only a few exceptions, al-Mawsuli will use the term "sultan" rather than "king." For Arabic-speaking Christians, "king" suggested Biblical associations where the "king" was a personal sovereign; sultan suggested a distant and alien ruler. For al-Mawsuli, the Christian/Spanish monarch was as alien to him as the Muslim/Ottoman sultan. See for the use of these terms, Bruce Masters, *Christians and Jews in the Ottoman World* (Cambridge: Cambridge University Press, 2001), 181.

23. The regent was Queen Mariana of Austria. Carlos II was a sickly child, and despite physical incapacitation, married twice before dying at the age of thirty-nine.

24. The *qirsh*/piaster was a unit of currency used in the Ottoman Empire.

25. This was Marie Françoise Louise, daughter of the Duke of Nemours (m. 1666).

26. Don Pedro had assumed the regency in November 1667.

27. See the study on non-Catholics going to America in Louis Cardaillac, "Le Probleme Morisque en Amerique," *Melanges de la Casa de Velazquez* 12 (1976): 283–306.

28. Mariscotti was an able cardinal who nearly became pope in 1700 but for the objection of France.

29. As it appears, the permit was for al-Mawsuli to go to Portobelo and Peru. Had he sailed on the *flota*, he would have gone to Vera Cruz, from where he would have continued into New Spain.

30. "All travellers and immigrants to the colonial empire were subject to control by Casa de la Contratación; their orthodoxy had to be established and whether they were of Spanish nationality had to be proved. Foreigners . . . were in principle forbidden entry to the colonies," Magnus Mörner, *The Political Activities of the Jesuits in the La Plata Region* (Stockholm: Victor Pettersons Bokindustri, 1953), 23.

31. As the list of *galeones* leaving Spain published by Henry Kamen shows, the *galeones* of 1675 left on February 14. See Kamen, *Spain in the Later Seventeenth Century, 1655–1700* (London: Longman, 1980), 133.

32. France's War of Devolution against Spain (1667–68) was ended by the peace of Aix-la-Chapelle, to which Louis XIV was forced to accede.

33. This was Cartagena de Indias, the richest and most populated city on the Spanish Main.

34. This is equivalent to ten million piasters.

35. See the description of such trading fairs in A. C. Loosley, "The Puerto Bello Fairs," *Hispanic American Review* 13 (1933): 314–35.

36. Mar Ilyas al-Hayy is a reference to Elijah, who is widely venerated in Eastern Christianity as a saint/*mar*. Elias is a variant of Elijah. His story, which includes his ascent to heaven (thus the epithet *al-Hayy*, living), is told in 1 Kings 17–19 and 2 Kings 2:1–11. I am grateful to Elias Touma for this information.

37. This is the only occasion where al-Mawsuli seems to fantasize.

38. The inns, *tambos*, were about twelve to twenty-four miles apart. In some locations in South America, they stood on the same spots where the Indians had built them. See the reference by D. Alonzo Enriquez de Guzman to the inns as early as 1535, "one called Capira, the second La Junta, and the third La Venta de Chagres," quoted in Clarence Henry Haring, *Trade and Navigation between Spain and the Indies in the Time of the Hapsburgs* (Gloucester, Mass: Peter Smith, rep. 1964), 183, n.1.

39. In 1668, the Welsh pirate Henry Morgan plundered the city and left it ruins. Three years later, in January 1671, he attacked the city again, aided by 1,200 of his men. See Peter Earle, *The Sack of Panamá* (New York: Viking Press, 1981).

40. Rabbat mentions that some of these lines are taken from the *Thousand and One Nights*, 20 n. They occur in the second journey of Sinbad.

41. A *miskal* is equal to 4.68 grams.

42. This is a reference to the mountains of Cotopaxi.

43. This is one of the over three hundred *obrajes* that were spread around Peru—textile factories as well as factories producing candles, cordage, hats, and shoes.

44. *Paramo* means a high and steep mountain.

45. A *cacique* is an Indian chief recognized by the Spaniards as an official of an Indian town.

46. The Franciscans had arrived in 1534, followed by the Dominicans, Augustinians, Mercedarians, and Jesuits (who arrived in the 1570s). "These five holy orders provided the bulk of missionaries who served on the front lines of the spiritual conquest, establishing *doctrinas,* or evangelical units, at the parish level that were designed to proselytize and 'civilize' the natives through methods that combined both persuasion and coercion"; Peter Flindell Klarén, *Peru* (New York: Oxford University Press, 2000), 55. For a study of the Franciscan *doctrinas* in Peru, see Antonine Tibesar, *Franciscan Beginnings in Colonial Peru* (Washington, D.C.: Academy of American Franciscan History, 1953), chapter 4.

47. The archbishopric had been established in 1546 and administered the affairs of the entire church in the viceroyalty of Lima; see Klarén, *Peru*, 56. Al-Mawsuli uses the Orthodox term for archbishop, "mutran," metropolitan. Despite being a Catholic, his ecclesiastical language was Eastern.

48. It is interesting that al-Mawsuli uses the noun that is associated in Arabic history with the conquests of early Islam. See al-Ghassani's reference below to the Mount of Conquest, *jabal al-fat-h.*

49. Atahualpa (1500?–1533), the last Inca ruler of Peru, fought and defeated his half brother, Hascarinca (Huascar) in 1532, after which he put to death all the royal family. In that same year, he was taken prisoner by Francisco Pizarro, the invader of Peru, and in either July or August of 1533 he was garotted (despite converting to Christianity) in Cajamarca.

50. *Maristan* is a Persian word meaning "hospital."

51. This is the mountain sickness *soroche.*

52. St. Alexis was known as "the man of God" (fifth century). On his wedding day, he and his bride agreed to part, whereupon he left Rome and went to live in Edessa as an anchorite. He died in 430.

53. Sentence missing in the BL ms.

54. *Shabaqat* is the Arabized plural of *chapeau.*

55. Schools were established to educate especially the children of the caciques. "The Spaniards realized the importance of gaining the support of influential people among the Indians"; see Tibesar, *Franciscan Beginnings*, 83.

56. The scribe in the BL ms. copied the same passage twice.

57. The dowry perplexed both Christian as well as Muslim travelers. Both ambassadors Hajj Mohammad Temmim (in France) and al-Ghassani (in Spain) found it strange. In Islamic law, it is the bridegroom who pays a *mahr* to the bride as part of the marriage contract.

58. Actually, by the time al-Mawsuli was visiting, the production of silver had declined dramatically from what it had been forty years ealier. See Mark A. Burkholder and Lyman L. Johnson, *Colonial Latin America* (New York: Oxford University Press, 1998), 139; and Lewis Hanke, *The Imperial City of Potosi: An Unwritten Chapter in the History of Spanish America* (The Hague: Nijhoff, 1956).

59. An engraving by Johann Theodor De Bry in 1600 shows the hollow interior of the mountain, with long ladders leading to the bottom. Naked Indians dig and shovel, while Spaniards outside the mountain lead silver-carrying llama away, presumably towards the port cities that will carry the silver to Spain. The 1700 illustration by Philip Lea of "The Silver Mine of Potozi" shows a small village, with the Jesuit monastery at the bottom of the mountain, the river, and the new mining site, "Young Potozi." Lewis Hanke, The *Imperial City of Potosí* (The Hague: Nijhoff, 1956).

60. This is a brief description of the forced labor (*mita*) of the Indians in the mines, first started in 1573. While some Indians worked in the mines, others led the train of pack animals to Arica, where the silver was loaded on ships. See Gwendolin B. Cobb, "Supply and Transportation for the Potosi Mines, 1545–1640," *Hispanic American Historical Review* 29 (1949): 24–45.

61. Clement IX was pope from 1667 to 1669.

62. Mules were valuable and were bred widely (along with horses) because they were needed for transporting mercury from Huancavelica to Potosi and silver from Potosi to the Pacific port of Arica.

63. Buenos Aires was the Atlantic rival to Lima. Illegally, contraband was imported from Europe to Buenos Aires and then carried to Upper Peru in exchange for silver.

64. The personal effects of priests and members of religious orders were among the few stipulated exemptions from inspection (Morner, *Political Activities*, 28).

65. By the time al-Mawsuli visited Lima, the expenses incurred by the treasury for defense against pirates had risen from 25 percent of the total budget in 1650 to 43 percent in 1680. See Klarén, *Peru*, 83.

66. The scribe in the BL ms. copied the same sentence twice.

67. The *audiencia* was the "second most important branch of royal government in America." It was composed of judges who had judicial and investigative functions,

and who oversaw the observance of royal laws, Klarén, *Peru*, 87. The *presidente* was the viceroy, the *alter rex*, who represented the power and authority of the king.

68. *Chiaoses* is the Turkish word for "messengers."

69. John 14:27.

70. Rom. 12:14.

71. This is Angelorum Civitas (now Puebla).

72. This incident occurred on December 9, 1531.

73. The attack occurred in May 1683 and was led by an English captain and five Dutch captains, one of whom was Laurens de Gaaf.

74. The island was discovered in 1542 and settled in 1564.

75. Julfa is near Isfahan, Iran.

76. This is a reference to Wan Li (1573–1619), who encouraged Jesuit activity.

77. St. John Chrysostom (c. 347–407) was the golden-mouthed patriarch of Constantinople, and was exiled by order of the emperor to Armenia despite the intervention of Pope Innocent I. He was a severe critic of ecclesiastical pomp and imperial vanity, especially of the empress Eudoxia.

78. France had seized Courtrai and Dixmude, as a result of which Spain declared war in that year, 1683.

79. Although Cadiz was the port for loading and unloading, Seville remained the location for the House of Trade and all its administrative machinery until 1717. See Kamen, *Spain*, 132.

80. Innocent XI was Pope between 1676 and 1689.

3

SPAIN

Rihlat al-Wazir fi Iftikak al-Asir
(The Journey of the Minister to Ransom the Captive)

Mohammad bin abd al–Wahab al–Ghassani
(1690–1691)

THE JOURNEY TO SPAIN of the Moroccan *wazir* (minister) Mohammad bin Abd al-Wahab al-Ghassani (al-Andalusi al-Fasi) took place at the beginning of the Islamic year 1102 (October 1690). Mulay Ismail sent him to negotiate with the Spanish monarch, Carlos II, for the release of Moroccan captives and the return of Arabic manuscripts that had been seized from Muslim libraries in Andalucia.[1] Ismail sent a letter with al-Ghassani, dated September 20, 1690 and addressed to the "Great One of the *ruum*, and prince of the Spanish regions and the lands of India," in which he informed "Don Carlos" about al-Ghassani and his assistant, Abd al-Salam Jassous. He was sending al-Ghassani with this letter, he wrote, in response to the letter the king had sent him in regard to one hundred Christian captives (including six priests) who had been seized at the liberation of al-'Araish by the "soldiers of Islam." Al-'Araish had been besieged on November 1, 1689, and on November 11 had fallen to the Moroccan forces.[2]

Ismail had earlier decided to free the Spanish captives, but then "some reasons" prevented him from doing so. Evidently, after the fall of the presidio, many of the Spaniards tried to escape "on the waves," where they met their death. Meanwhile, Ismail consulted with jurists, who assured him that the captives were part of the booty [*ghaneema*] that was rightly theirs (Moroccans') by religious law, because the captives had been an invading force that occupied the city after seizing the previous Moroccan leader, Mulay al-Sheikh, son of Mulay Ahmad, and taking his children hostage; because of their "pressure" on him, al-Sheikh had handed the port city of al-'Araish over to them.[3]

Ismail continued his letter to Carlos II with a tirade on the treachery of the Spaniards in Granada, two centuries earlier: how the Spaniards had expelled 40,000 Granadans after they had assured them of safety; how they had betrayed their word in "every city and village." Had it not been for that history, Ismail would have been willing to release the captives. But the jurists were adamant against such a move as many recalled their ancestors (including al-Ghassani) who had suffered at the hands of the *nasara* (Christians). For Ismail to authorize the liberation of fifty captives, therefore, he wanted in return "Islamic books, select and authentic, that are stacked in the libraries of Seville, Cordoba, Granada and other cities and villages, as our servant chooses, copies of the Qur'an and others." Should there not be books enough, Ismail continued, he wanted ten captives for each Christian, "Muslim captives, in whatever condition they are, and from whatever country they are." Ismail wanted his ambassador to select the books, making sure that all copies of the Qur'an were included. He also wanted the return of all captives, the "woman and the boy, the adolescent and the aged from among our subjects as well as from among others." Furthermore, he wanted Carlos to allow any free Muslim in Spain wishing to leave the country to do so. The reason he wanted to secure the liberation of the Muslim captives was to receive the blessing of God. Should neither books nor captives be found, he continued, then the hundred Christians would join their captive brethren and "serve like them" in Morocco. He hoped that the Spanish monarch would cooperate and return the ambassador safely to Morocco.

The account that al-Ghassani wrote about his visit provides the first Arabic description of Spain by a Muslim after the expulsion of the Moriscos in 1609. The account focuses on the country, surprisingly saying nearly nothing about the captives. Al-Ghassani wrote about the agricultural and rural communities in Spain that he felt sometimes resembled the bedouins of North Africa; he also described the highly urbanized and sophisticated cities and apprised himself of Spanish history, dynastic changes, the role of the Inquisition, and the nature of the Madrid government. The detailed information he included in his account strongly suggests that he must have kept notes while traveling, for he recorded, among other things, the distances between cities; the number of columns in a mosque; the inner designs of churches and cathedrals; and the (unfamiliar) names of regions, rivers, valleys, animals, and imperial officers.

Al-Ghassani was not familiar with many of the Christian terms, and therefore confused them (convent and monastery, nun and monk) or used them interchangeably. His writing is full of repetition of the same facts but in different words and phrases. Often he used the third person plural pronoun without including a referent—suggesting a generalized source for his information. But he was sure of his antipathy to the pope, whom he denounced repeatedly as the perpetrator of all the violence that had been committed against the Muslims of the Andalus. Perhaps because of his anger that Christians were so mistaken in their beliefs (due to the misguidance of the apostle Paul), al-Ghassani did not develop—or at least did not write about—any personal friendships with his hosts in the manner that Ahmad bin Qasim or Abdallah bin Aisha did. The reason for his overall sternness was Spain itself: it was, after all, a country that had expelled his coreligionists and his ancestors (as his epithet, al-Andalusi, shows) and now kept his compatriots captive (and, until his visit, did not want to release them). Neither he nor his king could really come to like Spain or the Spaniards. Nor could he, of course, come to like their brand of Catholic Christianity nor the papacy that supported it—with the memories of expulsion and autos-da-fé still circulating in North Africa. Al-Ghassani's text is therefore full of formulaic denunciations of religious institutions and the representatives of those institutions whose legacy of brutality and xenophobia he still felt. Yet, as much as he inveighed against the Spaniards and other Catholics for "worshipping the Cross," and as much as he was unrelenting in his grim imprecations, he remained willing to read reverently the Christian Gospels and to treat Christ with deep respect—which is more than can be said for the majority of early modern Christians who traveled among the Muslims and who derided the Qur'an and anathematized the Prophet of Islam. It is important to note how frequently al-Ghassani quoted the Bible, and how he used it, and not the Qur'an, to refute his theological disputants.

Moroccan hostility to the Spanish monarch explains why al-Ghassani refused to refer to Carlos II as anything other than "despot" (taghiya) or the "great one." Such titles were intended to demean the Spaniard in comparison with the Moroccan ruler. Curiously, just about a century earlier, the highest title that Abu Faris al-Fishtali, scribe to Mulay al-Mansur, was willing to use to describe England's Queen Elizabeth was sultana. He did not use *malaka*, despite the great admiration al-Mansur had for her. In 1777, the Moroccan ambassador to France insisted on using "great one" and not "emperor": by so doing, he angered the French, who demanded that he change his mode of address. Evidently, the titles used in Magharibi official correspondence were intended to place the European monarchs below the Muslim potentates—and to indicate the level of amity or animosity that prevailed.[4]

Al-Ghassani's account was widely read and orally transmitted. Half a century after the journey, the historian Mohammad al-Qadiri reported that the ambassador "traveled to Algiers in 1103 [1692] . . . after he had gone to the land of the *ruum* [Christians]. So he went to bring back the Christians [erroneously for Muslims] who were in the hands [of the *ruum*] and to bring back some books."[5] When al-Ghazzal went to Spain in 1766 and Ibn Uthman al-Miknasi in 1791, both were aware of al-Ghassani's journey. So influential was al-Ghassani's account that al-Ghazzal specifically noted that he did not want to consult it in order not to be influenced by its views.

In writing *Rihlat al-Wazir*, al-Ghassani cataloged Muslim history in Spain while describing the social, religious, and administrative characteristics of Spanish life and culture. At the end of his account, he turned to write the story of the Arab-Islamic conquest of Andalucia. Despite this nostalgic recollection of this initial eighth-century conquest and lamentation over what has happened to the country since it was lost, the main purpose of the account is to provide an informative and empirically based description of the lands of the *ajam* (Spanish). Al-Ghassani nearly always used this term—*ajam*—and not *isbani* to register the illegitimacy of the Spaniards in the land—that once had been Muslim.

Al-Ghassani is known to have died in 1707.

NOTE: The translation below follows the manuscript at the National Library of Madrid, Gg. 192. I have also consulted the manuscript at al-Khazanah al-'Aama, Rabat, 11329, the edition of the *Rihla* by Alfrid al-Bustani (1940), and the French translation by Henry Sauvaire (1884). The Bustani edition, long out of print, is good except for the fact that Bustani excluded a whole section on Spanish priests that he felt would be offensive to his colonial readers (he lived and worked in Tetuan when it was under Spanish rule). He also omitted numerous denunciations of Christians by al-Ghassani. The French translator inserted explanations and clarifications as if they were part of the original account. He also deliberately ignored specific terms that al-Ghassani used: throughout the text, al-Ghassani used the word *despot* to refer to King Carlos II; the French translation uses *roi*. There are numerous similar alterations.

The Madrid manuscript omits sections in which al-Ghassani presented historical descriptions and poems about the Andalus—and which appear in the Rabat manuscript (and in al-Bustani's edition). I have followed the Madrid manuscript in my translation but added one of the sections which appear in the Rabat manuscript—the opening (and very verbose) section since in it al-Ghassani explains the purpose of his journey.

Henry Kamen mentions in the bibliography to his *Spain in the Later Seventeenth Century, 1655–1700* (London: Longman, 1980) an English translation of the text by H. E. J. Stanley, "Account of an embassy from Marocco to Spain in 1690 and 1691," *Journal of the Royal Asiatic Socitey* 2 (1868): 359–78.

PRAISE BE TO GOD who made possible the sojourn of minds and ideas in the gardens of histories and news, and who expanded the hearts to make choices, and to wander in lands and regions, and who ornamented countries with jeweled territories. We praise the Almighty for what He has said about travel, which fills notebooks and tomes, and we thank Him for uncovering through travel the secrets of wonders and the wonders of secrets. We pray and salute our lord and prophet, our *sayyid* [master] and *mawlana* [protector] Muhammad, the noblest over whom the heavens cast its shadow and whom the earth bore; he who has all the perfect honor; and we salute his purest of family and his chosen companions.

For now:

Our sayyid, the sultan and imam, the victorious and courageous, possesses virtues that rival the greatest achievements of predecessors and successors. His qualities have overflowed on humanity like benevolent seas, and his ambition aims at the highest achievement in protecting the lands, the believers, the religion, and the regions of Islam. He is dedicated to defending and affirming the *sunna* [the prophet's code of action] of his grandfather, prayer and peace be upon him, the truly bred and glorious potentate, the shadow of prevailing justice, Abu al-Nasr Sayyid Ismail, son of mawlana the shareef,[6] may God continue his victories, and elevate his palace and enrich his country. He is impassioned to revive the laws [of God] and eager to apply them with clarity. He has dedicated his energy to liberating the captives and bringing them back in exchange for Christian captives who are in his hold; he wants to win the reward for liberating the captive, which the messenger and prophet [Muhammad] had promised.

I was one whom God had chosen to serve his Porte and whom God had graced to be near his highness.[7] He [Ismail], may God preserve him, sent me to the land of the *ruum* to bring back the captives of Islam, and to search in the Andalusian libraries for books of jurisprudence that the Muslims had left—so I could enjoy the guaranteed reward with him, may God preserve his glory. [This mission was] the first blessing that I received from his highness. So I went, with God's help, to those lands, with his honored permission and command, sheltering myself under his majesty and glory, and I saw there wonders of wonders, things that stun the mind and dazzle the intellect. So I recorded some of [those sights] on these sheets of paper, so that they would not be lost, and I wrote them down for fear of forgetfulness. I hope that they will prove useful to all the brethren who may consult them, drawing on God for help and support, for in Him is goodness, generosity, and benevolence.

In the name of God, the Merciful, the Compassionate.
And God's prayers and peace on *mawlana* Muhammad,
his family and his companions.

INFORMATION ABOUT THE ANCHORAGE OF JABAL TARIQ [THE MOUNT OF CONQUEST]

It is known as the Mount of Conquest [Gibraltar], for it was from here that the conquest of the Andalusian territory began. Tariq [bin Ziyad], God have mercy on his soul, crossed [into Spain] after Musa bin Nusayr, God have mercy on his soul, had sent his troops in obedience to the order of his prince, Walid bin Abd al-Malik.[8] At that time, Musa was viceroy for Walid over Africa and Tariq was deputy for Musa over Tangier. There had been correspondence and contact between Julian, in the territory across the sea,[9] and Musa, in which the former had invited the latter to cross and invade the Green Island. So Musa wrote to Walid, who said, "Skirmish in the territory with a few detachments of cavalry." So Musa tested it by sending the aforementioned Tariq,[10] who invaded and gained booty and captives but then returned to the land of the Berbers because of the war with the infidels there.

When the Berbers became Muslim, after long battles and horrible captiv-

ities, [Tariq] again turned against the infidels of the Andalus. Having seen
the cavalry detachments return safely and richly laden, Musa decided to
send another detachment in the year after. It was said that when Julian invited Musa to the Andalus, Musa turned to the Prince of the Faithful, Walid
bin Abd al-Malik, and informed him about the intended initiative, but the
latter forbade him from pursuing it, saying, "Do not expose the Muslims [to
danger]."

So he replied, "Prince of the Faithful. I am only sending my servant Tariq
with the Berbers.[11] If they succeed, we gain from their success; and if they
fail, we lose nothing."

So al-Walid ordered him to proceed, while Julian arrived with his daughter from the palace of Rodrigo in Ceuta. Julian then went to Musa in
Ifriqiya,[12] and described to him the fertility of the Andalus and the proximity
of its towns, and described how easy it would be to defeat its armies and pre-
vail over it. So Musa said to him, "I will accept your advice, but there is nothing in me [that motivates me to pursue this venture] except the desire for
[spreading] the religion [of Islam]."

So Julian led the men who arrived with Tarif and attacked the region, and
they returned safely and loaded with riches. Musa was thus assured, and decided to send Tariq with the Berbers. So Tariq crossed over from the coast of
Ceuta and landed near this mount on a small island [Algeciras] that faces the
city on the mountain slope.[13] This island is small, one mile in length and
width, edged by a large river that descends from the Ronda mountain range.
These are high mountains that correspond to the mountains of Fahs and Ha-
bat and others in the [North Moroccan] lands of the Berber. This small region is called [Green] Island, but it is not an island because it connects with
the land of the Turks and other lands of the infidels, such as Flanders and the
lands of Italy and Germany. There are no buildings or houses in this Island
today.

The Gibraltar anchorage is spacious, with a wide gulf, at whose entrance
stands a strong fort built in the best of manners. It contains equipment and
cannons, since it is the residence of the patrol guards and their families. It
dominates the whole anchorage and its wall extends across the foot of the
mountain connecting the fort to the city: it is around one mile long and terminates in the city at the edge of the sea. The city, which receives many
ships, is medium sized, more on the small side, inhabited mostly by soldiers
and their families. It does not have many traders and builders, as other urban
and inhabited locations have. On the opposite side [of the sea], on the

Islamic side and at a very close distance, is Ceuta, with its buildings and residences. It is the nearest location to the Andalus, separated by a distance estimated at fifteen miles. Most of the guards in this [Spanish presidio of Cueta]
watch the coast line of the Mount of Conquest from the land of the Berbers,
for it is their only fear and always commands their attention. They have
learned in their histories and chronicles that none has ever been able to cross
the sea to invade Gibraltar except from the Berber side. Ceuta was not conquered at first and, lately, none of the kings of our Maghreb, may God have
mercy on their souls, has reached it except from the coast facing the Mount
of Conquest and of Tarifa.

This city is called Tarifa for the following reason: when Musa bin Nusayr,
may God have mercy on his soul, was viceroy over Africa for Walid bin Abd
al-Malik, and Tariq was deputy for Musa in Tangier, and when Julian the
convert came from Algeciras, Musa wrote to Walid, who wrote back, saying
that he should test it with some troops and not to lead the Muslims into a
land of many dangers. So Musa wrote to him, saying that there was no gulf in
this land. So Walid wrote to him, "Test it with the troops to verify if the situation is as you have described it."

So Musa gave a hundred horsemen and four hundred footmen to an ally
from among the Berber known as Tarifa, whose epithet was Abu Zar'a. They
crossed in four ships and landed on the Andalusian seashore in the location
known today as the island of Tarifa. It was named thus because he landed
there. He then launched an attack from there in the direction of the Green
[Island] and won booty and captives, after which he returned safely.

What stands across the Mount of Conquest in our country is Mount
Bilonch. It is known as Mount Musa but it is named Mount Bilonch after the
name of a city that was once there. Some of its walls are still there, as are the
trees that show where it stood. It is two miles to the west of Ceuta. To the
west of Bilonch there are sweet-water springs long known as the Fountain of
Life. It is claimed that it was the Fountain of Life from which the Khidr,[14]
peace be upon him, drank. Near those fountains there is a rock on which,
some historians claim, Moses' boy forgot the fish.[15] Across from Tarifa is al-
Kasr al-Saghir, near the borders of [the tribal region] Lanjara: the city is
nearer [to the Andalus] than any other city in the strait, at a distance of eight
miles. [Despite the proximity], the buildings from this side are not what the
infidels expect or fear, for there is only open space between the Mount of
Conquest and Tarifa; there are no urban residences.

We reached this anchorage on the evening of the day we had embarked,

Wednesday in the middle of the month of Muharram 1102 [October 18, 1690]. We had embarked from the fort of Fraga, overlooking Ceuta, may God return it to the house of Islam. We found a ship in the anchorage, ready with supplies, soldiers, and other necessary equipment. It had been sent by the duke who lives in Sanlucar and who is its governor in compliance with the order of his great one. This duke, who is in charge of all the coast, is a member of the nobility, for none can be in command of the coast facing our land except one who has noble ancestry and who carries the title of duke or count. The big ship had been sent by the aforementioned duke from the governor of Cadiz and weighed anchor in Ceuta, may God return it to Islam.

When the eastern wind blew, they [the Spaniards] could not stay near Ceuta nor its surroundings. They sailed back to the Mount of Conquest anchorage and waited there until the wind would take them back to Ceuta in order to meet us. When we arrived in the Ceuta fort, the inhabitants came out to welcome us, as did the son of the captain. They told us that they were awaiting the arrival of the ship that is at the Mount of Conquest. We told them that they should either take us there or we would cross the strait in small boats that are fast and light. So they prepared for us three small boats and filled them with soldiers and cannons for protection, and we got in them and sailed in the protection and safety of God. We sailed for half a day until we reached the aforementioned anchorage and then transferred from the small boats to the ship that was ready for us. We sailed toward the city of the Mount of Conquest and spent the night on the ship.

Around midnight, the sea became rough, and the waves broke violently. The ship swayed from left to right and wallowed like a beast. We grew afraid, and we stayed in that condition until dawn. We asked the ship captain to return with us to the anchorage where we had been, for it was like a lagoon sheltered from the wind and the sea. We weighed anchor where the violent waves were quiet, under the fort and in the shadow of the Mount of Conquest. We stayed there for eight days awaiting the eastern wind that would enable us to sail to Cadiz, our destination. There the Christians had prepared to meet us and had gathered in large crowds. While we were in the aforementioned anchorage, the mayor visited us and sent us fresh and dried fruit daily; he also apologized for his failures—until one of our companions smelled the breeze of the eastern wind on Wednesday midnight, the eighth [day] in that aforementioned anchorage [October 25]. The aforementioned companion was knowledgeable about the sea, having traveled frequently.

Meanwhile, the sea captain was asleep, so we alerted him and informed him about the wind, whereupon we departed instantly, leaving that spot. At dawn, we saw the city of Tarifa, which is medium-sized, in a plain at the edge of the sea. It was named after its settler Tarif, as was already mentioned, and faces al-Kasr al-Saghir on our side of the country, as was already mentioned. We continued sailing half a day until the noon prayer. We then saw the city of Cadiz, which is a big city standing on an island in the sea with a land connection. The sea surrounds seven-eighths of it, and it has a big, immeasurable anchorage with countless big and small ships.

Cadiz is a big city to which travelers and traders come from every region. Christians come to it from every nearby village and city to buy and sell and conduct business. Countless small boats gather there, bringing food, countless supplies, and fruit. When the governor of Cadiz saw the wind that he knew would bring us over, he [and the inhabitants] began their extensive preparations to meet us. They assembled the soldiers and horsemen who were there and brought out the sea and land cannons and went out to sea to await our arrival. When we were two miles away from the city, a captain came to us in the governor's boat, which he had decorated with all sorts of cloth, silk, and brocade and on which he had hung one of the flags of the despot [Carlos II]. He boarded the ship and presented a long salute and apologized on the governor's behalf [for his not coming himself to meet us]. We then transferred from the big ship into the boats and aimed for the city.

We found the city governor standing at the edge of the waves, accompanied by all the women, men, and boys of the city. The governor had not left a single entertainer or musician nor a single cannon on the city walls or in the large ships, but had brought them along. The aforementioned governor met us in the best of manners and rejoiced to see us. We then saw the captives who were in the city of Cadiz—men, women, and children who rejoiced and pronounced the witness, praying for the Prophet, God's prayer and peace be upon him. They called for victory to our sayyid and victor by the help of God. We talked to them and promised them all good, assuring them that our sayyid, may God make him victorious, would not desert them as long as God was benevolent to him. That day proved a feast day for them and they rejoiced for the good news from God at the hands of Mulay, victorious by God, especially after they realized that our sayyid, God make him victorious, had no other intent or desire in gathering the Christian captives in his dominions except to effect the liberation of the Muslims from the hands of the infidel enemy, may God destroy them. They rejoiced in the attention given to them by the king, may God preserve him and lengthen his life.

The aforementioned governor then led us into a big house that he had prepared for our residence. He had brought various kinds of supplies, and he and the rest of the dignitaries stayed with us all that day and night until the next day. Then he started asking us about our travel plans and whether we intended to stay there and rest for a few days. We told him that we could not stay anywhere until we reached the destination we sought and the despot to whom we had been sent. He replied, "That is the desire of our sayyid and great one. He is rejoicing in your visit and awaits your speedy arrival."

So we agreed to leave on the following day. He brought us two coaches and led us out of the city while showing it to us, neighborhood by neighborhood. We found it to be a big and prosperous city, its markets full of merchants and craftsmen, buyers and sellers. The city has no wall except in the direction of the anchorage; from the other directions, its wall is the sea, because it is so shallow and rocky that no ships can venture into it. On the following morning, the aforementioned governor, along with his assistants, prepared for our departure. As was customary, all the inhabitants of the city, along with soldiers and cavalry, came out to accompany us. The governor of Santa Maria had sent some of his assistants to learn on which morning we were planning to leave and when we would arrive [in his city] in order to prepare our place of residence. On the morning we were preparing to leave Cadiz, a priest of the Christians who had lived in Grand Constantinople came to see us, telling us about the victory that God had granted the Muslim army, and that Sultan Suleiman,[14] may God give him assistance, had recovered the city of Belgrade and its surrounding regions and dependencies. After the victory, [the sultan] started repairing what had been destroyed of the city walls and defenses, and hired 12,000 workers for that purpose. We rejoiced in the victory that God gave to the Muslims. The Christians saw in that victory and recovery of the city proof of the sultan's power and might, and thus referred to the sultan in the highest terms.

We went out to sea, having found the ship we had used just as we had left it. So we boarded it, God almighty protecting us, and sailed to Santa Maria, the distance [between it and Cadiz] being six miles. We sailed so fast that it felt like it was faster than an hour. As we approached the coast of the aforementioned city, we saw a cavalry unit of nearly a hundred men that had come out to meet us. They showed much happiness and joy, and as we weighed anchor in Santa Maria, we saw huge crowds of men, women, and children. The governor and the judge had come out to meet us, with two coaches for us. Upon meeting them, they welcomed us in perfect and undeniable appropriateness and accord. We entered the city and they took us around all its neighborhoods, markets, and streets.

It is a very large city, wide and spacious, its streets paved with stones. Despite being one of the urban centers of the country to which traders and merchants flock, it does not have a wall separating the sea from the city nor the city from the rest of the land. To the seaside there stands a large house whose entrance has been sealed. It is the house in which the Sultan al-Sheikh, son of Sultan Ahmad al-Dhahabi, stayed, the one who went to Spain. None lives or inhabits it now, for it is the custom of the Christians to respect the house in which a king has stayed. They have walled its entrance so none can use it. By so doing, they preserve its status, as they have done in Madrid to a house that has remained uninhabited since the time of Carlos Quinto [Carlos V], who had fought the king of the French, defeated, and captured him. He then took him to the seat of his kingdom and the residence of his authority, Madrid, and kept him in the aforementioned house. He remained in Carlos's hands for quite a time until the Spanish king released him.[17] The king honored him by leaving the house in which he had stayed as it was and sealed its entrance with a wall. It is famous and well-known.

When we reached our residence in Santa Maria, the inhabitants and dignitaries came out to greet and welcome us. Unlike others, they were full of smiles and were very friendly. The governor and the judge visited us continuously until well after the night had cast its shadow. On the next morning, some dignitaries came with the duke and leader of this coast town, who lived in the city of Sanlucar, to apologize on behalf of the welcoming officer who had fallen ill and who had been prevented from coming. We accepted his apology and left the city after its inhabitants had come out to bid us farewell. The aforementioned judge and the governor joined the cavalry captain and his detachment, and they accompanied us for three miles until we reached a boundary known to them that marked the limit between their territory and the territory of Jerez de la Frontera. The dignitaries and all who had accompanied us came down from the coaches and bid us farewell, apologizing for any failures and saying, "Here is the boundary separating us from the governor of the next city which faces us. If we could have continued with you, we would have walked for the whole day, in honor of the majesty of the one who had sent you."

They meant by what they said: to honor one, they honor a thousand.

We bade them farewell and they departed. We walked a distance and reached the city of Jerez. We crossed a vast region full of trees and rivers with orchards and vineyards and numberless plants. The city of Jerez is big and spacious with old urban ruins. Some of its walls have survived, but most have been destroyed: the Christians did not bother to build walls nor fortifications, except for cities near the sea, such as Cadiz, and Mount of Conquest, which is well-fortified and has a not-too-high wall because it faces the sea. The city of Jerez is known as Jerez de la Frontera which means Across [the Frontier]. They mean that it stands across the land of Islam, may God glorify it. Most of its inhabitants are originally from among the Andalusians, and from among the nobility who had converted to Christianity. They are farmers and tillers.

We passed through it in the morning and continued walking for the rest of the day. In the evening we reached a city called Lebrija, a small city, close to bedouinism.[18] The remains of its outer wall have also been destroyed. We met its governor and judge, who led us to a house that belonged to some of the affluent among them. They then began their formal greetings and welcome. Some of the Andalusians revealed to us their affiliation by discreet signs because they could not talk except secretly. Most of its population look like they are from the remnants of the Andalus but they have been too long in the affluence of infidelity. As a result, decadence has overtaken them, may God protect us.

On the following morning, we left for a city known as Utrera. We passed a spacious region with vast lands in which were strange plants and cattle. Most of the goats in the Andalus are black. To the left of the traveler from Lebrija to Utrera, two or three miles away, is the Grand River [Guadalquivir] descending from Seville in which the rest of the Andalusian rivers meet. Ships can sail this river from the big sea [the Atlantic Ocean] to Seville, which is forty miles away.

Utrera is a mid-sized city. Most of its inhabitants are from the remnants of the Andalus. We reached it in the evening and found that all its inhabitants had come out to pray for rain. They all carried crosses on their shoulders; they met us in that state because they could not delay [coming to welcome us]. We stayed in a large house overlooking most of the city. After they lay down their crosses, they came to greet us, smiling and showing friendliness. The inhabitants are of royal descent and most of them are handsome, both men and women. We saw two daughters, the daughter of the governor of this city and the daughter of the judge: both were very beautiful, attractive and perfect. My eyes did not see in all of Spain more beauty than theirs. They are of the descent of the Andalus and of the blood of the last king of Granada who had been defeated. He is known to them as the *el-rey al-chica* which means the Little Sultan. In Madrid, I was told by a man known as Don Alonzo, grandson of Musa and brother of the Sultan Hasan who was defeated in Granada,[19] that the two girls in Utrera are of his blood.

This Don Alonzo is a man of excellent conduct, handsome, strong, and courageous. He is well-known among the Christians and is considered one of their best and bravest horsemen who confronts evils and wickedness. He is captain over the cavalry and the Christians praise his courage. Despite [his status among the Christians], he favors whomever he meets from among the Muslims and tells him about his descent, and admires what he hears about Islam and its followers. He told me that when his mother was pregnant with him, she yearned for a couscous meal. So his father joked with her saying that perhaps the infant in her belly was from the line of Muslims, and he teased her that way often. They did not reject their descent because they knew that they were from the line of kings. We seek help in God against despair and error, and implore Him for success and guidance.

One of the great signs of the friendliness of the inhabitants of Utrera is that in that evening they brought to our residence some of the friars who sing in their churches. They brought with them their musical instruments, one of which they call the harp, which is coarsely shaped and with many strings. They reported that it was the instrument of the Prophet David, on him and on our Prophet be God's prayer and peace. I saw one like it in one of the statues they have in their houses and residences which they claim is of the Prophet David, peace be upon him. All their dates and religions are taken from the religions of the children of Israel and from the Torah, as they claim. But differences occurred between them and the Jews when the latter turned against Christ, as a result of which there has been enmity between them. Since that time, they have continued to innovate in their religions and to follow the false doctrines and whatever errors the pope in Rome upholds, may God send him to join his predecessors.

Between this city of Utrera and the city of Marchena are twenty miles of open and spacious land. There are no mountains in these Andalusian regions except for those on the right of the travelers, such as the mountains of Ronda and others. There is a big river between Utrera and Marchena, with a big bridge that has been standing in an excellent condition since the time of the Muslims. The famous battle of Sagrajas took place on the banks of this river.[20] There is a small church which has a wall carving depicting that battle.

The city of Marchena is medium-sized with ruins of an old urban dwelling. Today it is closer to bedouinism with very friendly people, some of whom lay claim to descent from the Andalus. From there to the city of Ecija are twenty-one miles of open and spacious land full of orchards, gardens and trees, most of which are olive trees. To the Ecija side of the city of Marchena are eight miles, all planted with olive trees, and each olive grove has a storehouse and residence for the workers and their supervisor. The road from Marchena that goes beyond Ecija for eight days is also covered with olive trees, right and left, front and rear. The Andalus is that part of the country which is most densely covered with trees and olives. Near Ecija, on a hill overlooking the city, there is an old building which people claim is the garden-tomb of a pious Muslim in whom they found great miraculous power. So they have left it as it was.

When we approached the city of Ecija, we saw a beauty and splendor we did not see in any other city in this country. Ecija is situated in a depression near the river called Genil. The Christians still call this river by its accustomed name. It is a big river that descends from Gaudix [Wadi Ash] and from Genil from the mountains and the region of Granada. There are countless parks, gardens, orchards, mills, and various kinds of agriculture near this river. Nowhere else in this country did we see a place more spectacular. The city, with its gardens, parks, and residences, sits on the bank of the aforementioned river, like a firmament of moving planets.

I was reminded by what I saw of the beauty of this river and its stunning pulchritude of the words of Hamda [bint Ziyad], the Andalusian poetess, who came from the Genil region:

> Tears have betrayed my secrets in a *wadi* [valley] whose beauty is striking;
> A river surrounds every meadow; and every meadow boarders every *wadi*;
> Among the gazelle, a black fawn stole my mind, after stealing my heart;
> She desires to lie down for a reason, and that reason prevents my sleep;
> When she loosens her tufts, I see the full moon in the black clouds,
> As if the dawn had lost a brother, and in sorrow, clothed itself in mourning.

This Hamda is one of the poetesses of the Andalus. She is famous in that region and among all the poets and poetesses of the country. She wrote:

> When the slanderers wanted to separate us, despite not
> having any revenge against me or you;
> They launched their attacks in our hearing, after which
> my protectors and supporters deserted me;
> But I attacked them with my eyes and tears, and with my
> breath [wielded] swords, death, and fire.

Upon seeing this city and its beauty, she recited a verse from al-Hariri and added two others:

> I judged, once my eyes saw its beauty, that there is none
> like it.

And these are the two lines of explanation:

> May God protect it, until the supreme religion is fol-
> lowed in it, [and may it be] protected from all turmoil.

As we approached the city, its governor came out in his coach with his children and with some of his officers on horses, which, they reported, were of the best Andalusian breed. He met us outside the city and welcomed us without omitting any expression of joy and good manners. He led us into the city, and we went around its markets, public squares, and streets. We found it to be urbanized, neither large nor small, and very clean. Its inhabitants are beautiful and well-mannered. In its center was the community mosque, strangely shaped, well-built, with orange trees in its *sahn* [courtyard in a mosque]. It dates back to the time of the Muslims, and has remained as it was. The governor then took us into his house, which was large and spacious. He accommodated us hospitably, showing us in his welcoming speech all the appropriate signs of respect.

We stayed in his house that night. On the following morning, we left the city and saw a marvelous bridge under which, and near to the city entrance, were numerous buildings and mills. We continued walking until we reached Cordoba, which is a big city, one of the capital cities in the country. It is one of the capital cities, an old royal residence where the governors of the

Andalus lived before the arrival of Abd al-Rahman bin Muawiya.[21] In 168 [A.D. 784], Abd al-Rahman moved from La Ruzafa, where he had lived, to Cordoba, and he turned it into the capital of his kingdom and the seat of his rule and caliphate. Previously, it had been the residence of the kings of the Umayyads—from the time of Abd al-Rahman al-Dakhil and all others who came before and after him.[22]

The city is on the foot of the mountain called Sierra Medena. It is on the bank of the river called the Guadalquivir, which descends from the mountains of Baeca, Jaen, and others. The Christians still call it by the name by which it was known in the time of the Muslims. This river is the biggest in the Andalus. Many rivers join it, and it is this river that passes through Seville and flows toward the sea in Sanlucar. Outside the city of Cordoba, there are numberless gardens, orchards, and vineyards. As we approached the city, its inhabitants came out to welcome us. Among them were the captives who were witnessing to God and invoking victory for our sayyid, victorious by God. The Christian children were repeating what the captives were saying.

When we entered, we saw a big and prosperous city, full of artifacts and industries. Most of its vendors are women. We stayed in the governor's mansion and on the following day, we left after having visited the grand and renowned mosque, whose fame is far-reaching. It is a very big mosque, perfectly built and designed. Inside, there are 1360 columns, all of white marble. Between each column and another there is an arch, on top of which rests another arch. It now has fourteen doors, since many have been walled. Its Islamic *mihrab* has remained the way it was without any change.[23] The only change [by the Christians] was the installation of a brass window with a cross in front of it. Every Christian who enters venerates the cross. They did not add anything inside it or to its wall, neither small nor big. This mosque has a very large *sahn* with a fountain in its middle. Around the *sahn* there are 117 orange trees [Patio de Los Naranjos]. Facing the *mihrab* across the *sahn* is the minaret of the mosque. It is a big minaret built of stone, but it is not as high as the minaret in Toledo or Seville. It stands above one of the doors of the mosque facing the "Place of the Goat." The ceiling and the doors of the mosque are still the same, and nothing has been done except what was required to repair the ceiling, which is nearly collapsing, and other similar repairs. The Christians built in the middle of this mosque—facing its *mihrab*—a large square-shaped cupola, and decorated it with windows of yellow brass. Inside this cupola stands one of their crosses; there they keep their prayer books, which they use when chanting to the accompaniment of music. The gates of the mosque are still the same since their initial construction, as are the inscriptions, which are in Arabic.

Facing the mosque is the grand citadel, which used to be the seat of the kingdom of Cordoba and the rest of the city's sultanate when there was unity—before the advent of *muluk al-tawa'if* [Dynastic Kings 1037–1086]. We implore God to return it to the House of Islam under His prophet, peace be upon him. The walls of the citadel have remained as they were—well built, high, thick, soaring into the sky at the same height as the mosque. One feature of the greatness of the construction of this mosque and the height of its walls is the presence of stones protruding from the same wall. Ten arm lengths separate one column from another in order to strengthen and buttress the walls. Around the whole mosque complex, there is a wall as high as a human being, protecting the aforementioned walls.

This mosque is one of the finest in Islam and its fame precludes lengthy description. It is said that it is the same size as the Aqsa Mosque. I copied from the book *Nuzhat al-Mushtaq fi dhikr al-Amsar wal-Aqtar wal-Buldan wal-Mada'in wal-Afaaq*,[24] where there is mention of the Aqsa Mosque. It says, "There is none like it on the face of the earth, not even the community mosque in Cordoba in the land of the Andalus." The author mentioned that the Cordoba Mosque ceiling was wider than that of the Aqsa, and the *sahn* of the Aqsa Mosque is 200 fathoms in length and 180 in width.

On the outskirts of Cordoba, near the river bank, there are countless farming lands and stables to breed horses. Christians consider the horses of Cordoba and its regions the best in all of Spain. As a result, the despot of Spain forbade the Andalusians to mate a donkey with a horse, and whoever is apprehended for such a crime is severely punished: his property is confiscated, or he is imprisoned, or given other punishments. The breeding of mules takes place in a region called Mancha, which means "mark." Mancha is a very large region, six-days walking, a rough and stony area producing nothing but wormwood and other dry plants. It is the region that separates the Andalus from New Castile. The mules in this country are similar to those in Syria [*bilad al-Sham*], and somehow resemble them.

The inhabitants of Cordoba are tillers and farmers. There is little water in all the Andalusian region except in the aforementioned rivers. The inhabitants have not exerted themselves in building canals and drawing water, and all their farming is therefore done without irrigation—except what we have heard about in Granada and its regions, where water flows and runs in every place. There are many well-constructed bridges on this river, including a big bridge at the entrance gate of Cordoba, under which are the remains of another bridge. It was reported that the Muslims had built the lower part, which was destroyed by a seasonal flood ten years earlier. The Christians built another bridge on top of it, with seventeen arches.

From Cordoba, it is fifteen miles to El Carpio, a small town on an elevation and also near the Guadalquivir. There are waterwheels that carry water from the river to orchards below the town. The people are peasants and tillers and close to bedouinism. On both sides of this river, there are countless villages and towns.

It is twenty-one miles from El Carpio to a city called Andujar, an ancient urban center, also on the banks of the Gudalaquivir. Above the river and near the city stands an old bridge from the days of Islam. The city is surrounded by very fertile fields, orchards, gardens, and olive trees, along with vast cultivable land. The inhabitants are peasants and farmers, mostly from the remnants of the Andalus. The majority are descendants of the Serraj [family], who converted to Christianity during the reign of Sultan Abu Hasan, the last ruler of Granada—or so Christians claim. [25]

They tell in their histories that some of the Granadans, children of Ibn Zakary of Granada, had reported to the king that one of the Serraj men had had an intimate conversation and relationship with his daughter-in-law. The king became angry with the Serraj family, who were with him in Granada, and killed their elders at a time when the Serraj men were the strongest defenders of the Muslims, still retaining control of their region of Andujar after the infidels had conquered Cordoba and its surrounding regions. They were fighting to defend it, but once they heard what had happened to their kinsmen in Granada they became so zealous, furious, and hateful that they went immediately to the [Christian] despot and converted at his hand. They then left him for Granada: they attacked it and then joined the despot in his wars on Granada and its surrounding regions. May God protect us from ignorance after knowledge, and from going astray from the straight path.

Most of those Christianized in Andujar are of the elders of the city. But they do not have the same titles, such as duke or count, that other Christians have by inheritance. The highest honor they have today is to be descended of those people who had converted, so they can inherit the [honor of] carrying the cross on their shoulders, and putting its mark on their clothes. That is the badge of nobility among them. The positions the remaining aforementioned people fill are those of scribes, magistrates, and police [officers], all of which do not bestow much status or importance—unlike [the positions of] governors of states, large regions, cities, and capitals, such as Seville and others. At any rate, they are quite numerous in these regions—innumerable: some of them claim [noble] descent while others do not and reject such an allegation. Those who reject that descent and repudiate it claim descent from the Navarra Mountains, which are far away from Castile. Many Christians fled there after the Muslim victory over the country. They are proud to be descendants from the mountains and the surrounding areas. If any of them, however, has a governorship or a postion in official administration, he does not reject the [Serraj] descent.

One day I met a man in a coach in Madrid (whose name I forget now), accompanied by young and older women. They were handsome and beautiful. He stopped and greeted me lengthily, showing, with his women, joyous welcome. We reciprocated appropriately, and when he was about to leave, he introduced himself, saying, "We are Muslims by origin, descendants of the Serraj family." I inquired about him afterward and was told that he was one of the scribes of the court who oversee petitions, depositions, and similar things.

There was also another group of Granadians living in Madrid who had authority and power and who came to visit us. They were friends of Don Alonzo, who was a descendent of the King of Granada, while they were descended from those who had been in Granada but had been defeated. May God protect us. They often asked us about the religion of Islam and matters in that regard. When they heard our answers about our religion, about the purity of judgments on which Islam was based and many other things, they liked what they heard and listened carefully and thanked us—in the presence of Christians, and quite heedless of them. Throughout our stay in Madrid they visited us repeatedly, showing much love and affection. We ask God Almighty to lead them to the straight path and guide them to the true faith.

From Andujar to a city called Linares it is twenty-four miles. Three or four miles beyond Andujar, the traveler leaves Guadalquivir to his right as it flows down the mountain. Linares is a medium-sized town with ancient urban ruins. A small portion of its population is a remnant of the Andalus. On the outskirts, there are numerous mineral deposits—especially lead, which is exported in large quantities from Spain.

When we reached this city, its inhabitants came out, as usual, to welcome us. Among them were some friars who welcomed us and, on behalf of the nuns, asked us to visit and see them—which we decided to do the following day. As we were leaving the city in the morning, we stopped at the convent [kanbant] where they were. We entered and found them in a building near the church attending mass. There was a brass window looking into the church, through which they see the church and hear the mass. They were deeply respectful and quiet, from the little seven-year-old girl to the old virgin women. One of their customs is that whoever desires the monastic and ascetic life, whether young or old, enters the appropriate convent and vows that she is entering the convent after having renounced all desires and wants in the world and with no lust for a man, neither by looking at him nor by going out or coming in. She enters the convent and puts on a coarse habit. If she has money, she receives installments from it; if she does not, she serves another nun and lives and eats with her; otherwise, she depends on the income that accrues from the religious foundation. This convent for nuns (known in the *ajami* [Spanish] tongue as *monqad*) is completely prohibited to men. Old women oversee it and if one [of the nuns] becomes sick, a doctor is called who enters the convent and examines her in the presence of four other old women, one in front of him, one behind him, one to his left and one to his right. They surround him from the moment he enters the convent door and do not leave him until he departs.

A woman's entry to a convent is like her death, for she will have no more desire for the world. But if a girl is admitted before puberty at a young age, she will stay there until the time when she is asked to choose and given responsibility for herself. If, after reflecting privately, she finds that she likes the place and declares that she has no desire to leave or marry after she is released, a decision is confirmed, after which she is asked to make a commitment to stay there and neither to desire nor yearn for anything in the world. If she desires to leave and get married, she is not prevented and is permitted to leave. Some prefer to stay there for companionship while others stay there because they believe themselves to be following a righteous path, while others stay because they are afraid of shame and dishonor since they would have been thought to have already become nuns.

In most cases, a woman enters the convent because she does not have the necessary dowry to give to a man upon marriage, for one of the customs is for the woman to pay the dowry from her own money. This dowry has become so high that many women are no longer able to afford it except those who are rich and have a large inheritance. When they do not have money, they enter this place, which is prepared for that purpose. Some are of the nobility, with much wealth, but claim to become ascetical and indifferent to world, status, and honor: they want to leave honor and status to their sisters and to others in their families; they thus enter the convent. Most of them are virgins.

Because their mothers or fathers want to protect them from the iniquities of the world and psychological changes, some are sent to the convents to protect their chastity until they reach marriage time, whereupon they are taken out. In a convent of monks [sic] in Seville, I saw a tall girl of great beauty with a face as bright as the dawn, who was fourteen years old or thereabouts. She was not, however, dressed like the rest of the nuns, so I inquired why she was dressed differently, and was told that she had been entrusted there for the protection of her chastity until marriage. Her father had entrusted her there before she had been weaned at the age of twenty months.

These nuns have as many orders and *turuq* [Sufi ways] as the friars. Some are called discalced nuns because they do not earn or own a *fils* or a *dinar*. They live on offerings that Christians claim as charity. There are some female friars who follow a very harsh and narrow order. When a woman decides to join such a convent, she is asked for commitments, covenants, and statements in which she declares that she no longer has any interest in the things of the world and that she will never look at anybody outside the convent. Even if her father and mother decide to see her, she puts on a veil that prevents her from looking at them. These nuns are extremely ascetical, unlike others in different orders; even the windows between them and the church from where they hear [the teachings of] infidelity are very small and located in dark corners. These windows have nails and spikes on the church side to prevent [anybody] from coming too close, despite their very small size. The windows are located in dark places so that nuns can neither see nor be seen through them. Some nuns of this [harsh] order in the city of Carmona requested to see us, and the governor asked and requested us to go to them. We found them in this condition: extremely ascetical. After we had conversed with them and were preparing to leave, one of them said, essentially, "God has given you and us the path of salvation. But He has not shown us where He intends to lead us."

"To hell and damnation," I said to her.

This order is extremely ascetical and monastic. [Nuns in other orders] are tightly imprisoned and do not leave, or marry, or enjoy clothes and other things of the world. There is a big difference between them and this order. They are like the friars [*farayila*] in their asceticism. But some of the friars use their monasticism as a trick to enrich themselves with things of the world. If a friar has a government position, he collects thousands from the foundation income, claiming that it is for his livelihood. Others turn to monasticism in order to find ease and avoid the toils and troubles of the world; others still become friars in order to protect and shield themselves from people's criticism: none can talk badly about the friars or malign or accuse them of evil even if they personally witness their misdeeds. The friars are the ones who have gone astray and lead others astray from the correct path. They have gone astray and have led others astray; may God clear the world of them and sustain it by His praise. What we saw of the friars has driven us to mention all this.

Let us return to Linares, where we saw the friar [sic] nuns. As we have already mentioned, Linares is a medium-sized city, with evidence of urbanity and full of friendly people. To exhibit their friendliness and generosity, men and women assemble around a musical instrument. Their custom is for a man and a woman to dance together: the man who wants to dance stands up and chooses a woman, be she young or old, removes the sombrero on his head and bows in her direction. She cannot refuse him. Most of the inhabitants of this city are farmers and tillers, for it has not been a city either of trade or other means of subsistence; and it cannot become one because it is not considered a capital.

We continued from Linares to a village called Torre de Juan Abad. It is a big village whose inhabitants lean toward bedouinism. Their bedouinism is similar to the bedouinism of our Berbers in the Fahs Mountains and nearby regions. They all came out to meet us as we arrived, with some of their women carrying cymbals and tambourines like the Berbers in our country. Their singing is different from that of the city inhabitants among the Christians. We reached this aforementioned village on the day we left Linares, which was the day we left the Andalusian region and entered Mancha, which we have already mentioned. The terrain is rough, mountainous, rocky, and full of difficult paths. There are withered trees and dried river beds because this region, called Mancha, is very arid. It is dry in comparison to the rest of the Andalus, which has very little water. Its soil is red and its buildings are dilapidated, unlike the rest of the Andalus.

From the village of Torre de Juan Abad (and the word *torre* means fort), we reached a house that was prepared for our stay, off the road and at the foot of the mountain, near a city called Socalana. This is one of the customs in all the lands of the Andalus and elsewhere in that region: at each two or three distances, they erect a hostel [*funduk*] or house for guests and travelers. When a traveler arrives at one of them, he stays there, and finds all the food that he desires and can afford—each to his budget. He also finds hay for his animals and a mattress for himself. He eats and rests and feeds his an-

imals and whether he arrives in the daytime or at night, all he has to do is to
ask for what he needs or desires.

When he is about to leave the hostel or the house that is designed for ac-
commodation, the wife or the daughter of the keeper approaches him with a
bill of his expenditure on food, hay, and rental of the residence and mattress.
The guest has to pay all that is calculated for him, with no bargaining. The
owner of the hostel or the house pays an agreed-upon sum to the despot, so
that no traveler in this country, whether traveling far or near, finds himself
having to sleep in the open or wherever sleep comes to him. Rather, travel is
timed and covers a specific distance, so that if a traveler leaves from one location, he knows that his nighttime stay will be at a designated place. The
traveler does not carry on his journey any food or edibles; he just needs to
take money with him. Expenses during travel, however, are high because
prices are always exorbitant. A man in Spain economizes on his food, drink,
and living expenses and refrains from prodigality. Even so, he cannot save a
single *riyal*. Meanwhile, if somebody likes to enjoy his food and drink, his expenditure will be high and his needs many.

Despite all the hamlets, villages, cities, and towns in Spain, no one can
travel alone for long distances in the Sierra Medena Mouuntains or all of
Mancha for fear of robbers. The Christians who were escorting us on the
road were always prepared and on the alert during our travels. They did not
want any of our companions to travel ahead of us nor lag behind for fear of
accidents. Whenever we came across three or four travelers, we asked [our
guards] why they were traveling in small numbers. They told us that these
[small groups] were dangerous because if they found an opportunity in this
desolate region, they would do what robbers do, and no trace would be
found of them. In regard to [our encounters with] these robbers, there is
nothing to report—except one rare episode.

On our way out of Madrid toward Torre de Juan Abad, a man from a village called Orcera, which is a few miles away from Torre, came to us. He
saluted and welcomed us, and mentioned that there was great love and deep
friendship between him and Don Alonzo, the grandson of the King of
Granada. He reported that Don Alonzo had written a letter to him from
Madrid asking him to accompany us in this dangerous region and urging him
to stay with us throughout our passage through the land in which they always
fear attack. This man was considered one of the strong and courageous robbers of the mountain. It was mentioned that while he was involved in robbery, the despot of Spain sent a regiment of three hundred riflemen to

capture him, but he disappeared into the mountains and they were unable to find him. And when they left, he returned to his house in Orcera, where he still lives, unafraid for his life and possessions. Nevertheless, he wants to get a pardon from the despot and hold it in his hand, thereby ensuring his security and safety. But on his own, he is not afraid of anything.

We saw his farms and his horses grazing in acres of land near the city, roaming and feeding. He told me about himself and about the robberies he had committed in the mountains. But now he appears to have discontinued those activities. He said, "Had I been ready for travel, I would have gone with you to Mulay Ismail and asked him for a letter to the Sultan of Spain so he would grant me a pardon so I can feel safe. When somebody comes again from your land, I will accompany him." He wanted to stay with us [for the rest of the journey], which was the reason he had come to meet us. We told him, "We do not need you. It will be propitious for you to return to your house." We tried to send him back, but he refused and insisted on accompanying us. So we agreed, in light of his persistence and his friendship to Don Alonzo. Along with a friend of his, he continued with us for another day until we urged him to return to his house.

The hostels that are prepared for travelers and their companions have horses for the use of government emissaries and postmen who cross long distances in a single hour. When a postman approaches a designated place, which they call in their language *venta*, a saddled horse is brought out for him. He is met at the door of the venta with a glass of wine and two chicken eggs, which he consumes, and then exchanges his horse with the one that has been brought out for him. The venta overseer sends with him another rider so that when they draw near the next venta, the latter blows the horn, which serves to announce their arrival. As soon as they arrive, they find the horse ready along with the customary wine and other things. He hands over the horse to his companion to return it to its owner, and then takes another horse and another companion. He does this repeatedly, thereby crossing long distances to faraway lands in a single day.

When we were staying in the city of Sanlucar on the coast of the Great Sea [the Atlantic Ocean], we used to receive letters from Madrid and from the cardinal, along with communications from the Spanish court that had been sent three days before. We were stunned, since the distance was more than three hundred [miles]. This postal service prevails in the rest of the land of the *ajam* [the Spanish]. But for the postman to fulfill his duties, he needs to be given at the outset a note from the sender and the name of the country to which [the letter] is sent: only after showing these to the venta overseer will he be given the necessary companions and horses. Once the overseer of the first venta gives him what he needs, the overseer's action protects the postman from being mistakenly taken for an escapee or a fugitive from the law: this action is required of the overseer, who would be punished if he failed to do it. After crossing the first distance, the postman does not need any further introductions nor investigation. The hourly payment for renting a horse and hiring a companion is fixed. The overseer of the venta makes all the arrangements [for the postmen] based on a preagreed-upon contract that entitles him to designated payments from taxes and other revenues of the despot. The postman hands over what he is obligated to pay at every stop, and the owner of the hostel gives him what he has to in accordance with a commitment made at the beginning of each year. Most of the income of the *ajam* is from taxation and similar sources.

From this house west of Shaklana, [travelers] customarily go to another venta called the venta of St. Andres. There are contiguous villages and prosperous towns nearby from where people came to see us—men and women, along with their governor, who had grown-up daughters of great beauty and many children. They came from a distance of three miles. They were closer to bedouinism than to urbanity because they are far from cities and capitals.

Four miles from this venta, there is a small river and another venta for travelers. There is also a church, to which Christians come from every village and city. This church has a wonderful orchard with a fountain of sweet water. It is in a spacious region, open as far as the eye can see. Once a year, a market [*souk*] is held here at the beginning of the month of ———.[26] Travelers, traders, and others come to this place from every corner and region and stay without constructing any buildings. Fifteen days later, the people disperse and nothing is rebuilt again until one year later, on the appointed day in the same month. They call it in their language *feria*, which means *souk*.

From this souk, [we continued] to a city called Membrilla, a city with old buildings. But most of these cities are today called villages because they have grown empty and no longer have the significance associated with cities. The Christians, may God destroy them, do not care to build walls, and when a wall collapses or crumbles, they do not rebuild it. That is why the cities are now villages. The soil in Membrilla is good for farming and tilling, but its water supply is little except for the streams in the orchards and groves.

A mile away from this city lies Manzaranes, whose fields are joined to those of Membrilla. It is a medium-sized city but bigger than Membrilla and more urbanized. As we approached it, we were met by some dignitaries from a city nine miles away from Manzaranes called Almagro. They were the in-laws of the Aleppan Christian, the translator sent from the despot of Spain as ambassador. They came from their aforementioned city and stayed at the house of a cleric, a cousin of theirs. Among Christians, the cleric is the student who has acquired learning; he is not a friar, though like the friar he does not marry. His habit is different from the friar's and from other Christians. These clerics [*clericos*] are the ones who conduct the *misas*, which means masses, play a musical instrument in their mosques, and recite and chant their prayer books in melodious voices. Some are castrated in order to refine their voices and improve their singing. I saw two eunuchs, student youths, in the palace of the despot in Madrid. They reside there and melodiously chant the prayers to the accompaniment of music—in the manner that people like.

The people who came to see us from Almagro were the dignitaries of the city. They came to welcome us and saluted us and took us to the house of their aforementioned cousin. They had prepared another house on which they had spent a lot of money for accommodating the Christians who were with us. When we reached the city we found it attractive. At its edge was a small well-built citadel with a high wall and turrets. Encircling the wall was another shorter wall and encircling both was a deep moat in an excellent condition. The city itself does not have a wall. We entered the house of the cleric, who was extremely happy to see us. He showed us all the paintings [icons] he had and explained their meanings since he was very proud of them. He implored us repeatedly to drink with him a little wine, which he praised highly, saying that it was a vintage of many years. We told him that our religion prohibited us from doing so, and our laws did not permit us. He then offered us pure cold water which we drank. We spent the night at his house and since he was celibate, he brought women who were his cousins and sisters [to help him]. On the following morning, his cousins accompanied us to the outskirts of the city, after which they returned to their homes and lands.

From this city called Manzaranes [we continued] to a city called Mora, which means Muslim. The reason why it is named thus is known only to God, but perhaps because it became Christian much later than its neighboring cities. Between the two cities there are countless vineyards among which we traveled all day; there were no trees, only vineyards. Because the distance between this region and Madrid is short, the inhabitants increased their planting of grapes in order to produce wine. They drink wine at all times and with all their meals. Wine is their principal drink. One rarely finds anybody drinking water in all that country; but despite drinking so much wine, one rarely finds anyone who is drunk or unconscious. Whoever drinks too much and gets drunk is judged to be false and without self respect. Some of them who drink this wine mix it with water while others drink a little bit undiluted. Because wine is drunk in large quantities, and because Madrid has a large population of inhabitants and visitors, settlers and traders, the price of wine is very high. A tax is levied equal to two-thirds its price at the city gate, but nobody cares because they [Madrid inhabitants] cannot but use wine on all occasions. They all drink it: men, women, and children; males and females; nobility and commoners; monks, priests, deacons, friars, and others. All drink it, and none can do without it.

The city of Mora is medium sized, rather small, and its people are as urbanized as those in Manzanares. After we left it, having stayed the night there, we walked for fifteen miles until we reached a big river, which they call the Tagus. It passes through Toledo, which is six miles to the left of the road. The city can be seen by the naked eye from the road, for it is situated on a hill. On the bank of the aforementioned river, and in that spot through which we had passed, stands a large mansion belonging to the despot, which he visits when he comes hunting near this river and its surroundings. To the right of the traveler on both banks of the river are thick trees and woods that constitute a hunting sanctuary for the despot. They are guarded, and none can enter or hunt there. The road on which we were traveling led to Madrid and Castile and other cities. But there was no bridge for the crossing, so the people tied some wooden logs with ropes to the two banks of the river. When a group of people, caravan, wheeled coach, or wagon approaches, the raft is pulled up to the edge of the river and the animal steps on it with no difficulty, and then one man pulls it from one side of the river to the other. A traveler in his coach or on his animal can barely feel that he has crossed the river and reached the other side. They pay a small, insignificant amount of money for the passage. The river is beautiful to look at, wide and big, with many buildings, villages, mills, and farms on its banks. Fish are caught in the river, but in very small quantities.

Six miles on from this river, there is a village called Bargas. It is a bedouin city with no buildings and with people who are bedouin-like. We spent the night there after we had crossed the river and then we left for Madrid, which is twenty miles away. Just before reaching Madrid by six miles, we passed a big city called Getafe. It is a very big city but because it is near Madrid the latter has become in this time the capital city, where the despots of Spain reside. So the urban population of this city of Getafe, as well as of all other big cities in Spain, moved to Madrid.

We reached this city of Getafe at noon, and we met a man from among the principal servants of the despot. His name was Carlos de Castile, and he was known as the count. He was using the despot's own coach and had been sent to meet us. This count is charged by the despot to meet delegations that arrive from Islamic and other kingdoms. This is his only function; he has no other. He draws a salary of three thousand *ecus* per year.[27] When we met, he descended and greeted us on behalf of his great one and then seated us in the coach he had brought—after he had shown much courtly friendliness. He led us to Madrid, but a mile before [arriving there], we saw multitudes of people who had come to meet us, among whom were some in coaches, others on horseback or on foot.

We reached Madrid, which we found to be on a hillock near the bank of a deep river that flows from heavily snow-capped mountains. These mountains separate this region from Castile, known as Old Castile. Madrid is in the Castile they call the New Castile. The river overflows during the cold season because of the melting snows from the aforementioned mountains. The river is called [Rio] Manzanares, over which are two bridges, one excellently built, and the other destroyed by flood. The people are now rebuilding it and have put up the foundations and covered them with hardened timber so that coaches, wagons, and travelers can cross. We entered the city and found it very spacious, with beautiful buildings, and a large population.

We met there some of the captives who were happy and joyful, proclaiming in a loud voice the witness and praising the Prophet, may God's blessings be upon him. They also hailed our sayyid, victorious by God almighty. The Christian children repeated what they were saying. As we were entering the city, we passed by the mansion of the despot, and we saw him standing at a window looking from behind the glass. We were told, "There he is." The captives followed us, shouting in joy. We were taken through wide streets all paved with stones until we reached a mansion near the despot's, a big mansion that serves as residence for those who visit from distant countries from among the non-Christian lands. Their custom is that the visitors stay in the mansion for three days while searching for living quarters if it is their intention to stay [for long]. It is the custom of the *ajami* kings to send to their fellow kings messengers, called ambassadors, who serve as intermediaries among kings in regard to correspondence and other matters. As for those who arrive from other [non-Christian] nations, they reside in that mansion until they depart—as was the case with the Turkish delegation that came to Spain, as it was said, forty years ago.

[Members of that delegation] had claimed to be from Istanbul but they had been, more correctly, from among the underlings who wanted to create confusion for the king of Constantinople. Three years before, a delegation had arrived from the lands of Moscovy, far away lands near the North Pole. It came to the great one of Spain to ask his mother for the hand of a niece of hers in the lands of Germany in marriage to the King of Moscovy. Her parents did not want him to marry her, so they delegated responsibility to her aunt, and they sent the delegation to Spain. That is the reason the Moscovy delegation came to this despot, as has been mentioned.

When we entered the mansion, we found it very large and spacious, full of furniture, wall hangings and all the necessities. We found an overseer who was a servant of the despot and responsible for the royal bed. He saluted us warmly on behalf of the king, and we stayed there twelve days. We entered Madrid on the evening of Saturday, the seventh of the prophetic month of Rabi in 1102 [January 6, 1691]. During the twelve days, the count who was making arrangements for us, along with the overseer of the residence and other dignitaries, used to visit us, mornings and evenings, to convey the greetings of the despot. They said, "He wanted you to rest from your travels, and he is preparing to grant you audience, getting fully ready and fully attentive." When the twelve days had passed, the count who was responsible for us came to tell us that his great one was preparing for the meetings. He inquired about our protocol of salutation so he could convey it [to the court], for he had not met before with any of our religion, may God almighty elevate it. We told him that we had one way for saluting those of our religion, and another for saluting those who were of a different religion. The latter salutation was the following, "Peace be on the follower of guidance"[28]—with nothing added to it.

He left us to go report it, wondering about the salutation he had never encountered before. He could not but act in accordance with it as he recognized our determination and insistence that not a single word more be added. The aforementioned count returned with a piece of paper on which was written the manner in which we would enter, the dignitaries appointed to welcome us at the door and who would walk in front of us, so that we take cognizance of them. He said, "The *mayordomo*," which means deputy, "will meet you at the so-and-so door, and with him will be such-and-such dignitaries. He will have such-and-such soldiers of the guard, and at so-and-so door, such-and-such dignitaries will meet you from among the dukes and others."

On the next day, he came to us at an appointed time, after his great one had prepared for the meetings. He led us to him. We found that all the city community had gathered, men and women, so that we did not reach the despot's mansion without great effort because of the multitudes that had assembled. As we approached the door, we found the deputy accompanied by many dignitaries and soldiers. He saluted and welcomed us, and admitted us to the mansion, which they call *palacio*, which means palace. We walked past groups of dignitaries who stood up to salute us, each at his designated place, until we reached a large, domed hall. At the door, we found the chief scribe of the court, an aged man who was so old that he was bent over. Along with a group of dukes and counts, he greeted us warmly, and then admitted us to another hall with a cupola, where we found the despot standing on his feet. He had a chain of gold around his neck: it is one of the customs of *ajami* kings to use it instead of a crown. To his right was a gold-inlaid table, which had been made during our stay: after our arrival, the sultanic letter was laid on it, in recognition of the majesty and glory of its sender, may God almighty elevate him. To the right of the table stood one of his ministers, the constable, who has authority over all the revenues and expenditures, and who oversees the affairs of the palace and all the private affairs of the despot that pertain to his family and mansion. He is one of the dignitaries of the court. To the right of the aforementioned minister was the wife of the despot, with numerous ladies and daughters of dignitaries. To the left of the despot stood other ministers. When we entered, he welcomed and smiled and did not hide his politeness and warm reception. He asked numerous questions about our sayyid, victorious by God almighty, and when he mentioned him, he took his sombrero off his head in majesty and respect. We told him, "He is well, thanks be to almighty God." And we handed him the blessed sultanic letter after kissing it and placing it on our head. He received it with his hand and kissed it and laid it on the table that had been prepared for it, after he had also uncovered his head.

He then began to ask us about the journey, and the difficulties and obstacles we experienced. We told him that everything had gone well, and thanked him for all that he and his servants, who had escorted us on the road, had done. He was pleased and satisfied. After further talk, he said, "God be praised for your safety. We will discuss the purpose of your visit on another occasion." We left him accompanied by others who were there, and returned in the direction of our residence.

The despot is a young man, about thirty years old, white in color, short in stature, his face longish, his forehead wide.[29] He is known as Carlos Segundo and the meaning of *segundo* is second. It means that he is the second to take the name of Carlos, after his predecessor. He is originally from Flanders, the country of the Flemish, and is not of the lineage of the Spanish despots who fought the Muslims and conquered the Andalusian lands, Castile, and other parts, may God destroy them all and cleanse the earth of them and rebuild it to the glory of His name and oneness. For one of the earlier despots, whose name was Fernand Santo, and who defeated Granada and all the Muslims in its environs,[30] was living in the city of Seville, may God return it to the house of Islam. When he died, he left a son called Fernand, after his father, who is known as *catolico*, who reigned after his father for a few years and died leaving no male heir.[31] His wife Isabelle reigned after him, daughter of the King of Aragon, since Aragon is one of the capital cities of this country and a seat of kingship.

She reigned for years and used to go out and in, ride her horse, run, and act like men. It was during her time and reign that some Spanish sea commanders discovered lands in India that are in their possession today. They saw how the inhabitants were disorganized and lived like animals, without weapons, for their tools of battle were poles in which they inserted flint stones. When he saw them in that condition and learned about their laziness and indolence, he returned to Spain and told Queen Isabelle about them. She gave him three ships with cavalry and cannons, and he set off to the same place he had earlier seen, and where he had landed. The inhabitants of that land fought him, but he defeated them and became their master. He also captured their king. They still possess many countries and vast regions in India from where they annually bring vast riches.

By capturing these Indian lands with the abundance and wealth that is brought from them, the Spanish people have become now the richest among the Christians, enjoying the highest income. But opulence and urbanization have overcome them, for it is rare to find one of them who trades or travels to other countries for the purpose of commerce, like other peoples from among the Christians, such as the Flemish, the English, the French, the Genovese and others. Furthermore, they refuse to take the manual professions that the lowest and meanest outcasts take and they see themselves as superior to other Christians.

The French constitute the highest number among those who perform these base jobs in the lands of Spain.[32] Because work opportunity and income are tight in their lands, they migrate to Spain to work and earn and save money. In a short time, they amass large sums of money. Some give up on their native country and settle in this country; despite the high cost of living here, there are many opportunities for making good incomes.[33] The majority of the Spaniards see themselves as part of the government or the army: they refuse to work in industry or trade in order either to be viewed as members of the nobility or to be able to bequeath [a title] to their descendants if they themselves fail to get one.

It is one of their customs, may God destroy them, that all those involved in crafts, industries, and trade do not ride in coaches in the city of the despot. If anyone desires to join the nobility or to participate in government and become part of it, he leaves those crafts and trades with which he can be reviled and hopes that if he does not succeed [in reaching his goal], his descendants will. But on his own, he cannot secure a position in government, try as he does, unless he is a very rich merchant who does not use a weighing balance or sit in a store—like the rich merchants who have large businesses and enormous wealth that allow them not to buy and sell in stores and markets. Only after leaving trade or never even practicing it can one rise in status and nobility.

Nobility among them means that they can embroider a cross on the shoulder of their garment, designed in a style common among them. [Such a cross shows that the members of the nobility] have reached a high status; those who attain this status are very Old Christians who can count back seven grandfathers, and for whom other Christians would attest that they have known their fathers and grandfathers, or had heard from others and from old people that so and so is from the Christian lineage of so and so, and that he is a descendant of a Christian back to the seventh grandparent. None of them can be suspected of having any blemish or tinge of Jewishness; otherwise, he is a non-Christian. Only after all of this will it be ordered that the cross be embroidered on his shoulder. To reach this goal, he has to pay high sums of money to the officers of the court and the friars, who then grant him permission to do so. He will follow them in their ancient belief and doctrine. And this sign of the cross can only be achieved, as we have already mentioned, by those who have pure Christian origins or those who are descendants of the Andalus and had been dignitaries over their community, and then converted to Christianity for personal reasons; they are given that sign to show their Islamic origin, and their noble status in this corrupt religion. May God protect us.

Let us return to this despot in order to introduce him. We mentioned his ancestors and how it fell that he became king of Spain and of other countries such as Flanders and all the regions under him. He is, may God shame him, Carlos Segundo [Carlos II], son of Philip Quarto [Philip IV], son of Philip Tertio [Philip III], son of Philip Segundo [Philip II], son of Carlos Quinto [Carlos V], son of Philip el Hermoso who was a great count from Flanders where he has fame, reputation, and authority. When Fernand the Catholic died—who had been living in Seville, as we have already mentioned, and who did not leave a male heir to reign over his people after him—his wife Isabelle became queen. This Isabelle had a daughter, called Joanna, who married a Flemish count named Philip el Hermoso. The meaning of Hermoso is "handsome one," for in his time, much was said about his beauty and elegance. He thus came to be known as Hermoso.[34]

When Queen Isabelle died, her daughter from King Fernand was already married in Flanders. They sent for her to inherit the kingdom of her ancestors. She came with her husband, Philip el Hermoso, from whom she had a little boy named Carlos Quinto, by which they mean "the fifth," to carry the name of Carlos in view of those who had preceded him. He was the first king of Spain of that cursed lineage, may God cleanse the earth of them. By virtue of being the first, the grandson of his grandson will be called Segundo, which means "the second."

The daughter of Fernand reigned over Spain with her husband. This son of hers, Carlos Quinto, grew up to be one of the worst despots among the despots of the infidels—may God destroy them, a man of might, deceit, malice and intrigue. From the time he attained manhood, he did not rest a moment until he assumed power and rule. He started subjugating and conquering other countries of the lands of the infidels, may God destroy them. He moved and campaigned and led armies by sea and land. They calculated his maritime journeys and found them to be more numerous than twenty. He was the one who attacked Algeria with a huge fleet of ships and galleys, more than three hundred in number.[35] He took with him on his ships construction equipment, building stones, lime, and laborers. He anchored in Algiers at night, and the Algerians did not see anything until they found a tower hanging over them, firmly built and defended with cannons and mortars. He proceeded to destroy their walls and tear down their fortifications and houses. They were in great difficulty and danger, and he was about to conquer them, but God almighty refused but to favor His religion and to show its superiority over all other religions. The sea grew rough and the waves crashed, and all the vessels on which he had sailed sank. The despot survived in one of the seven of the ships that had carried his people and suffered with them great hardship at sea. It is said that he then took off the crown from his head and threw it into the sea, saying, "Whoever wishes to wear this crown, let him come and conquer Algiers." Only he and those who were on the seven ships escaped.

On that same journey to Algiers, this Carlos Quinto also laid siege to Tunis.[36] As for the tower he built in Algiers, it is known today as the Tower of Mulay Hasan; it is still standing in perfect condition, overlooking the city. It is near the city, a cannon shot away, to the right upon exiting from Bab Azzoun. This despot conquered many regions of the Andalus and other regions in the lands of France, Germany, and Valencia [Venice]. He was the one, as we already mentioned, who fought the King of France, captured him and brought him to Madrid, and then released him for a ransom. It is told about this despot that after he took possession of all the lands and conquered Germany he grew old. He had a son named Philip Segundo, which means "the second," to hold that name considering that his grandfather was the count who came from Flanders and who gave him kingship over Spain, Flanders, and Milan. Carlos had a brother named Fernand, to whom he gave possession of Germany and the title of emperor. This present despot, may God destroy him and cleanse the earth of him, is a descendant of that emperor. After he [Carlos] appointed his son and his brother, he became a friar and joined a convent of friars and became one of them [in 1556].

He claimed to have become a friar and an ascetic in a city called Plasencia, in the province of Castile, fifty-four miles from Madrid. Before becoming a friar, his wife had been Isabelle, the daughter of the King of Portugal, sister of Sebastian al-Kharij,[37] who invaded our land [in 1578] accompanied by the one who had appealed to him, the son of Mulay Abdallah. When this Philip Segundo became king [in 1556], he proved to be one of the most evil despots of his time. He attacked countries and laid siege to one of the capital cities of France,[38] setting up cannons and mortars, hoping to destroy it. It was reported that a church he had besieged in the city, and which was named after a friar called [Saint] Lorenzo el Real, stood between the city and the cannon range, as a result of which he could do nothing to the city. When the siege grew long, there was no alternative but to destroy this church, which had prevented him from hitting the city. He vowed to build another, greater church and name it after this Lorenzo. So he turned his cannons against the church, destroyed it, and then attacked the city. When he returned, he built the church as he had vowed to do. It is known among them as Escorial. The Escorial is at the foot of a mountain near Madrid. It is an amazing building that we will describe later, God willing.

They claim that this Philip Segundo met with his maternal uncle, Sebastian, the despot of Portugal who invaded the land of the Maghreb during the reign of Sultan Mulay Abd al-Malik [1576–78], son of Sultan Mulay Mohammad al-Sheikh [1555–57], accompanied by the son of Mulay Abd Allah [Al-Mutawakil, 1574–78]. When this Philip heard of his uncle's invasion of the land of the Muslims, he approached him and talked to him about that. He advised him to restrain himself and not to expose himself and get embroiled in the land of the Arabs. He tried to dissuade him as much as he could, warning him not to heed the appeal because he did not know the land and because leaving his country for another country was not something he should do, and because he had no capability for fighting the Muslims, as the Moroccans had a king.

They reported that the one who had appealed to him sent him letters from some of the Moroccan tribes who had sworn allegiance to him.[39] The despot of Portugal would not but follow his own opinion, and he did not heed his nephew's words or advice. So God gave the Muslims in that invasion a great victory, the first to be seen in a long time. On the day of that blessed victory, Sultan Abd al-Malik died as a result of illness that had struck him as he was on his way to fight the Christians, after he had heard of their invasion. The Christians recall his bravery and strength and say that he fought with his sword, despite his illness, until the illness overcame him and his high fever prevented him from fighting any more. So he died, God have mercy on his soul.

On that same day, his nephew, Mohammad, son of Abdallah, was killed, and so was Sebastian.[40] All the Christians who were with him perished, and only a few escaped, so few that they were not worthy of being counted. The number of the Christians, as it is known to us, was 80,000. The Christians [however] claim that the number of the army that was with Sebastian during the invasion was 18,000: 12,000 Portuguese and 3,000 English who had joined him during the period of peace between them [England and Portugal], and 3,000 Spaniards, sent by his nephew, Philip Segundo. The correct number is what is confirmed by the Muslims.

Because the despot of Portugal did not accept his nephew's advice, and because he got embroiled in the lands of the Arabs, he is credited with stupidity and folly. It is because of that blessed invasion that the Portuguese have remained weak to this day, may God destroy them. Sebastian was killed and the Portuguese suffered as they did, since their despot had left no son to inherit his throne. They reported that he had two brothers, one a cardinal and one who reigned after him for a few days and died without issue. When the line of their kings ended with the death of these two, Philip Segundo inherited the kingdom of Portugal through the line descending from his mother Isabelle—in accordance with their customs and canons that female succession is legitimate if there is no male heir.

During the time of this Philip Segundo, the remaining Andalusians revolted after the Christians defeated them in Granada and its surroundings.[41] They heard of the arrival of ships brought from Algeria by Habib Rais. He landed near Almeriyah, which convinced them that he was going to help them, but what he did was to carry as many of that city and surrounding inhabitants—as many as he could in his ships—and crossed over to his country. The Andalusian rebels were thus unable to resist the Christians, who fell on them with their swords. Some converted under force after others had fled. They remained in that situation—converted and defeated—for forty years until the time of Philip Tertio, son of Philip Segundo.[42]

They report that the King of the Turks sent a letter to the minister of Philip Tertio asking him to find means to send out the remaining Andalusians of the country who had been defeated; he would view such an action as a sign of amity and cooperation. Treacherously, the minister advised his master to expel all the remaining Andalusians who were new to the religion. "Most of them," he said, "are still alive and their numbers are higher than the numbers of Christians. We cannot be sure that they will not revolt again. Better that they evacuate this country, and be transported across the sea to be dispersed in the lands of the Berbers. Staying in this country where they have lived is dangerous." The despot agreed to what his minister advised him, and he ordered that they be gathered and taken across the sea—except for those who had converted willingly to Christianity, and who were more numerous than those who were forcibly converted, those who had been given protection, or those who had gone into hiding and about whom nobody knew anything. At any rate, since the number [of those who stayed] was very high, it was not easy to locate them because they intermarried and forgot Islam. Most of those who left the country in that period were of the rebels from Granada and its surroundings. Their number was high. After the minister advised his great one to expel those who had converted to Christianity, many Christians slandered him by accusing him of being Jewish because he failed to urge the expulsion of the Jews, who had been considered Christian.

Christians are quite frequently secret Jews. As a result, there is in Madrid a court/tribunal [*diwan*] with numerous senior jurists of the [Christian] religion. They call it the Inquisition, and for the smallest reason, they search out anybody who has a trace of Judaism. They apprehend him and put him in jail after seizing his money, property, and all his possessions. They then divide everything among themselves while leaving him in jail for a year. They then interrogate him about what he is accused of, and if he denies the accusation, they tell him that he can prove his innocence by informing on those who betrayed or accused him. He then gives three names, and if the betrayer is one of the three whom he has named, he explains that there has been enmity between them for such-and-such time in regard to such-and-such a matter. If they believe him, he finds the means to protest and defend himself. The case against him stretches out in time, until the accusation is forgotten, and the only thing he wants is to save himself. He will then be released.

If, however, he is convicted of what he had been accused of, or to what he had confessed, they force him to abjure his Judaism and to convert to Christianity. If he abjures it and converts to Christianity, they take him out and parade him in the market places, placing a yellow cross on his shoulder to signal that he had been a Jew but has converted. After six months of keeping the cross, he removes it and becomes one of the Christians. If he insists on his Judaism, or if he is convicted on the basis of the evidence, and if he does not abjure his belief, they burn him without permitting any intercession for him. That is why there are no Jews in all of Spain and Portugal.

This aforementioned tribunal is designed to investigate this and similar matters that undermine their religion—especially when someone's faith is in question, or when there is a smell of something shameful. None can challenge the tribunal or accuse [its members] of falsehood or avarice; so the members look for any reason and means to pounce on and destroy [their victims]. None can effect the release of anybody in their hands, not even the king himself. If somebody is accused of something of that sort [being Jewish] and even if he seeks the protection of the king, the latter cannot show him respect, nor will he be able to prevent them from seizing him even if he is one of the king's servants or commanders. If they detect any of that smell on him, they seize him wherever he may be, whether he is with the king or in church or anywhere else.

During our stay in Madrid, they accused one of the king's and the ministers' officers of Judaism. They apprehended him and then jailed him in Toledo, where he still is. While we were there, they also accused another man who oversaw the collection of one of the king's revenues. They pounced on him, his wife, children, family, and servants, and threw them all in jail. They seized all his money and all his household property. They are still in jail despite once having large amounts of money. One of the members of this tribunal is a man sent by the pope in Rome, may God shame him, an envoy who represents the pope in all these and similar matters. They call him, in their language, *al-nuncio*.

The people accused of Judaism are of numerous nationalities, but most of them are Portuguese. The majority are descendants of the Jews who inhabited this country during the Andalusian period. They had been protected as *dhimmis* in that time. But when the Muslims were defeated, they sided with the Portuguese and merged with the Christians. It is said that there are many more of them in Portugal than in Spain.

After the aforementioned Philip Tertio died, during whose reign the remaining Andalusians were expelled from this land,[43] Philip Quarto, which means he was the fourth to use the name Philip, succeeded him. He was an evil despot among the despots of the infidels, may God destroy them. During his reign, the Portuguese nation revolted and called on a man named the Duke of Braganza to reign over them, the father of the present Portuguese despot. His wife had been a sister of a duke from among the notables of Spain, high in nobility, the duke of Medina Sidonia. They claim that his grandfather [ancestor], Don Alonzo de Guzman, was the governor of Tarif when Tariq [bin Ziyad], may God have mercy on his soul, conquered the city. Until today, the family carries the surname of Guzman.

When the people of Portugal called the Duke of Braganza to reign over them, he consulted his wife about the matter, and she advised him to accept the offer, saying, "A king for one night is better than a duke for fifty years." So he accepted their offer. He then reached an accord with his brother-in-law who was living in the city of Sanlucar. Between Sanlucar and Portugal there is a city called Ayamonte, where there is a powerful marquis, one of the nobility of Spain, known as the Marquis of Ayamonte. He entered with them into an accord, along with another duke known as the Duke of Yjar.

Each of them wanted himself to become king. Philip Quarto discovered [the plot] and summoned those three who were his subjects and in his kingdom and sent them off to Madrid before they found out what he knew.

There he had them tortured in many ways to force them to confess, for he had secretly read some letters that had been exchanged among them, revealing their plans. Meanwhile, the Duke of Medina Sidonia confessed quickly since there was affection [*mahabba*] between him and the despot. So he was released and exiled to a city called Valladolid. He was removed from office after he had been the commander of the fleet that patrolled our coast, may God protect it. As for the other two, they were put to painful torture, but they did not confess anything. The king took them [out of prison], along with all their servants and Medina Sidonia's servants, who were privy to the plan, to a plaza in Madrid and had them all killed.

As a result, war broke out between Portugal and the despot of Spain, lasting for twenty-six years. It ended with the death of Philip Quarto in 1666 in their Christian era, and in ours, 1077. [44] The king of Portugal then paid [a certain sum of money] to the Spaniards.

The despot of Spain, Philip Quarto, had many children, but according to the laws, none could inherit the throne because they were illegitimate. Philip had married the cousin of the Emperor of Germany[45]: he had brought her over in order to marry her to one of his sons; but upon her arrival, the son who was to marry her died, and then his own wife died too.[46] When she [the young German girl] reached puberty, he took her as his wife. She bore him a son, Carlos Segundo, the despot who is ruler today. But when Philip Quarto died, he left [Carlos] a child,[47] so his mother took over as regent. As for the other children who had no right to inherit, it is said that most of them became friars, including the friar who is the mufti of Malaga, known in their language as *sobisb* [*obispo*/bishop], which means mufti. He had another son named Don Juan of Austria whose star rose among them because of his bravery, wisdom, and cunning. He commanded the armies and waged wars and crushed rebellions. He assumed this responsibility throughout the time his father's wife was regent and as long as his brother from his father was still a minor. He became so powerful that he did not allow anybody [to present a different] opinion or point of view, and he started laying down rules and initiating actions unlike any known before. He prevailed over the members of the court and the queen, his father's wife, saying always, "I am only one of my brother's servants, and I will continue to serve him until he grows older." But members of the court and the queen were very suspicious that he wanted to become king himself.

The queen had a man by the name of *duende* who served as her agent.[48] He reproached Don Juan for what he was doing and was subsequently

imprisoned in a well-defended fort on the highest hill in the country, overlooking a village known as Consuegra.[49] It was eighteen miles from Toledo,
on the road from the Andalus. The fort is well-built and quite strong and
dates back to the days of the Muslims. Because of its elevation, it overlooks
many villages and cities in the region of Toledo. The castle has two high walls
and within it, there is a big church with a few friars. I entered this fort and I
saw how well-built and fortified it was, noting the attention that its builders
had given to its construction, may God rest their souls.

After the duende was imprisoned in the aforementioned place, Don Juan
ordered that he never be freed. He then began to monitor members of the
court—the decisions they took, the opinions they expressed, and the actions
they carried out. He approved what he thought was good, and rejected what
he thought was bad. He also diminished their status and reduced their incomes. He said, "This one does not deserve to merit this [royal treatment],
and why should that one eat up all [the money]?" He got to the point where
he allowed the queen expenses only for her essential needs. When his
brother became fourteen, he took him one day to the kingdom of Aragon
and presented the throne to him. He then returned with him to Madrid and
[Don Juan] started to serve him as his deputy, equal to a servant. He continued to wield power over his brother's mother until he exiled her out of
Madrid to Toledo, where she remained for a year and a half.[50] When Don
Juan of Austria died,[51] the queen returned to her seat. The duende was released from prison and left for India [Philippines], where he still governs a
large region.[52]

Carlos Segundo grew up in the court and married the daughter of the
French great one.[53] She died without issue. After her, he married his maternal cousin who is the [paternal] cousin of the emperor in Germany.[54] He has
been married to her for a year, but until now, he has no children. He has not
traveled anywhere, nor has he led an army nor waged war. He likes the seden-
tary life and does not ride horses or any other animals. Instead, he always
rides a coach with his wife and goes out to his hunting fields in his coach. He
always goes to church and worships in accordance with all their rites.

When we left him on the day of our meeting with him, we had given him
the sultanic letter which he handed to the Aleppan Christian, the translator,
to translate into their *ajami* language. Once it was translated and he saw what
the Prince of the Faithful, God be on his side, had mentioned about deliver-
ing to us five thousand books and five hundred captives, he felt the weight of
the Alawite [Moroccan ruler],[55] and he did not know how to respond to the

request, knowing full well that it was a demand from the king, may God grant him victory. Both he and members of his court could not but feel anxious in their hearts given the great reputation of the Alawite Imamate and the king's grand position, may God protect him by His grace. He and his courtiers fell into discussion and saw that it would be better for them and indicative of their cooperation to respond to what Mulay the Imam had demanded and to conform to his command, may God almighty glorify him. They deliberated for days and we had other meetings with him in which we were invited to see him. After they became cognizant of the sultanic command, they reported that the Islamic books in Spain had been burned and they brought to the discussion with us the chief court secretary and the cardinal who is the head of their religion and the successor to the pope in Rome. He is the final arbiter in religion and politics.

Mulay the Imam, may God keep him and sustain him, had proposed an alternative in his noble letter to them: if they are unable to find books or they are unable to procure them, they can provide instead a thousand Muslim captives. They tried to reduce the number from a thousand, but found no way of doing so and could not but abide by the command. When the victorious Mulay the Imam, may God grant him victory, agreed to that, they started looking for captives and gathering them together. Meanwhile, and while the despot was sending out to all regions for captives, he continued to look after us and ordered that we be taken to his parks and hunting areas and to his palace complex to see the living quarters, residences, and gardens. By so doing, he wanted to provide us with recreation, so that not a single large mansion of his courtiers and servants in Madrid did we not see. We also saw their parks and gardens, and whenever we met him, he smiled and expressed his joy, and he did not fail in honoring and hosting us throughout our stay with him.

There are many parks in Madrid. The despot has a large mansion called El Retiro which is his summer residence, consisting of a beautifully designed orchard with beautiful streams and rivulets. In the middle of this orchard there is a big river with beautiful buildings standing on its two embankments; near it are domed buildings, built in the best of style, to provide shade in the summer time. There were also boats and small ships that the despot used for his excursions. During the cold season, this river freezes so that a man can walk on it. So, you find the Christians walking on the ice with great skill, but most of those who do so have had some experience and are Flemish or English; for their countries are to the north, where snow and ice abound in all regions, especially in rivers. They reported that Flemish women slide on ice by putting iron sheets on their soles; they go for long distances in the mornings in order to earn their living, buying and selling, and in the evenings they return to their homes. I saw some Christians walk on ice in this river: the man stands on one leg and raises the other and stands straight so that he does not sway to either side and then he passes as quick as lightning.

Many people visit this river during the snow period to look and wander about. There are so many Christians and so many coaches filled with men and women that the aforementioned park cannot hold them all. When the summer season arrives and the despot comes to reside here, no one can enter except those who have permission. In this park, there is a big marble pedestal with the statue [sura] of a big horse made of red brass. The horse has a brass saddle and is rearing on its hind legs. On the horse sits the statue of the father of this despot, Philip Quarto, made of brass too, with a rod in his hand. It is one of their customs, which they call baston. We were told that at the time of horse mating, they bring the mare and position her in front of the statue and then activate the horse so that it moves and makes sounds and neighs just like a horse. Then they bring to her a stallion they have selected and chosen, so that the female will produce foals in the likeness of the statue. We saw something similar to that in another mansion of the despot, outside the city. The mansion is in a park on the river embankment—the same river that passes through the city. The horse is like another one, under a similar statue of the father of the king, Philip Quarto.

[Carlos Segundo] has many orchards and parks outside the city of Madrid, and many locations designated exclusively for royal hunting and shooting: other than he, none can hunt there, no matter of what rank. One day he sent the count who was assigned to attend to us and ordered him to take us out to the hunting grounds and gave us permission to hunt there. The grounds were six miles from the city of Madrid, wherein stood a large mansion called El Pardo, which his father had built. It is a huge mansion that overlooks the river Manzanaris, which passes through Madrid. This hunting ground has many wild animals, like deer, hog, and rabbit: they are great in number because none but the king can hunt there since the ground is protected for his use. He does not even permit anyone of his inner circle to hunt. We were told that the permission granted to us was special, never before granted to anyone else. They reported that the French and German ambassadors had asked for such a permission from him, but he refused to grant it.

In this hunting ground, there are wolves much bigger than the wolves in our country. They are big yellow wolves, strong and ferocious. We tried to get a glimpse of them as we were hunting there but could not. One day, when the despot went hunting, he killed a wolf and brought it back to his residence. He then sent it to us so we could inspect it since he knew that this kind of wolf did not live in our country. They call this kind of wolf *el lobo*; the small kind which is in our country they call *el zorro*. They describe the large species as powerful and fierce; perhaps this is the species, as nearly big as a tiger, about which [stories are told] in the land of Egypt.

This city of Madrid, despite being the seat of the ancestors of this despot [Carlos Segundo], was not always as urbanized, big, and wide in its streets. The monarchical seat of the despots before his father and grandfather was a city called Valladolid, which is three days away from Madrid. As soon as his grandfather settled in Madrid, buildings, houses and construction increased with the increase of inhabitants and the general population. Most of the Christian nobility of Spain live there with the despot, and whoever rules another country or governs another city leaves somebody in it to represent him. The markets of this city are spacious and full of people buying and selling, along with merchants and craftsmen, men and women. All the inhabitants of the villages and towns near Madrid come to this market. There are many villages near Madrid whose inhabitants bring to it all that can be sold of foods and edibles and fruit—even bread. Only a small amount of bread is baked in Madrid, and most of what is consumed in the city comes from the surrounding villages.[56] Women arrive with the bread on animals, and then stand in the marketplace to sell it off the animals' backs. Some of the women deliver bread to houses in accordance with what each house needs because it is a custom of the Christians not to bake bread in their houses. All their supplies come from the market.

There are many shops in the market that cook and prepare food for strangers, guests, and travelers who have no regular residence. A man enters the shop and talks to the woman inside, telling her what he desires of meat or chicken or fish or anything else he likes and desires. He then eats and drinks and pays the woman what he owes her. In this market, you find a countless variety of wild meats, game, and birds, dead but not slaughtered; others are alive for those who want to collect the blood and eat it. You also find abundant dry and fresh fruit: apples, grapes, and pears are sold all year round, until the other seasonal fruit appear. Most of this fresh fruit is brought from the mountains of Granada and Ronda: despite the distance between Madrid and those aforementioned locations, the high prices in

Madrid ensure that every kind of product is brought to the city from other regions. Also found in this market are large quantities of fresh fish from Alicante and from the direction of Portugal, a distance of seven days from the sea. In the center of the market, there is a large square with big shops; above those shops are houses and rooms and residences, six stories high, inhabited by people from the market and elsewhere. It is reported that there are in this plaza 14,000 families. There are many craftsmen, artisans and traders in this market, both men and women, and they call it the Plaza Mayor, which means the big market. In the middle, there are women who sell vast quantities of bread, vegetables, fruit, fish, and meats of all kinds.[57]

In this plaza, they have their feasts and festivals, such as the festival of oxen and others. One of their customs is to select strong fat oxen in the month of May, on the tenth or in the middle of the month. They drive them into the plaza and decorate them with silk and brocade and then sit on the roofs overlooking the plaza. They then release them into the center of the plaza one by one, and then any man who wishes to show his courage goes in, riding a horse, to fight the ox with a sword. Some [fighters] die, while others kill the ox. The seating place for the despot in that plaza is well-known so that he, his wife, and all his staff can attend. Meanwhile, all the people assemble at the windows. The rent [of a window] for that one feast day is equal to a whole year's rent.

I attended there in the plaza a feast that celebrated a friar whom they call San Juan.[58] They reported that he was a friar, and he became so devoted to the teachings of their religion that his life was exemplary. They believed that he saw what Satan made him imagine, things they call *milagros* [miracles], which means demonstrations. He lived about one hundred years ago. In this year, they reported that the pope had reached a determination about him, and permitted that he be paraded so that people could see and know him. They designated that day for his celebration, after decorating his church with various kinds of silk and brocade. They dressed his effigy with magnificent clothes covered with pearls and diamonds and they decorated all the streets leading from his church to the plaza. They also decorated the plaza with numerous ornaments and hung up diamonds, precious jewels, and priceless inlaid golden crucifixes.

The despot celebrated the feast and ordered us a seat opposite the one prepared for him and decorated in the same manner as his was. He then invited us, so that we could socialize and be entertained. We went to that place and found so many people, men and women, mixing together, that the place could barely hold them, despite its size. After struggling through the crowd, and there were more people in the markets and alleys than had assembled in the plaza, we reached the place that had been prepared for us. We went up and sat down, and saw the despot across from us, who greeted us profusely by removing his sombrero from his head. He then sat down with his mother and wife, his staff and ministers surrounding him. They then paraded with their crucifixes and effigies and the effigy of friar Juan for whom the pope had decreed that numerous churches be built in every city and village; each city and village instituted a feast for him in accordance with its status. The friars in his order [the Brothers of Charity] attend to the needs of the sick, treating, serving, and performing other duties. In his days, some friars used to serve in that way, and they have since established hospitals [*maristan*] in the churches, in which they attend to the sick in the best of manners.

There are countless hospitals in Spain. Madrid has fourteen hospitals, quite large and clean, offering residence of bed, food, drink, and pastries, and attendants who serve the sick. They have placed old women to attend sick women, and old men to attend sick men. They are very careful in treatment, and ignore nothing that the patient needs, be it large or small. I visited many of the hospitals and saw some patients who had wealth and status. In every hospital, there were places of storage, filled with what each hospital needs of oil, vinegar, pastries, drinks, and a kitchen. I found various kinds of meats: mutton, chicken, pheasant, rabbit, pork, and other kinds for the patients. When the doctor checks on a patient, he feels his hand and knows how his condition is; then he writes a prescription, which he hands to the superintendent of the patients who in turn hands it to the female cook so that the patient will receive what the doctor has prescribed. In another house, I saw the patients' belongings. When a patient is admitted to the hospital, his clothes are removed and stored in a designated room. They make a list of the items and add a label with the owner's name, and then they give him other clothes that are made there for patients who are to stay in the hospital. They give him a bed with two thick covers, two sheets, and a pillow. Every eight days, they wash his clothes and give him new ones. If he recovers from his illness, they give him back the clothes in which he had come, and he goes on his way. If he dies, he is shrouded with hospital cloth, and they try to locate his family to give them the clothes he had left there.

Every hospital has an assigned doctor whose home is near the hospital. Its rent is paid from the revenue. Its rent and all the doctor's supplies, along with all essentials and living needs that pertain to the doctor and to his staff—everything—is provided by the [revenues from the] religious founda-tions so that the doctor can be present at all times, and not absent himself or worry about his living needs. Most of the people who serve the sick belong to the [order] of the friars of San Juan, for that is one of their articles of belief.

Some of our companions fell sick while we were staying in Sanlucar. [Fri-ars from this] order came to visit us every day. When they saw a sick man, they asked that he be moved to their place in order for them to be able to look after and treat him. I prevented them from doing that, which surprised them. They said, "We wanted to do good and we did not think you would prevent us." They insisted on taking him but I refused to give in, so they con-tinued to visit him until he recovered. One wishes, given their convictions and gentle manners and humility, that they had been on the straight path [of Islam]. For in their good manners, they are the best among the religious or-ders. "But God guides whomever He chooses to the straight path."[59]

There is a place in the Madrid market for letters and messages that are sent from all countries, regions and lands. Every Friday, letters from a specific country arrive: whoever expects the arrival of a letter goes to the shops that are designated for that purpose and inquires whether anything had reached him. If he finds a letter, he pays a fixed amount, as much as a quarter of our country's ounce. Similarly, he who wants to send his letter to another country, writes it and leaves it in the designated place but does not pay anything. He who receives it has to pay for it. This practice applies to regions that are half a month's walking distance or less. But if the letter is from a faraway land such as Italy, Rome, Naples, Flanders, France, England, or other distant countries, the payment for a letter arriving from one of these countries is its weight in silver. A large amount of money is generated by these letters.

In the month of February, the postman arrived from Italy and Rome with a weight of fifty-three quarters of letters so that thirteen and a quarter ounces of silver were generated. This [postal] service is in the hands of a count called *condiyati*, to whom, they maintain, it had been given by the des-pot for his livelihood. All the postmen are under his authority. It is their cus-tom that the postman who is going to such-and-such country carries as many letters as he can and then travels without diversion or interruption, notwith-standing fatigue or delay. He changes his horse in each of the hostels that are provided on the road for travelers and postmen, as we mentioned earlier. The distance at which the horse is changed is nine miles, above which the horse cannot continue. He travels halfway through the country to which he is going until he meets another postman. Each gives to the other the post that he brought from his country and then returns to the country from which he had started. Every day, news is available about all countries.

In Madrid, there is another way for spreading news beside letters. In the case of news from distant lands, there is a house with a writing mold which is run by one man who is given this job by the despot in return for paying a certain tax at the beginning of each year. Whenever he hears a piece or shred of news, he collects it and puts it with other news in the mold, from which he prints thousands of papers which he sells very cheaply. You find a man carrying many of them and calling out, "Who wants to buy news about such-and-such country, or such-and-such country?" Whoever desires to learn the news buys a paper from him, which they call *gaseta*. The reader finds many items of news, but there is always exaggeration and inaccuracy stemming from [the desire to satisfy] people's curiosity.

With the postman who came from Italy and Rome, as we already mentioned, came the news of the death of the pope in Rome, may God send him to join his predecessors.[60] No one had replaced him until today. When we stayed in Sanlucar, it was reported that another man had filled his position. This position is a very important one among the worshippers of the cross, because he who fills it decrees religious matters and legislates canons: he commands Christians to do what he likes and prohibits them from what he dislikes, in accordance with his own will. Christians cannot disagree with him and cannot but abide by his will, for in disagreement with him, they believe, there is deviation from religion.

The way in which the pope assumes his position is the following: he has under him seventy-two friars who are among the most learned, known as cardinals. Among Christians, the position of a cardinal is inferior to the pope's. When the pope dies and goes to hell and into its fire, each of the seventy-two goes into his house and shuts the door, and sits, as he claims, to meditate, without conferring or talking with anyone. Meanwhile, he is given the food he needs and remains thus for four months. After the four months have passed, each decides on one man from among the seventy-one who appeals to him because of trustworthiness, knowledge, honesty, and religiosity. So, he writes his name on a small piece of paper and puts it in a closed box, where neither he nor others can see it. Each one of the aforementioned [cardinals] writes on a piece of paper [the name of] whomever he chooses, and puts the ballot in the prepared box. After the assigned days for this [election] have passed, as well as the writing and the reasoning, the cardinals assemble together and open the box and count the ballots. They then give the position to him whose name appears most on the ballots. They demand of him that he abide by the covenants and agreements in accordance with their regulations of sincerity and truthfulness. He then repeats the covenants that are known to them and thus becomes the pope. It is their custom, may God destroy them, not to select a pope who is not above eighty years old. The one whom they chose now is younger, and they claim that he is seventy-five years old.[61] They repeatedly say that he is young, and that no one has ever become pope who was of his age.

Another custom prevailed a few years ago, which was that no one was chosen for that position except a man from Italy, from the region of Rome and its surroundings. The reason for that was that they found that some [popes] who were French had filled that position and then started to collect money and secretly send it to their country. So the cardinals decided at that time that no one from France or Spain could assume the position because of the strong sense of [national] solidarity [*assabiyya*]. Rather, the pope would be a man from Italy and the region of Rome; no one other than such a man could oversee the affairs of Italy. The pope they chose this year after the death of the previous pope is from the region of Naples in Italy. But Naples is in the hands of the Spaniards. This rule has now been broken, as the papacy has been given to somebody from a Spanish [-controlled] region.

It is the pope who imposes the fast on certain days for a reason he explains to them. He prohibits them from eating meat on Fridays and Saturdays, and interprets the reasons in accordance with whatever opinion he likes. He also prohibits the people of the cross from marrying their relatives—[a man cannot marry his] paternal cousin or aunt, or maternal cousin or aunt—unless the pope gives his permission and makes it *halal*. Much money is spent in procuring that permission from him if one wants to marry his relative—expenses to intermediaries, and on travel, if one is far away. None can procure that permission unless he has money and status; if he has them, he finds the means to get the permission to marry. The pope has permitted marriage between relatives if assignations had occurred [between the couple] and adultery committed, leading to pregnancy. If the woman is a relative of the man, the pope will grant his permission without having the man go to him.

I saw in Madrid a young woman of beauty and status from among the Spanish nobility. Her uncle had married her, and his name was Don Pedro de Aragon. He was one of the sons of the kings of Aragon, so he married his niece with the permission of the pope, may God shame him. He was old and was afraid to die without issue, and he had none to whom he could pass on his inheritance, so he sought permission from the pope and married his niece. He died soon after his marriage, leaving her an incalculable amount of money. Some nobles tried to win her hand in marriage after him, but failed. For she was from the people of Spain, a daughter of a duke called the Duke of Medina Celi. He was a minister to the despot and was also his chamberlain, and could enter even when the despot was in bed.

This duke already had a large inheritance, which he and his father had received from an ancestor since they were descended from the kings of Spain. Whenever he greeted the despot, he said, "We will succeed you." He meant that they would get the crown if there was no heir to the throne. It was reported that like his ancestors, who had maintained this attitude to the king's ancestors, the duke maintained this attitude until nine years ago. The despot was troubled by the words he heard, which hurt him deeply, because he did not have a son. So one day, he leaned over [and said] to the duke, "Those words which I often hear from you hurt me deeply, and I want you not to say them again, nor to look forward to it [succession], neither you nor any of your descendants after you." The duke discontinued saying the words, as he could not disobey the king, but he continued in his ministerial position until the despot ordered him to perform a certain task; but the minister liked to contradict him, so he did not obey him nor did he do what he had been ordered. The despot thus concluded that the minister was determined to oppose his will. The minister had a key which enabled him to go wherever the despot went. So one day, the minister came as usual but found the door closed from the inside. When he tried to open it, he could not. So he knocked on the door and the despot came to see who was knocking. When he opened the door and saw who it was, he shut it in his face. The minister furiously went back to his house and stayed there. Not long thereafter, he became sick with what we call *al-nuqta* [epilepsy] and he was sick for around eight years. He died and went to hell the year we were in Madrid, leaving a son who is an ambassador in Rome, representing the despot of Spain to the pope.

One of their customs in Spain is to send ambassadors to each other—a custom of the pope as well. He sent a distinguished man from among the learned of his religion whom they call *el nuncio*. He is the successor [*khalifa*] of the pope in matters of courts and laws. There are many ambassadors now in Madrid, including one from Germany and another from England. Earlier, a man had come from England and settled in Madrid. He fell in love with a woman who became pregnant, so the Englishman had to convert to [Catholic] Christianity and follow the religion of the people of the cross since the English do not worship crosses. As soon as the English heard that he had converted to Christianity, they sent another in his place. He [the former], however, stayed in Madrid, got married, and now receives an annual salary of 12,000 riyal from the despot. But he has lost everything that he owned in his own country—which does not seem to bother him.

There are also in Madrid the ambassadors of Valencia [Venice] and Portugal. They are settled with their children and wives. Other diplomats come to perform certain missions, after which they return to their countries. A little while ago, the ambassador of France was in Madrid, but when conflicts and war started between various Christian nations, as we shall explain later, God willing, he returned to his master.

The cause of the present enmity between [Spain and France] is twofold. First, the French [king] raised his nose and stuck to his opinion, arrogantly seeking to extend his borders into the other countries. He had a neighbor, a duke, who was governor over a province that was not under any king, but was one he had inherited from one of his predecessors. The custom among the kings of the *ajam* is the following: if the king has many children, the eldest inherits the throne, and the next [in line] becomes a duke over a certain and specified region of the country, a known supporter who does not challenge or covet the throne.[62] If the brother who had inherited the throne dies without an heir, then the throne goes to him [the duke], for in their customs of inheritance, a brother inherits his [dead] brother if the latter has no children. And anybody from the lineage of the brother can succeed to the throne, be it a grandson or great grandson, nephew or niece.

This aforementioned duke was governor of one region of the country,[63] but he was not French. The French [king] wanted to remove him and appoint somebody else in his place. The duke was unable to resist the French, so the pope opposed the king on the duke's behalf, but the king did not care and persisted in his action, not heeding the pope nor his denial.

All the worshippers of the cross see themselves under the authority of the pope in whom all their canons and decrees are finalized. From him they seek guidance about their religious duties and rulings, and from him they take their doctrines, which are a deviation from the way of truth and guidance and a venue to falsehood and untruth. He innovates for them laws in accordance with his will and whim, and they support him in those matters in which God has decreed their misery. They never resolve anything in their religion without his permission and consultation, thereby obeying him in ways relevant to their worldly affairs and leadership.

When the pope opposed and resisted the French king, a quarrel broke out between them because the French king did not heed the pope and disobeyed his resolution regarding this matter. He had broken rules that they do not break by removing men who had been born to their inheritance and office. Disagreement and enmity ensued. Meanwhile, negotiations took place between the French king and the emperor of Germany in regard to the truce between him [the French king] and the King of the Turks, may God give him strength. The German emperor called on him to end the truce and withdraw his support, but the French king ignored the emperor and his request. So they fell into disagreement because of that. Due to the aforementioned [disagreement], the rest of the Christians condemned the French [king] for opposing the emperor and for not agreeing with him to end the truce. The emperor was respected and honored among the various nations of Christians because he always confronted the Muslims and fought with them at all times. That is why he is called emperor, and why others support him in his war. The nations that obeyed the pope and were of the party of the emperor became hostile to the French king,[64] and wrote to him, saying,

> Learn that by continuing in these actions, you oppose the pope, whom we all look up to. By deliberately breaking the established custom and removing those who are destined to their office, you have opposed the head of this religion intentionally, and you have done so knowingly. You have also reached a truce with the Turks that you have kept although you know of the wars that are raging between them and the emperor, wars that you cannot ignore. In accordance with our religion and beliefs, it is our duty to help and support him. Either you end your truce with the Turks and join us and the emperor in the common cause, or we will assemble in a council to declare enmity and war against you.

They thought that once he saw their assembled decision to fight and go to war against him, he would not be able to resist them. He would then become penitent and feel guilty; but if he persisted in opposing them, they would unite to fight him by land and sea. They would break his back and crack his thorn. When he learned of their decision, he listened to himself only and decided to fight them. He wrote to them, saying, "I have learned of what you have agreed upon. I want you to write to me and include the signatures of the kings so that I can reflect and decide on my own." They agreed and wrote to him. When he saw what they had agreed upon, and when he read about their decision to go to war if he did not end his truce with the Turks, help the emperor against them, and stop his opposition to the pope, he knew for certain that they would fight him.

So he wrote in his own hand at the bottom of the letter, below the signatures, "These nations are enemies to the French and the French are enemies to these nations." And he sent the letter to them. When they learned that he was intent on maintaining his enmity to them, they found no alternative to war. So war broke out among them, by land and sea, which is still flaring and ongoing.

These aforementioned nations are: Spain; Germany; Italy; Susa, which the Christians call Sweden; and the Savoy. The only detractor from this league of war is Portugal, whose despot was invited to join, but refused to become part of, either the league or the war. Similarly, the Genovese did not join them; their ruler is a duke who is called Grand Duke, which means the great duke, because of the provinces and regions that are under him. He did not entangle himself with those nations in the war but maintains a truce with the French [king] that had been negotiated earlier; he pays him a specific amount of money, keeps a specific number of ships at sea, which the French king uses when he needs, and he [the Grand Duke] maintains his truce with the other nations. Earlier, neither the Flemish nor the English nations had entered the war like the other Christian nations because they were not viewed by them as Christians, given the difference between them in not showing obedience to the pope as do other Christians who worship the cross.[65] The English and the Flemish are alike and reject many things that the people of the cross had innovated in their ignorance. All are following ignorant ways from which we ask God for protection. That is why those Christians call the English and the Flemish "heretics," which means "rejectors."

The despot of the English had died during the conflict among the Christians,[66] and had not left a son to succeed him, but he left a brother called Ya'qoob [Jacob/James]. This James and his wife secretly followed the [Catholic] religion of Christianity without any of their people knowing it. When his brother died, and the matter [of succession] fell to him, there was no alternative for him but to assume [the throne] and to replace his brother. So they called on him to reign over them, but he deceptively feigned refusal; so they persisted, and he saw that they had no other choice since there was nobody else who, by right of inheritance, could succeed to the throne. He said, "I will not cooperate in what you ask of me and tell me to do unless you agree to do something that is not harmful to you—which is: whoever loves his religion should follow it." So they agreed and supported him and gave him the crown and made him king. But not long after, they found that he and his wife had started hanging crosses; they also brought a friar from among the Christians and went to church and prayed the prayer of Christians. Whoever was of his cloth and had known about the matter joined him since he desired to make his people follow his religion.

When the English nation saw what happened to them in having a king who resisted their religion and followed the religion of the people of the cross, they feared that the disease would so spread and infect the people that they would not be able to terminate it. They repudiated what the despot had initiated about religion and convened in their council, planning to kill him. As soon as he sensed the danger, he and his wife fled to the king of France and sought shelter there [December 1688]. The French, hating the English and wanting to spite them, agreed to support and protect him. The English communicated with the French king and continued to do so until he said to them, "You are all enemies to me, just like the rest of the Christians. So prepare to fight me, until I return the fugitive to his house and kingdom against your will."

After the English king departed and war broke out with the French, the English brought the Prince of Orange to reign over them[67]—the same who reigned over the Flemish nation, since both nations had the same religion and differed from the people of the cross. The prince took over, and they gave him the title of king and prepared to fight the French by land and sea. The country of the Flemish and Holland were contiguous to the country of Flanders—the country of Flanders being originally Flemish—and all were of the same opinion and belief in religion and doctrine. Flanders fell to the Spaniards after the removal of the count, the son-in-law of Fernand who was in Seville, as we have mentioned; then all of Flanders and its cities fell to the despots of Spain, who wanted to force the Flemish to become Christian and be of the religion of their rulers. The French king rose in that year and sent his son, the dauphin, may God remove him, to battle. He then caught up with him, and reached the [Spanish] seat/capital city of Mons, and besieged it for a few days, firing canons and bombs, and humiliating the inhabitants and making them suffer very much.[68] There were in the city 12,000 Spaniards who, when they saw what happened to them from the siege, feared death and surrendered. The French king took over the capital city, along with all that was associated with it of villages, cities, and towns: they reported that over seven hundred towns and villages belonged to it. After defeating it [Mons], he marched into it on Easter day in the middle of April of this year. He left the dauphin, his son, in charge, and returned to Paris, the seat of his kingdom and the capital of his country.

His son continues to oppose the Prince of Orange, who has been made king over the Flemish and the English nations. They say that the number of the Prince's armies is 75,000 and that he has a fleet at sea confronting the French fleet. They reported that the English fleet defeated the French fleet and destroyed forty ships.[69] The French have also fought the Spaniards by land and sea: on land, [the French] laid siege to Catalonia in the region of Barcelona [sic]. Defending the city is a Spanish army led by the Duke of Medina Sidonia, known as Guzman. During our stay in Madrid, the Spaniards feared for him from the French, and they sent him a small insignificant army and then awaited the result. They reported that in this month he [the French king] laid siege, and pointed his canons and bombs at Catalonia and Barcelona, too, destroying thereby many houses. So the people of Barcelona rose up against all the French who were in their country and ordered all who were unmarried to depart, leaving only those who were married. After the French ships attacked Barcelona, they continued to a city called Alicante, where they destroyed with their bombs more than six hundred houses.[70] As a result, the people of Alicante rounded up all the French in the city and killed them. Not a single one escaped. They reported that three thousand souls were killed in Alicante.

When the Spaniards heard of the approach of the French fleet on Alicante and Barcelona, while the Spanish fleet had gone to the Great Sea [the Atlantic Ocean] in search of the India [American] fleet, of which there had been little news, and which was unusually late in arriving, they sent for the fleet to return toward Alicante and Barcelona to fight the French fleet. The fleet did not arrive until after the French had destroyed what they had destroyed and done what they had done and left. They did not find any ship of the French fleet there.

The French have also fought the people of Venice, Italy, Germany, and Savoy. Savoy is in the hands of a duke called the Duke of Savoy who had joined the league of the people of the cross in their enmity to France. In this year, French forces attacked Savoy and caused its people much suffering. They conquered all of Savoy, and all its cities and villages, so that the duke who ruled was left with only the city in which he is now besieged. The forces are still there surrounding him.

Because the French are fighting the [German] emperor, for the reasons already mentioned, it is reported that the French king also assists the king of the Turks, may God give him strength, and they claim that he extends to him military supplies, such as cannons and others. It is because the French ambassador resides in Istanbul that such claims are made, but the truth is the following: the French are a people of trade and commerce, and most of their trade is in the Istanbul area. Traders and commercial agents have a special place in the eyes of the French despot, may God destroy him. For all these years, these traders had been members of his court and entourage, and, unlike kings of other nations, he used to assist them in all that promoted their trade and commerce, which brought considerable revenues to him. Among the Spaniards, and unlike other people, the trader is considered nothing, as a result of which the number of Spanish traders has declined. None are found traveling for purposes of trade, except those who are going to India.

Most of the traders and commercial agents in Spain are English, Flemish, Genovese, or others. The cooperation between the French court and French traders is a result of what is seen as mutual benefit; for the Turks seek help and strength from God almighty, and not as these people of ignorance and confusion claim. The French have gone to war against the emperor, who is fighting the Turks because last year, the Turks reconquered Belgrade and its environs. God upholds His religion.

News has arrived this hour that the king of the Turks, may God assist him, has gathered large numbers [of troops] and is intent, with God's help and will, on the city of Vienna, which is the capital of the German [Emperor] and his seat of government. They report in their [newspaper] publications this month that the vizier of Sultan Suleiman appeared with his force consisting of 125,000 fighters and was joined by the army of the Tatar [Hungarians], consisting of 80,000 fighters. They happened to reach a location used by the forces of a captain in the service of the emperor, who had 6,000 fighters. The Tatar fought the forces of the aforementioned captain and captured 4,000 of his followers, and killed many. Only a few escaped, not worthy of being counted. The Turks included the forces of a count called [Emmerich] Tekli, who used to be a *dhimii* [tributary] to the king of the Turks.[71] He then changed his mind and wanted to become independent, but when he saw what happened to the city of Belgrade, Tekli reverted to the support of Sultan Suleiman, may God be with him, and committed such deeds on the followers of the cross that they continue to mention them in their histories.

They reported that the emperor often tried to draw Tekli away from the king of the Turks, but he failed. Later, some of the emperor's forces attacked Tekli's people and captured many, including the wife of Tekli and some of his children. The emperor threatened to kill them if Tekli did not break with the Turks, but Tekli did not. The emperor wanted to kill them in order to bring Tekli back to his side, but Tekli did not cooperate. So the Emperor threw Tekli's wife and all who were with her in jail, where she still is. But Tekli has grown stronger in his defiance and courage against the followers of the cross, may God destroy them.

The emperor, may God mutilate him, continued to plead with the people of the cross for help, and promised truces to those neighboring the Turks in the hope of bringing them over to him to help him against the Muslims, may God give them strength. Among these peoples were the Poles. Poland is a Christian nation with regions that neighbor the lands of the Turks. The Poles, may God destroy them, have a despot who is also at war with the Turks.

They reported that the Emperor wanted to bring with him into the war against the Turks the nation of Muskovy. They are in a land to the north. He persevered and they cooperated but then disagreement and hostility ensued because they reported that a group of Tatars had attacked some of their own compatriots who were tributaries under the protection of the despot of Muskovy. They claim that they are vast in numbers, may God eradicate them all from the earth and preserve it in His eternal praise and preserve His religion of oneness and rectitude.

The Spaniards have a custom that whoever wants to rise in status and join the nobility but does not know how to do so or does not have any connections with the government so that he can live comfortably without turning to trade can go to Germany or beyond. There, he takes part in the war against the Muslims, may God magnify them, and he secures in his hand proofs and documents of his service, cooperation, and effort. When he returns to Spain, he presents the evidence in his hand, and shows proof of his service and honest commitment. He thus attains status, just like those who have ancestry or those who have money and connections. This is a custom of the soldiers who covet the status of nobility. If the Spaniard is a descendant of one of the privileged families and his father had an important title such as duke, count, marquis, or other lower titles, and if he has no right to inherit his father's title, he joins one of the armies, most of which are in Germany. He takes part (or does not take part) in battle, and when he returns, he brings with him a document from the campaign chief, showing that he had been with him in such a battle in such a place, and that he had performed honorably and done this and that, regardless of whether or not he had done anything at all. He requests a title or a stipend to improve his conditions.

One of their inheritance customs is that the firstborn, whether male or female, is the one who inherits everything. If a titled nobleman dies, he bequeaths it [his title] to his firstborn along with his possessions so that none of the siblings can inherit anything, even if they are many. They will not have anything other than what their father gives them during his life, in gifts or presents, or in a dowry to the girl: for one of their customs is to give dowries to girls. If the girl is the main heiress of her father and she marries somebody who has a title as a high or higher than hers, he takes over all her inheritance and she will assume the title of her husband. And if she marries an untitled member of the upper class without a right of inheritance from his father, he will assume her title by his marriage to her. That is why many men without inheritance delay their marriage in the hope of marrying the daughter of a nobleman with a right to inheritance. And if she does not have an inheritance, it is their custom that her father give her 100,000 riyals, [a sum] fixed by the despot and not to be exceeded.

The Spaniards have other and different customs for bequeathing titles of nobility. One of the Spanish despot's ministers is called Count Constable, and is known for his noble status. The custom which has been practiced for generations is that if he dies and leaves no male heir, his title and wealth do not go to any of his family but to an outsider from among his servants: to the earliest in his service. When he [the count] dies, they look to see who of his servants has seniority in service, and then he takes over the title, wealth, and ministerial function.

If there is disagreement as to who is most senior among the servants, an hour is appointed when those who are most known for their honesty and piety leave the residence [of the deceased count]. The first man who passes in front [of the arbitrators] is called and given the title, be he of the nobility or an average person. They take the man to the despot, where he kneels for an hour before him. After an hour, the despot orders the man to rise and stand to his right, where the dead minister used to stand. He then orders the man to cover his head as he assumes the position and takes over all the count's possessions, property, regions, and lands. This is the custom among the *ajam*, where noblemen who possess regions and cities that they seized after their victory in this land acquired the right to them. None can take any possession away from the descendants who inherit it from their predecessors.

This count has a niece, but she does not inherit anything. He also has an illegitimate son who also cannot inherit; he is the governor of Cadiz, may God shame him.

They have another custom. A man called the *princeps* in Barcelona near Catalonia died and left a daughter, one of the most beautiful in her time, and he left her money and possessions and jewelry, and countless hamlets, villages, and cities, and many other posessions. But he stated [in his will] that she could marry only the man who defeats his rivals in a duel. When her father died and the news of her inheritance was reported among all the nations of the cross, many of the sons of the nobility and dignitaries came from every region seeking to duel in front of her in order to win her. The duration of the duels was fixed for six months. When a man who wanted to duel others arrived, he stayed outside the city, after passing by her, whereupon she saw and met him. The contestants then went to the duel site on a set day. Each contestant rode his horse after donning as much as he could bear of a suit of iron and armor, and he carried in his hand a lance topped with a diamond imbedded in the iron [of the lance]. They then charged, one against another, each aiming at the chest of the other with the lance. Whoever unhorsed the other was the winner—until he was defeated. He then withdrew but stayed on at the woman's own expense until the designated period [of six months] was over and there were only two winners left. Then these two winners dueled each other. Whoever became the final winner won her as a wife, along with her inheritance.

They reported that a group of noblemen came and dueled. The daughter liked very much, and at first sight, one of them, the cousin of the French despot. She sent him a present and extended hospitality, exceeding that which she had shown to all others. Her heart felt for him all that it could feel. Such an example, and many others that occur in the absence of a single law, are their inheritance customs. Each does what he wants before he dies.[72]

A man has complete control over his inheritance, possessions, and money. If he chooses to give it all to a male or female stranger and disinherit his children, he can do so without embarrassment. If he bequeaths his possessions to others, or if somebody with a title inherits him by marrying one of his daughters, or if his daughter is the one to inherit him but her husband is without a title or has a title that is beneath his wife's, the husband will take the father-in-law's title, and all his possessions and property. The sons of the man with the inheritance will assume titles other than their father's.

Because women inherit in such a fashion, the Spanish nation is expecting the French to rule over them by one of two ways.

By inheritance—if their despot does not have a male heir. The French despot had married the daughter of Philip Quarto,[73] the sister of this despot from his father. She had a son called the dauphin [Louis the dauphin], may God shame him, who was more devious and evil than his father, may God destroy them both. If this despot, Carlos Segundo, dies without an heir to the throne of Spain, the throne will pass to the son of the French despot by right of his mother.

Or by war. As of now, the French king is at war with them and has advanced in person with his forces against them. The Spanish despot has not been able to rise against him since he has never fought in any war, and thus he is unable to go to war and fight. For these two reasons, and because they expect the French to rule over them, the Spaniards have started learning French and teaching it to their children in all places and at all occasions—without caring or bothering about their despot.

What happened this year in killing the French has stoked the fire of hatred and enmity between them.

They reported that before the pope died this year, may God remove him, he had been trying to arrange a peace between the warring monarchs. But then he died. Since the French king had quarreled with the pope, as already mentioned, he started making decrees and taking decisions without consulting the pope.

The cause of the conflict between the Flemish and the English [Protestants] on the one hand and the [Catholic] followers of the cross on the other has been reported thus: some friars quarreled with the pope, who subsequently had them imprisoned for years. After they were released, they rejected the pope and joined the French despot and started innovating religious doctrines that suited his whims. They even decreed that he could marry a woman who had been his mistress and declared it legal for him to marry her alongside his wife, the queen. The pope had forbidden him from getting married as long as his wife was alive, but he disobeyed the pope and did what he desired and what his heart wanted, despite the fact that their religion prohibits them from marrying more than one woman.[74]

The followers of the cross cannot disobey the aforementioned pope in anything, be it big or small. For he decreed their doctrines and beliefs, including eating restrictions during the fast days and other practices in which they differ from the Christians of the east. All, however, are lost: may God increase their ugliness and eradicate them from earth.

During their fast, we saw them eat all day long while still claiming to fast.

At the end of the month of February, they have feasts and celebrations in which they prepare for the fast. The first day of March is the first day of their fast, which goes on for forty-six days—the same number that had been imposed on the people of Israel with an additional six Sundays that are in those fast days. That is how they calculate forty-six days. This fast of theirs does not entail fasting from food, drink, or sexual activity: it is a fast from eating meat, as they claim, but the nobility are excluded from this fast. Whoever is ill is also excused and eats meat in obedience to the pope's decree. The rest of the common people eat fish throughout the days of the fast. The pope has also decreed it legal for them to eat chicken eggs during their fast, after seeking permission from the friars and paying a fixed sum: [to get the permission] young or old have to pay the equivalent of a riyal. A large amount of revenue is raised this way, one-third of which goes to the despot who spends it on his fleet. You thus find a poor man who does not own a *dirham* begging in the streets so he can collect enough to pay for the *bolia* [Papal Bull], that is the permission to eat eggs. During the fast, they eat all day long.

When a Christian wakes up in the morning, he drinks a cup or two of chocolate with as many biscuits—which is dough mixed with sugar and egg yolk. In the middle of the day, or an hour later, they eat ravenously: the nobility, who have no constraints or who are excused because of sickness, eat whatever meats they want. If a person is not of the nobility and is intent on fasting, he eats fish and eggs and drinks as much wine as he wants, diluted or undiluted. And he drinks whenever he gets thirsty. When it is midnight, he eats a little, half a *rotl* [a unit of weight varying between one and five pounds], as he claims, and then stays home till the next day. When he wakes up, he drinks as is his habit—and so on, for the rest of the fast days. The friars are permitted to eat during fast days half an hour before noon, and their justification is that they spend all night in what they claim to be meditation and prayer. But all other nonfriars eat only after noon.

During their fast days, they have one day other than Sunday when men and women listen to [the preaching of] infidelity and go to church: it is Friday. They view it as an act of piety to walk on that day: the man leaves his horse and coach, and walks for an hour, and when he gets thirsty, he drinks. They continue in this aforesaid manner of fasting for thirty-eight days. Then the feasts and celebrations for which they had prepared during the fast begin, coinciding with what they claim happened to Christ. On the thirty-ninth day, they celebrate Sha'neen [Palm Sunday].

The feast of Sha'neen is the day in which Christ entered Jerusalem,

according to the Gospel used by them. When Christ entered Jerusalem, all
the people of Israel went out to meet him, covering the roads and paths with
tree leaves and branches. But there were those among the people of Israel
who wanted to capture and kill him. On that day, many people believed in
him, as it is mentioned in their Gospel, so his enemies could not capture him
nor plot anything against him on that day because of the multitudes that believed in him. The Christians have turned that day into a feast day [*eid*]: they
meet in church and listen to a sermon and recall what happened to him.
They bring out a cross and circumambulate with it in the streets while carrying in their hands a palm leaf or an olive tree branch or any other branch
from soft and malleable trees such as myrtle or its like. They then return the
cross to its place.

I saw the despot that day go into a chapel in his own mansion and listen to
[the preaching of] infidelity (God protect us), which the minister of the
church preached to him and to others who were present. He then left along
with all the priests and friars, the bishop, which means the mufti, and the
nuncio, who is the successor of the pope. On this occasion, the friars dressed
up in magnificently jeweled clothes, and carried a palm branch and a silver
cross in front of them, with a statue on the cross covered with a piece of silk.
There were young friars who were good at singing to the accompaniment of
musical instruments, carrying in their hands papers from which they read
their hymns. Behind these friars were their superiors, and then the nobility
from among the inner circle of the despot who came behind them, carrying a
palm branch covered with flowers in his hands. They circumambulated with
the cross the despot's mansion and then returned the cross to its place in the
church. They repeated this parade in every church so that on that day and
later, every Christian carried in his hand a palm leaf or an olive tree branch
or some other tree.

On that day, the despot attended the Palm Sunday celebration alone,
without his wife. He sent us an apology for her absence in regard to an illness
that prevented her from coming. We took note of that. It was his deputy who
apologized to us. On the morning after, they congregated in churches and
delivered sermons and recalled what had happened to Christ after Palm
Sunday with the people of Israel who plotted and devised schemes to capture and kill him.

On the forty-fourth day is the feast of breaking of the fast, which is called
Fis-h [Easter]. On this day, the despot lays out food for the poor and invites
thirteen poor men into his mansion. The archbishop, the mufti, and the nun-

cio, who is the successor of the pope, assist the despot as he serves food to the aforementioned poor with his own hands. He offers them plates and then takes them away, just as a servant serves his master. He gives to each of the thirteen poor men thirty plates of food which contain no meat at all, because they do not eat meat during the fast. Despite it being the day of breaking the fast, they have added it to six days in addition to the forty, as we have already mentioned. The despot offers them fish of various kinds and adds to the thirty plates varieties of fruit, both dry and fresh, until he finishes feeding them all. He offers them drink and wine, too. Once they finish eating, the head of the church enters with a washbowl of water, followed by the nuncio, successor of the pope, while the despot washes the feet of all those poor men. He then dries them with cloths especially made for that occasion. When he is finished drying their feet, he kisses the feet of each of them, gives them clothing and money, and they leave with all they had received including all the food that had been left and all the plates. You will then find them selling that food in the streets to the multitudes who believe that the food is blessed. Similarly, his wife and his mother each feeds thirteen poor women in the same manner as he fed the poor men.

They claim that in their gospel this washing is an act of piety and a *sunna* that Christ performed on the day of Easter.[75] When it was Easter, Christ wanted to break his fast and was asked by his disciples, "Where do you want us to prepare the Easter meal?" And he answered, "Go to such-and-such place," which he named for them, "where you will find a man carrying a jug of water. Follow him into the place where he goes, and tell the master of the house that the teacher wants to celebrate Easter with him." So they went and found the man with the jug of water and followed him to the place he had described and said to the master of the house, "The teacher says, prepare for him the Easter [meal] so he can eat it with you."[76] The man prepared the meal, and Christ came with his disciples, and they were thirteen men, and they ate the Easter meal together. When Christ finished, he went down on his knees, after tying a towel around his waist, and started washing the feet of his followers, one by one. When he got to Sema'an [Simon] al-Saffa, the latter said, "Are you washing my feet?"

Christ answered, "What I do now you cannot understand now, but you will later."

Simon said, "You will not wash my feet—ever."

Christ said to him, "Truly I say to you if I do not wash them, you will not be with me [in the kingdom]."

Simon then said to him, "Sayyid, do not just wash my feet, but my hands and head too."

Christ said to him, "If I, your sayyid, have washed your feet, you should do the same and wash each others' feet. I have done this to set an example for you. As I have done to you, you must do to others."[77] This is the reason why the feet of the poor are washed. Dignitaries, members of the nobility and wealthy people also do the same.

They also reported that when Christ was eating the Easter meal with his disciples, he said, "One of you will deliver [betray] me tonight." So each of them started swearing his innocence. But there was among the thirteen disciples a man called Judas Iscariot who they claim was one of the disciples. Satan whispered to him to strike a deal with the Jews who were against Christ and to sell him to them for thirty pieces of silver.[78] He delivered [Christ] to them the night he was captured in the garden where he was praying. Judas went with the soldiers to capture him.

On Easter, and besides feeding the poor, all the Christians, priests and friars, and all the nobility and the commoners, gather together and bring out the crosses and statues that they worship and circumambulate with them in the streets of the city while carrying countless lighted candles in the daytime. None can refuse to carry a candle or to walk in front of the crosses and statues. They go from one church to another, showing sorrow and sadness. They claim that this had been done with the crucified. A statue of Christ is passed before them, showing him at prayer in the garden, with the statue of an angel coming down to him with the cup of death, which he receives in his hand. Then another statue passes, showing soldiers whom they claim plotted against Christ. Then they bring another statue of Christ showing him after his lashing, with blood between his shoulders; then Christ carrying the cross on his shoulder. They then pass with Christ crucified, and then Christ in a coffin after being taken down from the cross.

One of the Christians imitates the crucified and covers his face in order not to be recognized. But behind him, he will have a servant or a friend who looks after him lest he faint from the lashes on his back as blood trails down to his feet. Another crucifies himself by tying his hands and head to an iron post and then goes through the streets during the procession, again covering his face lest he be recognized. On the next day, they parade a statue of the crucified on the cross, and then another statue of him having been taken down the cross, and then another showing him buried in the tomb. They chant sad melodies as they enter the church and leave him there, after extinguishing all lanterns and candles, and then they hang black cloth on the church and close the church doors. They neither ring bells nor ride a coach or horse throughout the days of the procession. Instead, all these days they use their feet, both the privileged and the common people. I heard them say that John of Austria, brother of the aforementioned despot, was the one who forbade them from riding during the procession.

On the following day, the third day of Easter, at noon, they open the churches and light the candles and remove the black hangings and replace them with colorful ones. They ring the bells and celebrate, and they print pictures on little pieces of paper that they claim are those of angels. They write between the words letters in Chaldean, which are *halleluja*, which means, rejoice, rejoice. When the bells chime, the pictures are thrown down at them which they catch and then exchange as gifts among each other, joyous and happy at what they think is the news of his resurrection, as in their false beliefs: the crucifixion of Christ, his burial and his resurrection from the grave.[79] "But they did not kill nor crucify him: only a likeness was shown to them; and those who differ are full of doubts, without certain knowledge; they follow only conjecture, for it is definite that they did not kill him. For God raised him to Him: God is exalted and wise."[80]

They have followed error in what they uphold of their false doctrine and flagrant error and deviance from the right path and the clear argument. Satan has used their pride to lead them astray from the right course. They have persisted in their infidelity and the pope, may God ruin his labor, has led them to a wrong path. It is because of him and whoever follows him in his way and belief that the common people have been infected by this incurable disease, which can only be cured by the sword. For there are among the common people those who speak with Muslims and learn how Islam is the right path: they listen and are grateful and do not turn away from listening, as we saw on many occasions.

The novices and friars are the most hostile, the harshest and the most determined in their infidelity, may God protect us. We met a group from among their novices and friars and we discussed their claims about Christ, may God be absolved of their words; we found them the most corrupt and implacable in their [false] beliefs. I met in Madrid a priest from among their priests who had returned from the Orient. He spoke Arabic and had been exposed to some of the doctrines of the Muslims because he had lived among them. So we discussed various things until I said to him, "What do you say of Christ?"

He said, "He is [an emanation] of God."

So I said, "How? If you say that he is like a part from the whole, the Almighty is indivisible. And if you say he is like a child from a father, you necessitate a second child, and a third and a fourth, with no end. And if you say he came about by means of change, then you necessarily imply corruption. But the Almighty does not change and does not shift from one state to another. Nothing is left except that he be of the Creator like all the creation which is the indubitable truth." But the infidel persisted in his opinion, may God punish him for his belief and for the belief of the pope; and may God destroy them for believing in change, for God is higher than all their sayings.

On another occasion, some priests who knew only *ajami* and no Arabic visited us. We started talking to one of them through a translator who translated our words into the *ajami* language. After an hour, one of the priests said, "By God, what you have said is acceptable to reason and unobjectionable to the ear. But a miracle and one of the great events that takes hold of the mind is this: Christ was man but was born without a father, and performed wondrous miracles in his time, healing the sick, recuperating the disabled, raising the dead and other actions. None can deny these facts that we believe." This friar was the superior of his order, and many members of the order used to come and visit us. After he left, he forbade them from coming again, in fear for them.

One day, on meeting one of them, I asked him why he did not visit us anymore, and he replied that his superior forbade him. He did not permit any of them to visit us until it was time for us to leave Madrid. He then came and bade us warm farewell in the best of manners.

The reason why these infidels, may God shame them, continue in their error is because the pope teaches them their religion and sets their laws. He guides them into the way of error of earlier people such as Paul, who recounted the Gospels they now have, falsely attributing them to John, Mark, Luke, and Matthew, who, as they claim, were disciples of Christ—all of which displeases God. They pretend that Paul was one of those who persecuted and put to death the followers of Christ. As he was going to Jerusalem to continue his search for them, a light appeared to him, and he fainted. When he regained consciousness, it said to him, "Saul, until when are you going to reject me?"[81] He found that he had lost his eyesight and he decided to repent. It said to him, "Go to such-and-such a place in Jerusalem and seek out so-and-so saint [*qiddees*] and he will give you back your sight." Immediately, Paul went to the place, and upon recovering his sight, changed his ways completely. He considered himself an envoy of Christ and he narrated the Gospels the way he wanted with errors and impieties, may God protect us. It is from his false teachings that they continue in their [erroneous] beliefs. We ask God to help and protect us in our true religion and straight path.

These friars have led Christians into error by the false doctrines that they have fabricated and that are offensive to the ear. There are so many friars and clerics that you rarely can find a Christian house to which a friar does not go daily to spread his impieties. These friars force people to confess the sins and faults they have committed and have thus established a custom that old and young have to follow. It directs that everyone has to reveal to the friar, who has authority, what sins have been committed, saying, "I committed on such-and-such a day, in such-and-such an hour, such-and-such a sin; Satan misled me and suddenly overpowered me, and I did such-and-such a thing." Only the friar is authorized to hear this admission and know of these acts. Then he says to the one who has confessed, "You must repent, stop committing the sin, and never repeat it. Firmly decide to repent and not to do it again; perhaps God will forgive you." After the sinner decides to repent, the priest draws the sign of the cross on him, saying, "By the power of such-and-such words of infidelity that they pronounce, your sin has been forgiven." The friars obligate men, women, and children to confess, no less than once every week.

On Sunday, women go to church for confession. The name of the man to whom they confess is the "confessor." As for the woman who does not go to church, the friar goes after her in her house and makes her confess: he enters with her into a secluded corner of the house, and then the two of them shut the door to the room in which the woman had entered with the friar. He remains with her until God decides! Then she emerges purified of all sin, with reprimands and penances to perform. If the husband returns home and finds her alone with the friar, it is not possible for him to go near her nor to disturb them as long as they are not yet finished with what they are doing. No one can bear any accusation against the friar for anything, even if somebody saw a shameful deed with his own eyes. Add to this that these people are by nature not jealous about those women who are forbidden others: men can visit the wives of others, whether the husbands are present or not.

The pope, may God mutilate him, requires all the peoples of the cross to confess another time during the Easter season: men and women go to church during all the days of Easter for this purpose. Old and young, woman and man, boy and girl, all confess the sins they committed and resolve themselves to renew their repentance. They receive cards showing the number of persons in the household who have confessed, the such-and-such church where they confessed and the such-and-such year. As the days of Easter arrive, the friar goes to each house and collects the cards, one by one, after confirming the number of people living in the house, and inquires whether they had been confessing or not. If, as he is collecting the cards, the friar discovers that somebody had lost his, or he finds that some members of the household had not confessed, this is a major abomination of which the sinner is guilty. The sinner is obligated to pay a specific sum of money, after which he confesses and receives absolution for his sins.

For doctrinal support of what they do [confession], they rely on the Gospels that they have from the mouth of Christ, God's prayer and peace upon him and upon our prophet, who said, "Be thankful to whoever does good to you, and whenever somebody asks God to forgive you, you in turn ask God to forgive them."[82] The leader of error, the pope, explains these words incorrectly, saying to them, "Forgive God." He thus gives them permission to do so—and while some may be denied that permission, it is not denied the friar who is over forty years old, knowledgeable, trustworthy, and honest. Meanwhile, if a Christian discovers among those friars any vice or abuse of confidence, it is a big sin in their eyes to proclaim it or level an accusation against any of them, even if he witnessed [the misdeed] and verified it. Rather, he is obliged to find an excuse for the friar despite the certainty that many Christians have about their sins and failures. More than once, some of these friars have given proof of their shortcomings and deceptions, committing deeds that both reason and nature abhor. They continue living in their customary tranquility and peace; but man is by nature subject to error and failure.

For instance, a friar withdraws with a woman into a house and shuts himself in for an hour to hear her confess her sins of adultery or others; for she does not hide any of her deeds or conceal her sins from him. When a woman admits to a sin of adultery or other similar deeds, how is it possible that the friar will have any scruples toward her, given the ease with which women deliver themselves to adultery in these lands? That such actions are committed by the friars is not surprising given what happened this year in Madrid: the pregnancy of an unmarried young girl. When she was questioned, she admitted to a relationship with a cleric. He was apprehended and condemned to the [slavery of the] galleys.

One who confided in me told me that in the village of Ceuta, may God return it to Islam, a young girl of great beauty was deflowered by a friar, her uncle. The affair was exposed and she has not been able to marry since, and remains so now. She is still there. There are many similar stories; no need to mention them all.

These two examples provide proof of how little jealousy there is among these people. And actions of this kind happen frequently. What further provides proof is what I heard from the mouth of a woman of great beauty in the city of Seville. She had come to visit us, along with her mother and her two sisters. As the conversation turned to the subject of friars and clerics, and in the presence of a large number of Christians, she sighed and said, "Be damned if you trust them." When we asked her for the reason for her words, she answered, "I know them better than anyone else, and I don't need to explain myself."[83] Her words made us even more surprised because there were many clerics there, but their presence did not inhibit her, despite the authority they have among Christians and the rank they occupy in society. They are the leaders of prayer and to them all men and women confess their sins. Despite all this and their large numbers, there are men among them who are good-natured and who one wishes would take the straight path. We ask for God's help.

In the large church known as the Escorial, I met an old man with reputation and honor who showed friendliness, charm, and affability that I cannot [sufficiently] describe. He was the superior of that church to whom all affairs and decrees were reported—including all the decrees pertaining to the hamlets around the church and the nearby villages that belong to it. He left his position, proclaiming that he no longer wanted anything of the world, and ascetically renounced the desire for dignity and status, and conferred his responsibilities on one of his pupils, named Don Alonzo. This friar, who is now in charge of the Escorial, showed affability, friendliness, and good conversation. After we met him, and throughout our stay in Madrid, he continued to visit us every time he came to see the despot. We also used to receive his letters from the Escorial.

The Escorial is a church that had been built for reasons mentioned earlier. Its builder, Philip Segundo, had laid siege to one of the French cities [Saint-Quentin] and had set his cannons and bombs at it. Across from the cannons stood a church that was dedicated to a friar called Lorenzo el Real. So he vowed to build a church greater than it because he destroyed it as he was bombing the city. When he returned, he built the church as he had vowed at the foot of the mountain that separates Old Castile from New Castile. It is twenty-one miles from the city of Madrid. This church, and everything of the despot's mansion, were built of solid stones similar to marble quarried from a mountain overlooking the church. The stones are large and quite heavy.

It was reported that at the time of construction, a wooden bridge was built extending from the top of the mountain to the location of the church. They used rollers to facilitate bringing the stones over the aforementioned bridge and putting them in their places without having to go through the difficulty of carrying them; for the stones are very big. Nothing has remained of the aforementioned bridge to show where it stood, but they said that all of it had been of wood, which is why it has not survived. The aforementioned mountain is very high, rising steeply from the church. This Escorial is quite magnificent and elevated into the sky. There are three doors on its western side: the middle door is the entrance to the church and everything within. Above the door is a stone statue that they claim is of Lorenzo el Real, after whose name the church was built.[84] To the right and left of that door are two doors that lead into two large residences for the young student friars [novices] who learn their sciences and study their books. The student friars in each group wear a distinguishing badge on the shoulder, blue and red, to signify how advanced they are in their arts.

Their first topic of study is philosophy and related material. There are in these two residences a large number who come to study from all over Madrid and elsewhere. But they report that the main place for learning is another city called Salamanca, which is three miles [sic] from Madrid. It is widely known among them that he who does not finish his studying and learning and acquire a degree in the city of Salamanca is really not an achiever. Most of the material they study in their youth is the infidelity that the teachers dictate. They memorize the material that is placed before their eyes. Then they learn arithmetic and geometry in the Latin tongue, for Latin is what grammar is to the Arabs. Not all Christians understand Latin unless they study it in their youth. Thus, there are Christian children being taken by their fathers to places specialized in its teaching, such as the Escorial, Salamanca, and others.

The middle door that opens into the church is enormous and contains many and numerous designs and decorations. Facing the door is a huge open space, *sahn*, surrounded by very large pillars, on each of which is a big stone statue. The statues are dressed in clothes made of the same stone. It was reported that all these statues are of the same stone. The statues number five, which, it is reported, was the number of the kings of the people of Israel. On the first statue was written: This is the Prophet David. On the statue's head was a crown of copper plated with gold and weighing five quarters. David held in his hand an instrument that he invented, and that they claim he used when he recited his psalms. They called it a harp [irba]. This harp is a big instrument of wood, as tall as a man. It has around forty-six strings and produces beautiful melodies in the hands of a good player.

These Christians use it often, and teach their women, children, and girls how to play it. Rarely does one find a house where all its [female] members do not play the harp, especially to welcome and entertain visitors. It is most frequently used by the daughters of the nobility and dignitaries and their descendants. They also use it in their chapels, churches, and other places of their infidelity. It is the most commonly used instrument for musical pleasure [tarab]. They have no knowledge of the instrument we call the lute [oud], but they know of another instrument that is similar to it, the guitar. It is a little smaller than the lute, and has two more strings. The harp is the most beautifully designed of the instruments of tarab.

To the right of the statue on which is written the name of David the Prophet is another statue on which is written: This is Solomon, son of David, peace be on both of them and on our prophet. There is a copper crown plated with five quarters of gold on this statue's head. Solomon holds in his hand a staff of copper plated with gold weighing three quarters. To his right there are three other statues. Written on each is the name of one of the great kings who ruled in that time. Inside the sahn there is a large court, to the right of which are schools for the residence of their students and friars. The number of the schools is fourteen, each of which includes many buildings with classrooms on top. Each of the aforementioned schools has a fountain, a big stall, and numerous columns, about twenty. Each school opens onto the other. To the left of the sahn leading to the church and facing the school gates is a door leading to the despot's mansion. It is big and everything—walls and ceiling—is built of the same stone as the church and in the same style, with the same size, height, and thickness as the church.

This mansion has three entrances. One is from the interior of the church, the other from the outside, and the third is from the garden near the church. It is customary for the despot to reside there for a month during the summer season because of the coolness of that place at the foot of the mountain. The church itself is huge with columns and courts. As you enter you see the statue of the crucified, which they worship and which is made of silver plated with gold. In the center of the church there is a high and thick cupola, very well designed and structured, rising on four huge columns, each of which is twelve arm lengths in width. Near every four columns there is a section decked with silk and brocade where friars sit during prayer and worship. There are also many lanterns of gold, silver, and gold-plated copper inside the church. There are many kinds of valuable jewels and precious stones and ornaments. In the upper level of the church where they pray and chant their hymns, and which they call *missa* [mass], there is a musical instrument called an organ. It is a huge instrument with big bellows and pipes of plated lead, producing strange sounds. In this and other locations of the church, and in accompaniment to this instrument, they chant what they claim to be the psalms of David, peace be upon him, and the Torah, which was revealed to Moses, on him and on our Prophet, peace and prayer. Their adoption of the Torah is based on the ten words [commandments] in which they concur with the Jews, and which they claim to preserve, which are: forbidding killing, robbery, adultery, [shedding of] blood, money, and others.

In this church, there are about two hundred senior friars who celebrate mass, along with a large number of junior friars. Above the church there are nine high and enormous minarets, in each of which there are machines that indicate the hours. The bells that strike on the appointed times are numerous and can be heard for miles as they strike one of various tunes. To the right of the church are libraries for books of science and religion, along with other valuables that belong to the church foundation since the time of its builder and henceforth. No one can take anything out of the libraries; one can only add to them. It was to these libraries that they transported the books of the Muslims from Cordoba, Seville, and others, and reported that they had all been burned by fire ten years ago. We saw the place that had been burned in the libraries and we saw how the fire had damaged them and the church extensively. Until now, the despot continues to repair what the fire destroyed. Had not the church had a ceiling of stone and had it not been without wood, which fire can consume quickly, the whole place would have been destroyed completely. Despite that, the fire climbed to the top of the church minaret and toppled many large blocks of stone, which fell into the garden around the church. They are so huge that they cannot be returned to their place.

To the north of the church there is a burial site for the ancestors of the despot, starting with the father of the one who built the church, Carlos Quinto, who became a friar. There is also Philip Quarto, the father of this despot. Both tombs are in a crypt below ground, to which one descends by many stairs made of the most exquisitely crafted and designed red marble.

Their tombs are caskets of marble plated with gold, each of which is raised between two columns, and on each is the name of the despot who is buried in it. There are five rulers and their wives buried there. It is their custom that only the despot who succeeded to the throne of the kingdom is to be buried there. Those who die without heirs or have no right to inherit the throne have another burial site, which is different but near by. Such are their burial customs, may God destroy them.

The administration of the church and all its services is conducted here: matters relating to the people, construction of mills to grind food, cooking facilities, dyeing facilities, and everything else needed by city dwellers. The church complex also has stores and depositories of medical ointments and lotions, and [medical] potions. Water is abundant, as surrounding the church is a spacious garden with amazing streams, rivers, and trees, all of which are for the friars' pleasure. There is also, around the church and the garden, a hunting ground for the despot, surrounded by a wall of such magnitude that they reported it to be thirty-three leagues in parameter. At every two intervals, there is a house and garden where the despot can rest during the hunt. I visited some of them when we went to the Escorial because the despot called us to meet him in a place he liked very much.

They consider this Escorial to be one of the wonders of their country. There is no other church of the same construction plan or greater in size.

Meanwhile, they do not deny the majesty and splendor of the Muslim mosques, such as the mosques of Toledo, Cordoba, Seville, all of which are famous far and wide. We have already mentioned the mosque of Cordoba, and we shall describe the mosques of Toledo and Seville at a later time, if God wills that we visit them on our way back from the city of Madrid.[85] We stayed all the time in Madrid where the despot wanted to entertain us and show us the places that were important to him, such as his parks; hunting grounds; orchards; feasts; mansions, with their interior residences and rooms; the armory, with his weapons and firearms; and other places. He repeatedly invited us to see all that I have just mentioned.

He held festivities for three consecutive nights in his mansion, to which he had invited us. He prepared for us a seating quarter under a high dome and on the same level as his and all his dignitaries, nobility, dukes and counts, and others of his inner circle. He came with his mother and his wife, along with the daughters of the nobility and dignitaries, all carrying candles in their hands. Once he reached his seating quarter, facing ours, he removed what he had on his head in the manner of their salute, then sat down, with his wife to his left and his mother to her left. Then the entertainers came, men and women, and performed what was customary in their entertainment and singing. They continued until midnight when they finished and prepared to leave. The despot stood first, and removed what was on his head after raising his head in our direction, and then each left to his place and residence. He always asked the servants who were serving us about us, inquiring about our pleasure, not wishing to ignore any of our needs. And he did that daily.

Among the parks and hunting grounds that he visited every year in the month of April, and where he stayed for nearly a month with his family and inner circle of associates and servants, is a place called Aranjuez. When he went there this year, he ordered his minister and chief of his court, the cardinal, to invite us over. Meanwhile, we were telling the cardinal, and urging him, about our desire to return. But the despot wanted us to go to where he was in Aranjuez, hoping for us to see and visit the place, as it was his best park. So, one day, he sent us the chief scribe of the court, who said that the despot wanted us to go there and enjoy the gardens and hunting grounds. We answered that we were very eager to leave and that we no longer wished to see parks or grounds because we were late in returning to our country. Our goal was to depart, which was our utmost desire. So he went away and reported our answer to the despot. Two days later, he returned with the order of the great one saying that he wanted us to go to where he was to enjoy ourselves and prepare to depart, for he was worried about what he had learned from him [the secretary] and others of his servants. He ordered the count who was responsible for us, along with the Christian Aleppan translator, to accompany us to where he was. For none could see him without his permission and express desire.

So we [began our return journey] on the morning we departed from Madrid. We walked for nine miles, passing through three villages. The first was at one distance from the city and was called Verde, which means green in their language, because of all its gardens and orchards. It was a small village, close to urbanity. After another distance, there was a village called el-Binta, larger than the first, and then a village called el-Moro which was larger than the two aforementioned villages. We found a house in it that was prepared for us, so we stayed in it until the day's heat had passed. In the evening we rode on, and crossed another nine miles until we reached the park known as Aranjuez. Nearby, we found horses that the despot had sent for us, and we received salutations and were told, "The despot had expected you at noon and had therefore prepared a festivity for you to attend upon your arrival. Because you were a little late, he sent you his messengers to welcome you."

We arrived toward evening without having anything with us for the overnight stay. They took us to a house overlooking that park and belonging to his minister, the cardinal. We stayed in it that night after one of his servants came to welcome and host us most lavishly on his behalf.

In the morning, he sent for us. We went to one of his parks there, surrounded by two big rivers which come together to form the Tagus river. The river passes through Toledo, at a day's distance from here. This park is beautiful in its streams and lined trees; it has flowers and blossoms, waterwheels, pipes, and water ponds on each side. It also has exquisitely designed seats overlooking the river on both sides. From this park we entered one of the houses of the despot after he had sent some members of his inner circle to meet us. When we stood before him, we found him on his feet, his wife to his left, with a group of nobles' daughters. To his right were his minister and other members of his inner circle and servants. We greeted them with our usual greeting, saying, "Peace to all who follow guidance." He saluted and welcomed us, as was his custom, and we found in his hand a letter that he had written to our al-Mansur, victorious by God. He kissed it and gave it to us after inquiring about us, having been concerned about what he had heard. We apologized by explaining that we could not be delayed any further from our sayyid, may God grant him victory. So he said, "Since you have your excuse for wanting to leave, we shall not keep you here. Convey to the Sherifian throne our appropriate salutation, and we hope well for the captives in his possession. Whatever his elevated position desires of us, we will accomplish with love and in honor of his majesty." He then asked the translator if there was anything that we needed. We declined the offer in the manner that is fitting for Muslims, God be praised.

We left him after he had bidden us farewell and given us the letter that he had written to the throne of our sayyid al-Mansur, victorious by God. He then sent a few of his inner circle to inquire whether we would like to stay in the park for a few days in order to hunt and relax. We answered him that our hearts were flying to our homeland and that we could not stay one more hour after that day. He wanted to return to Madrid on the following morning, so that evening and again in the morning, he sent us some attendants who looked after that place and who assisted in the hunt. We went hunting with them and found many deer and rabbits; so we abided by his wishes and returned on the next day to Madrid in order to prepare for our journey.

We left Madrid on the first day of blessed Ramadan of this year [1102; May 29, 1692]. The despot ordered the servants who were attending us to take us through Toledo to see its community mosque, which is one of the wonders of the world in its construction and the magnitude of its fame. On the day of our departure, we spent the night in a village near Madrid called Illescas, which used to be a capital of fame in this country and a seat of learning and wisdom. Today it is a dilapidated village but still shows the ruins of old Islamic buildings from the times of its prosperity under the Muslims—especially the main door leading into it. Today, it is closer to bedouinism than to urbanity. The distance between it and Toledo is twenty-one miles.

Toledo is a big city and a major capital of the country, the residence of old royalty. It rests on a hillock on the edge of a land overlooking the river called Tagus, the same one that passes through Aranjuez, the aforementioned park. The river surrounds it from three sides, while the fourth is the side that connects the road to Madrid. The fortifications of this city, along with its walls and alleys, are the same as they had been under the Muslims. It shows the remains of urbanization, but most of its roads are very narrow. Its buildings remain as they had been built by Muslims, with carvings and decorations in Arabic on the ceilings and walls.

Its community mosque is one of the wonders of the world; it is a large mosque built completely of solid stones strangely resembling marble, and its ceiling is a cupola of stone and is very high. Its columns are very thick and stunningly built and decorated. The Christians have added to the sides of this mosque some windows of yellow copper in which they have installed statues, crosses, and the musical instrument called by them an organ. They play it during prayer and accompany it with readings from books. Facing the window is the statue of the crucified made of gold, to which they turn during prayer. In front of the crucified are numerous lanterns of gold and silver, which are lit night and day, along with many, many candles.

The doors of this mosque are perfectly crafted and made. They have added on them statues, a custom they cannot renounce. Of the new additions to the sides of this mosque are many rooms with vaults containing large amounts of money and valuable colored stones of red, white, and yellow sapphire, along with emerald; there are also crowns decorated with pearls and priceless stones. Along with these treasures there are also a big crown of gold and two gold bracelets that they claim date back to the days of the Muslims, may God have mercy on their souls. To the right of these vaults is a vault with a big book written with gold water which they said is the Torah. They take very good care of it, for it never leaves the place it is in. They said that Philip Quarto, who is the father of this despot, wanted to take it away into his possession and was willing to give them in exchange a large city with its tributes and income, but they refused because of the esteem in which they hold it.

To the right of this vault there is another which has a big box full of precious items of jeweled gold, such as valuable fans, necklaces, chains, and rings. To its right is a [monastic] cell made of silver, higher than a man, the top and inside of which are golden and inlaid with colored precious stones. This cell [sawma'a] was built like that of the mosque of Toledo, in its exact shape and design: they view it as an ornament, and during their feasts decorate it and take it out with the crosses and circumambulate the streets as is their custom during the [Easter] procession or other similar festivities. The minaret in the mosque, may God return it to Islam, was modeled after that of Toledo, which is one of the most glorious buildings in design and height. It has three hundred steps, two hundred to the place of the call to prayer, and another hundred to the very top. In the place from where the call to prayer is made, the enemies of God almighty have installed nine large bells, so large that the parameter of each is thirty-six hand spans, while each of its edges is three quarters of an arm length. The minaret was all built of solid marble-like stone, from the same quarry as the mosque. We ask God Almighty to return it for the praise of His name and oneness.

Around these cabinets there are others full of gold and silver lanterns, inlaid crosses, and robes that friars, senior clergymen, deacons, and monks wear. All are decorated with very precious jewels. The friars who are in this church are all under the authority of the cardinal, who is today the greatest cardinal in Christendom, and who is himself under the authority of the pope, as has already been mentioned, may God destroy them both.

Since Toledo was one of the main cities of Spain, and an ancient capital of the kingdom, the cardinal who oversaw the administration of its church used to be higher in authority than all those who are called cardinals among the worshippers of the cross. The cardinal today is the head of the council of Spain and is the final arbiter in all matters relating to their loathsome religion, and to decisions and judgments in worldly matters. He consults with the despot, and the council follows his advice in all decisions.

There is in Toledo the remains of the citadel where kings used to live. Those who occupied it after its conquest built everything new in it.

With God is the command of the past and the future.[86]

Al-Ghassani continues from this point on with an account of the conquest of the Andalus, and the rivalries that subsequently occurred between Tariq bin Ziyad and Musa bin Nusayr. He also recounts some of the stories that survived about the Arab conquest, and refers to a book by Mohammad bin Musa al-Razi about the conquests carried out by Nusayr. Al-Ghassani and quotes from it about Nusayr assuring the Christian populations in the mountains of their safety with the understanding that they would pay the jizya.[87] Al-Ghassani continues by summarizing large parts of al-Razi's book about the relationship between the military conquerors and the Umayyad caliphs. He then adds a unit on the return of Nusayr to the Levant, in which he uses the account by Abd al-Malik bin Habib,[88] who had documented Nusayr's journey from Cordoba via Qayrawan. Nusayr, we are told, arrived with much of the booty of al-Andalus, which he then offered to the Prince of the Faithful. Al-Ghassani notes that Tariq contested Nusayr's claim to the conquest, but then, he repudiates that claim. The last words in the text confirm that "Musa was not a liar . . . and the conquest of the Andalus is credited to him." In this respect, al-Ghassani repeats the position of Abd al-Malik bin Habib and takes the side of the Arabs (Nusayr and his army, A.D. 712) against the Berbers (Tariq and his army, A.D. 711) in laying claim to the initial conquest of the Andalus.

Very strangely, al-Ghassani does not mention anything about the fate of the captives he had been sent to ransom. But it is known that he succeeded in liberating an unknown number of them (though whether it was the thousand asked for by Ismail is not clear). At the end of September 1691, the exchange of Magharibi with Spanish captives took place outside Ceuta, and on October 18, 1691, the liberated captives were paraded in Meknes.

NOTES

1. The background to this trip is fully described by Mariano Arribas Palau, "De Nuevo Sobre la Embajada de al-Gassani," in *Al-Qantara* 6 (1985): 199–289. For references to al-Ghassani, see E. J. Stanley, "Account of an Embassy from Marocco to Spain in 1690 and 1691," *Journal of the Royal Asiatic Society* 2 (1868): 359–78; and Henri Pérès, *L'Espagne vue par les voyageurs musulmans de 1610 à 1930* (Paris: Librarie d'Amerique et d'Orient, 1937), 5–17. See also Abd al-Majid al-Qadduri *Sufara Mahgaribah fi Urubba, 1610–1922* (Al-Dar al-Bayda': Jamiat Muhammad al Khamis, 1995).

2. A copy of the letter is reproduced in Abd al-Hadi al-Tazi, *Al-Mujaz fi Tarikh al-Alaqat al-duwaliyah lil-Mamlakah al-Maghribiyah* (Rabat: Matbaat al-Maarif al-Jadidah, 1984); a Spanish translation is reproduced in Tomas Garcia Figueras and Carlos Rodriguez Joulia Saint-Cyr, *Larache* (Madrid: Instituto de Estudios Africanos, 1973), 449–51.

3. This is quite a revisionist version, as Mulay al-Sheikh struck a deal with Philip III in 1613 to surrender al-'Araish to Spain, which he did, in return for the king militarily and financially supporting his claim to the Moroccan throne.

4. See for the last, J. Caille, "Les naufragés de la "Louise" au Maroc et l'Ambassade de Tahar Fennich à la cour de France en 1777–1778," in *Revue d'histoire diplomatique* 78 (1964): 256–57.

5. Muhammad al-Qadiri, *Kitab iltiqat al-durar*, ed. Hashim al-Alawi al-Qasimi (Beirut: Dar al-Afaq al-Jadidah, 1981), 2:298.

6. *Mulay/mawlana* was the title used by the Moroccan rulers; *shareef* indicates a descendent of the prophet's family.

7. Porte/*bab* was the name given to the Ottoman royal residence. From the end of the sixteenth century, Moroccan rulers called their residence, *bab*, in emulation of the Sublime Porte in Istanbul.

8. Al-Malik reigned from 705–715.

9. Julian was the ruler of Ceuta and known in Christian tradition as "the Traitor;" he was an enemy of the Visigoth King Rodrigo, whom the Muslims would subsequently defeat.

10. Actually, it was Tarif bin Malik that Musa bin Nusayr first sent to spy out the terrain, in 710.

11. The majority of the invading Muslim army was Berber.

12. Ifriqiya was the name given by the Arabs to the region of modern-day Tunis.

13. The crossing took place in 711.

14. The Khidr is a Quranic figure, similar to St. George.

15. Qur'an 18:60–82.

16. Suleiman II (reg. 1687–91). In 1690, the Turks drove the Austrians out of Bulgaria, Serbia and Transylvania. In that war, they retook Belgrade.

17. In 1524, the Spanish army invaded Provence and reached Marseilles. At the battle of Pavia, February 24, 1525, the French king, Francis I, was defeated and captured. He was held in Madrid—presumably in the house which al-Ghassani saw—until he signed the Treaty of Madrid.

18. Al-Ghassani often contrasts *badawa* with *hadara,* bedouinism with urbanity. These terms constitute the bases of Abd ar-Rahman bin Khaldun's theory of history.

19. This is Abu Abdallah, Boabdil (reg. 1486–1492).

20. On October 23, 1086, the battle of al-Zallaga took place between Alphonse VI and Yusuf bin Tashfeen; it ended in a Muslim victory.

21. He was also known as Abd al-Rahman the First (reg. 755–788).

22. Abd al-Rahman fled Baghdad after the Abbasid massacre of the Umayyad dynasty in 750 and established a new dynasty in Cordoba in 756.

23. The *mihrab* is a niche in the mosque, pointing in the direction of Mecca.

24. The most famous of Arab geographers, Abu Abd Allah Mohammad al-Idrisi (c. 1100–1166), wrote this book, which was known in the West as the *Book of Roger*, a detailed atlas/account of the world.

25. The story of Ibn Serraj became a popular topic among European writers: See Antonio de Villegas, *El Abencerraje*, intro. and trans. Francisco López Estrada and John Esten Keller (Chapel Hill: University of North Carolina Press, 1964); Lope de Vega, *El Hidalgo Bencerraje* in *Obras*, ed. Marcelino Menendez Pelayo (Madrid: La Real Academia Española, 1968), vol. 23; and Barbara Matulka, "On the European Diffusion of the 'Last of the Abencerrajes' Story in the Sixteenth Century," *Hispania* 16 (1933): 369–388.

26. This is left blank in both manuscripts.

27. An *ecu* is a silver or gold coin.

28. Qur'an 22:47.

29. Al-Ghassani is being generous in his description of this (possibly retarded) king. Compare the description by the papal nuncio a few years earlier: "The King is short rather than tall; frail, not badly formed; his face on the whole is ugly; he has a long neck, a broad face and chin, with the typical Habsburg lower lip, not very large eyes of turquoise blue and a fine and delicate complexion. . . . He is weak in body as in mind"; quoted in Henry Kamen, *Spain in the Later Seventeenth Century, 1655–1700* (London: Longman, 1980), 21. It is unlikely that al-Ghassani would have wanted to convey such an impression of the Spanish king, with whom his ruler was trying to negotiate.

30. This is San Fernando (d. 1252; canonized 1671).

31. Ferdinand V married Isabelle in 1469; he died in 1516.

32. According to the Marquis de Villars, the French numbered 66,000; see his *Mémoires de la cour d'Espagne, 1678–1682* (London: Wittingham and Wilkins, 1861), 285.

33. Al-Ghassani confirms the view of modern historians: the French "were a large and powerful minority with a decisive interest in Spain's economy. It is difficult to understand the significance of some aspects of seventeenth-century Spain without considering their role"; see Kamen, *Spain*, 183.

34. Philip the Handsome, who was duke of Burgundy (d. 1506), married Joanna,

the daughter of Ferdinand and Isabelle. By that marriage, the seventeen provinces of the Netherlands passed into Spanish hands.

35. The invasion occurred in 1541.

36. Al-Ghassani's information is not accurate here. The attack on Tunis had taken place in June-July 1535. During that attack, the town had been taken and brutally sacked. It remained in Spanish hands until 1569. It was occupied again by the Spaniards in 1573 and retaken by the Turks in 1574.

37. Al-Kharij (1554–78) was known as the invader.

38. This was the city of Saint-Quentin, 1557.

39. This was Mohammad al-Mutawakil, son of Mulay Abdallah.

40. This was August 4, 1578.

41. The revolt of 1569–71 was led by Fernando de Valor/Ibn Hamiyya against Philip II.

42. The edict of December 9, 1609 led to the expulsion of all the Muslim and Morisco populations. See above for the edict (quoted by Ahmed bin Qasim).

43. This was in March 1621.

44. Philip IV died in September 1665.

45. This was Marie-Anne of Austria, daughter of Ferdinand III.

46 His wife was Isabelle, daughter of Henry IV, the king of France.

47. He was born in November 1661.

48. The counselor Don Fernando Valenzuela was a poet, dramatist, politician, and the most trusted supporter of the queen; thus his title, *le duende de palacio*, the "palace elf."

49. Valenzuela was imprisoned on January 22, 1677.

50. Al-Ghassani confuses his facts here: Carlos II came of age on November 6, 1675. He had his half brother called to court on December 27, 1676. For a full account, see R. Trevor Davies, *Spain in Decline, 1621–1700* (London: Macmillan, 1965), ch. 6.

51. He died in September 1679.

52. He died in 1692 in Mexico.

53. Actually, Marie-Louise was the eldest daughter of the Duke of Orléans, brother of Louix XIV. She reached Spain in November 1679.

54. Marie Anne, daughter of the Elector Palatine. The marriage took place in 1689.

55. Mulay Ismail claimed descent from Ali, the son-in-law of the prophet Muhammad.

56. Al-Ghassani recognizes here the crisis of bread in Madrid. As Kamen has observed, bread was a "constant worry"; see *Spain*, 166.

57. The Plaza Mayor was the center of the city, with very high buildings for the rich population.

58. St. Jean de Dieu was the founder of the Brothers of Charity (1495–1550; canonized October 16, 1690).

59. Qur'an 2:213.

60. Alexander VIII, 1689–1691. He had died on February 1.

61. This was Pope Innocent XII (1691–1700).

62. This is a concise but confused explanation of the Law of Devolution whereby the children of a man's first marriage inherited everything, and children of a second marriage inherited nothing.

63. The War of Devolution started because Louis XIV laid claim to the Belgian provinces of Brabant and Flanders.

64. The triple alliance was actually Protestant (England, Sweden, and the United Provinces) and not from among the Catholic "worshippers of the Cross."

65. Al-Ghassani used the word *salibiyeen* which means "crusaders."

66. This was Charles II (d. 1685).

67. The reference is to William of Orange in 1689.

68. This was on April 9, 1691.

69. Actually, it was the French fleet that defeated the English fleet, June 30, 1690.

70. The French bombarded Alicante on July 25, 1691.

71. Emmerich Tekli was a Protestant who fought with the Ottomans against the Habsburgs under a Christian flag.

72. Islamic law is strict and detailed about inheritance, where none in the family is excluded from a portion of the inheritance.

73. This was Maria Teresa (b. 1638).

74. Was this the Spanish version of the Protestant Reformation which was relayed to al-Ghassani?

75. The *sunna* is the Muslim code of behavior, based on the teachings and practices of the prophet Muhammad.

76. Cf. Luke 22:7–13.

77. Cf. John 13:1–15.

78. John 13:21 ff.

79. The word al-Ghassani uses for "resurrection" is *rafa'*, which is the Quranic word used for the ascension of Christ.

80. Qur'an: 4:157–58.

81. Acts of the Apostles 9:4 and ff.

82. This is a variation on Matt. 18:21–22.

83. The number of affairs between priests and their parishoners was high. In

1680, as Kamen observes, eight prosecuted cases out of twenty-seven were "against women for sexual relations with a priest"; see his *Spain*, 172.

84. Lorenzo el Real was a Spanish martyr (d. 520).

85. Al-Ghassani does not describe the latter mosque in his account.

86. Qur'an 30:3.

87. A tax paid by non-Muslim subjects.

88. See the edition and translation by John Harris Jones, *The History of the Conquest of Spain* (1858; rep. New York: Burt Franklin, 1969).

A Paris Chez I. Mariette rue S.ᵗ Iacques aux Colonnes d'Hercules avec Privil du Roy

1. *Abdala Ben Aischa Amiral et Surintendant General de la Marine de l'Empire de Maroc, Ambassadeur de l'Empereur de Maroc en France en 1699.*
2. *Mahameth Touziris Capitaine de Vaisseaux Lieutenant de l'Ambassade.*
3. *Achmeth Soussin Docteur de la Loy Secretaire de l'Ambassade.*
4. *Esclaues Maures.*

Abdallah bin Aisha, Paris 1699. (Windsor Castle, Royal Collection)

4

FRANCE

Letters

Abdallah bin Aisha

(1699–1700)

ABDALLAH BIN AISHA, accompanied by his secretary/scribe Ahmad Sousan and his lieutenant Mohammad al-Thughiry, along with sixteen other members of the Moroccan delegation whose names Aisha refused to divulge, left for Brest on November 11, 1698 on a mission to negotiate a treaty with France. The visit attracted much media attention from the French newspapers of the period, especially *La Mercure Galant* and *La Gazette de France*. Although the negotiations failed, the visit provided Aisha and his retinue with the opportunity to see the grandeur and novelty of France and to mix with royalty and nobility.[1]

Aisha remained in Brest for two months, until discussions of his status—as to whether he was an envoy or an ambassador—were completed. It was a humiliating delay, but Aisha bore it with patience, standing adamant in his position, but willing to engage his hosts in their social activities and functions. Unable to speak French, but fluent in Spanish and English, Aisha always had to rely on translators and French commercial agents—the result of which was the development of a strong friendship that he confirmed by his repeated use of the word *mahabba*—love—in his later letters and exchanges. He stayed in Brest until January 12, 1699 when he was given permission by the French king to begin his journey to Paris. On the road, which took him through Rennes, Nantes, Angers, Tours, and the Loire Valley, he was welcomed by official parties that included women who flocked to engage him in conversation—something at which he was a

master. He was a poet, wrote the king's interpreter, and "fort curieux."[2] As
the entourage passed by the plain of Saint-Martin-le-Beau, the scene of
the last battle that stopped the Arab advance into Europe in A.D. 711,
Aisha was moved by the recollection of the martyrs of that battle, said a
prayer for them, and then picked up a dozen pebbles to take back with
him to his country.[3]

On February 9, 1699, he arrived in Paris, and on February 16, he had
his audience with King Louis XIV, accompanied by servants carrying the
royal presents: a Moroccan saddle, a tiger skin, five lion skins, and other
objects. Detailed accounts were written about him—both private, for the
perusal of the king, and public, for newspaper releases. Every move, every
place that he went to, every gesture that he made, the way he ate, prayed,
or smiled—all were noted. During his stay in Paris, he visited the Cathedral
of Notre Dame, the Royal Mint, the Royal Library, an observatory, from
where he took letters for astronomers in Morocco, the Saint-Antoine glass
factory, the church of Saint-Denis, and many other places. Such social excitement did he create that whenever he dressed up in his Moroccan
clothes and went for a stroll, Parisians flocked to look at him. For his protection, soldiers were stationed around his residence. Despite his openness
to the *nasara* (Christians), Aisha remained obedient to his Islamic codes,
and from the start ensured that the meat he and his delegation were eating
was *halal*.

Perhaps the most moving episode that occurred in Paris was his visit
to the deposed English king James II, who was then in exile. The story of
these two men has been shrouded in mystery. But the evidence suggests
the following sequence of events: Aisha confirmed that early in his life, he
had been captured by the English and taken to England as a slave, where
he had been bought by the Duke of York (James). It seems that he even
converted to Christianity, after which he had been given the name of
James. In 1671, he was taken to the Continent, where he met the Duke of
Florence and studied siege craft in Germany and the Low Countries. A few
years later, and for a still-unknown reason, James II interceded with his
brother, King Charles II, for the release of Aisha. Aisha was freed without
having to pay a ransom, returned to Islam, and then employed the military learning he had acquired in the numerous sieges of Tangier (which
was occupied, ironically, by the English). Later he became the commander
of the Moroccan fleet. Now, in France, after so many years, the two met
again: it was a moving scene, as the two wept together while recalling old

times.[4] As Pétis de la Croix, the French expert on oriental languages noted, Abdallah recalled the "bons traitments qu'il en avoit reçus, estant leur esclave, qu'il ne put s'empêcher de verser des larmes an abondance. Ces larmes rendirent le discours de ses yeux encour plus éloquent et plus pathetique que celuy de sa bouche, et en tirèrent également de la plus grande partie de ceux qui estoient presens."[5] Aisha visited James again, and after his return to Morocco, he told his master about him; Mulay Ismail subsequently addressed a letter to James II, promising him military support to regain his kingdom if he would be willing to convert to Islam. And if not to Islam, at least to Protestantism![6]

In Paris, Aisha made friends and stayed at the house of Jean Jourdan, with whom he would maintain correspondence after his return to Morocco. Jourdan (1667–1725) was a diplomat and an international trader who was married to Marie-Nicole Guillebon, and lived in Paris. Between 1695 and 1699, he was preparing for the establishment of a French colony on the Pacific coast of South America. In 1697, he founded the Compangie de la Chine, and by the time of Aisha's visit, he was already a wealthy man and a member of the Société de Salé. Aisha also wrote to Jourdan's wife, who had become very dear to him. During his stay with them, he met with many ladies of the court, and became particularly enchanted by Charlotte Le Camus Melson, possibly because she had been born English; the two could talk together without the intervention of an interpreter. A deep and intimate relationship developed between them "très vif et très spirituel"; and she gave him valuable presents that included diamonds and "une tabatière d'or."[7]

Many letters that Aisha sent were attached to shorter ones by his secretary and his lieutenant who included their warm regards to the addressees as well as to their friends. Not only Aisha, but all the delegation made friends.

The visit ended on April 26, 1699, when Aisha had his final audience with the king. Despite the failure of the mission, Aisha had won the respect and admiration of many officials with whom he had worked. There was praise for his piety and devotion: the month of Ramadan had fallen during his visit, and he fasted as was required; even when he had to attend official galas and dinners, he sat at the table, and while the French ate and drank, he counted his beads. On May 5, 1699, Aisha and his companions left Paris for Brest. He was in a hurry to return as he expected that Mulay Ismail was anxious about the results of the negotiations. On reach-

ing Orléans, he wrote his farewell letter to Mme. Le Camus and other letters of gratitude. He embarked from Brest on May 25, 1699 and arrived in
Salee on June 10.

Upon reaching Mekness, Aisha gave a full account to his angry ruler.
Ismail was unhappy that Aisha had been away so long, and he queried
him about every detail in the negotiations. The French king had sent with
Aisha a strong-worded letter to Ismail, boasting of his might and power.
Ismail was not intimidated and wrote back, saying that he did not care
about the king's threats. But Ismail was deeply concerned about his subjects: he wanted to prevent their captivity by French ships, and more so to
redeem those already enslaved on French galleys.

During the lengthy accounts that Aisha presented to his king about his
visit, he mentioned the beauty and charm of Madame de Conti, one of the
king's natural daughters. Fascinated by what he heard, Mulay Ismail
thought that perhaps the only way to cement an alliance with France (and
thereby protect his subjects while increasing trade) was by following the
traditional manner in both European Christendom as well as North
African Islam of contracting a marriage. He thus decided to propose a
Moroccan-French marriage in order to end all hostility—the marriage of
Madame de Conti to himself.

The Princess de Conti was born Marie-Anne de Bourbon on October
2, 1666, the natural daughter of King Louis XIV and Mademoiselle de la
Vallière. A year later, she was made legitimate by her father. She was married at the age of fourteen to the Prince de Conti, who died five years later,
whereupon the princess turned into "fille des plaisirs de Paris" (a "woman
of the pleasures of Paris"). Many poems were written about her and many
suitors asked her hand in marriage, but the princess was happy in her
freedom and charm. It was at the age of thirty-three that Aisha saw her
and described her to his monarch.

The letters of Aisha reveal the breadth of the interaction between himself and members of the French court. Specifically, they show the level of
intimacy that Aisha was able to enjoy among his addressees' families: in
the case of J.-B.Estelle, the French Consul in Salee, he had even participated
in the latter's wedding, and in the case of Jourdan, he had become so open
with him that he felt no qualms about addressing letters to Jourdan's wife.
The letters also reveal the amount of information about France that was
collected by Aisha and his delegation, and subsequently disseminated in
Maghrebi court and community. France made a strong impression on

him, and he always talked about it and about the people he met there to his wife, children, family, friends, and, of course, to his master. He had so admired what he saw—the luxuries, the artifacts, the novelties—that he repeatedly asked for samples for himself as well as for his master. The letters show the persistence with which he requested these luxuries, reflecting the desire of an underdeveloped society for the amenities of the modernizing world. Aisha, of course, knew full well that the only reason the French would send him presents was to secure the Moroccan markets for French traders.

NOTE: All the letters herein were originally written in Arabic. They were then translated by al-Salibi (as Aisha called him), the French official translator, Pétis de la Croix. Aisha therefore always realized that what he wrote would be read by the French and translated—although, because of his ignorance of French, he could never ascertain how accurate the translations were. Aisha was doubtlessly very circumspect, taking care to express his true feelings without jeopardizing negotiations or friendships. When he wrote from Mekness (he did not actually write, but dictated to Sousan), he had Mulay Ismail, a very suspicious and careful monarch, breathing down his neck. His language and choice of words could be seen to have been "censored" since his master most assuredly read the letters. Aisha had to be sufficiently praiseworthy to his master, while also being praiseworthy to the French—from whom he was seeking gifts, agreements, and clarifications. Private as the letters were, they were inevitably public, and had a wide range of intended (and unintended) audiences.

All the letters herein are taken from the Arabic original in Philipe de Cossé-Brissac, *Les Source Inédites de l'Histoire du Maroc, Deusxième Série, Dynastie Filalienne* (Paris: Paul Guethner, 1953), vol. 5: 420–426, 489–493, 506–508; and vol. 6: 184–187.

To Madame Le Camus
May 8–13, 1699

To reach the hand of the Madame de Signor Le Camus from your lover, and the one who yearns for your face and whose condition cannot be hidden. Finished.

Praise be to God alone. There is no strength or might
except in God the exalted and almighty.

I wrote this letter of love and sent it to you
And sang in the verses a predestined matter;
For there was fire inside me which I did not show.

O apple of my eye, how difficult it is to leave you
But in the core of my heart you are always present;

When the darkness of night descends, it brings upon me
your absence,
And when the morning comes, I awaken to sorrow.

Greetings to you and to whomever is with you.

Know that when I wrote to you, I was consoled by the letter you had sent
me. But when you said that you were in that house from whose door I had
returned, if I had known that you were there, I would have gone there on my
face, not my feet.[8] But I abided by the custom of the Arabs not to enter the
house of a man without his permission. Had the man who led me to you told
me, we would have left my house to go to you. But you sat in a place where
neither could we see you nor you see us. Everything got confused.

But I am yours and anything you demand of me I will fulfill [on my head].
May God enlighten you, and may He give me the joy of your love in this
world. I have put the letter you sent me in my luggage in order to show it to
my children and show them your love, goodness, friendliness, pure heart,
and overwhelming love. I have entrusted them with this charge—that should
I die, they would always continue the friendship with you, God willing.
Peace be upon you.

Servant of the palace, exalted by God, Abdallah.

To Jean Jourdan
September 16–25, 1699

*[In the margin, in French, "Letter of Bin Aisha, previously ambassa-
dor of Morocco in France, and at present, admiral of Salee; written to*

Mr. Jourdan on September 25, 1699; translated by Pétis de la Croix on November 20, 1699"].

Praise be to God alone. There is no strength except in God, great and almighty.

From the servant of God and slave of his follies, servant of the exalted throne and of the Prophetic Hashemite descendant, the sultanic sharif, may God elevate and protect him. Amen. The ever-happy Captain [admiral] Abdallah bin Aisha, may God assist him in fulfilling His will. Amen. Amen.

To our dear friend Mr. Jourdan: peace be to him who follows in the straight path and finds truth. We always inquire about you in *mahabba* [love], the effects of which we have seen in you. May God reward you with what He loves and desires. How is your wife, whom I view as my daughter, Madame Jourdan, and her two daughters from you, and your two daughters, whom I view as mine?[9] Greetings to them from me and my family. All our children inquire about you and always want to hear your good news since I have told them a lot about you, especially about how good you were to me, may God assist me in rewarding you. Amen.

Know, my friend Mr. Jourdan, that, with God's help, I reached my country and approached my master, victorious by God almighty. He welcomed me in great happiness, but then blamed me and turned his face away from me for having stayed too long in your country. He said, "As soon as you saw the people there change their attitude to you and no longer exhibit the same former emotions, you should not have stayed there so long and should have returned to us sooner." I begged and implored him, calming him and telling him about you and about the natural goodness of your countrymen. I also told him about the great qualities of your king, your master, and his officers and ministers, especially Mr. de Pontchartrain, Minister de Torcy, and Maurepas and other members of the court. He listened to me and heard some things but refused to hear others—as you know. I then turned to tell him about you and the *mahabba* you had shown, and all the valuable treasures from India that you had given to us. He mellowed and smiled at me, showing the happiness of his face. He charged me to write to you and thank you, and to assure you of your safety, as well as the safety of your possessions and ships wherever they are in our country and all the Maghrebi coast under the command of our master, may God grant him victory. All governors and sea commanders in those harbors will ensure the safety of your ships—and all this for [the sake of] your face and in consideration of all the good you and your children have extended to us.

I had written to you from Brest by means of Saint-Olon when I embarked on my return journey.[10] When you write a letter or a report, like the previous ones, let there be two versions, one French, and one Arabic. You did not write [and send] any letters, or else we did not receive them. Send them as soon as possible, as I have indicated. Attach to them everything you want from this country—and within the limits of divine law, our master, may God assist him, will make sure you are granted them.[11]

I am hereby sending you a report written in the hand of your factor.[12] Once you receive it, do not forget nor delay sending us what you had promised of the goods that would arrive on the ship from India;[13] send to us everything that you choose of the fine porcelain, ornamented in the most delicate designs and decorations. Do not mind the price, however expensive it may be, as long as you tell us about it. It must be done. It must be done.

Learn also, my friend Mr. Jourdan, that my master, may God grant him victory, still has me oversee all his affairs, at sea as well as in regard to the affairs of the various nationalities of Christians, wherever they are. Nobody has anything to do with them other than I. God is my witness, and you know that I speak the truth, I have informed my master, may God grant him victory, only of that which conduces to the good and to the establishment of harmony between [our] hearts. But nothing offended him more than when I told him that the king of France sought war with us and armed some of his ships to attack some coastal outposts. He replied with these words, may God assist him, "The sea belongs to the Christians—as it is said, the sea belongs to the *ruum* [Christians]. But if he wishes to wage war on land, he should merely inform us of the location, and we will give him ample time to assemble his armies and organize his forces the way he wants. And then he will see what the soldiers of Islam are capable of doing—what his eyes have never seen before, God willing." He was very reproachful in his words, saying to me, "You should write to the members of the French court, those members with whom you had been in contact and who had told you about this [imminent attack], answer them with what will prove satisfactory." He authorized me to work with them for the general good [between our countries]. Such is the bounty of God and the bounties of our master, may God grant him victory, despite the envy of all adversaries.

As for you, our dear friend, do not forget anything; tell me all that you hear about the affairs of your trade in our country, and bring some of your agents to live here in our city [Salee] or in any other. You will find everything to your satisfaction, and all our agents and servants will have complete and lasting security—by the power and will of God, and the goodness of my master, may God be with him. When our Master heard of the French desire to wage war and that some ships were intent on blockading our ports, he became angry and decided that no Christian from the French nation, neither trader nor anybody else, would remain on his soil. He then ordered to his presence the merchants who were in Salee and Tetuan and ordered them, "Get out of my country and from wherever you are." But they begged him for pardon and forgiveness, since merchants want only peace. They then asked me to intercede. So I implored him on their behalf, may God assist him, and apologized for them, trying to make him accept them. He rescinded his order to expel them from the country, and assured them of the safety of their possessions throughout the land. He pardoned them and ordered them neither to communicate news about us nor to receive news from their country, but only to pursue their trade; and none would see anything in our country other than kindness, with no evil intentions or consequences.

For you, my dear friend, as long as God's and my Master's blessing is on me, tell me your news, and whether your family grows bigger, thanks to Madame. I like to hear about everything there that brings you happiness and well-being. And from my side, I will tell you about God's bounty in keeping the favor and good will of my master, the Prince of the Faithful. What a blessing. I pray God to keep that grace on me and on all Muslims. Amen.

In brief, my dear friend Jourdan, send us twelve large eating pots,[14] as large as your factor mentioned in his letter, written by his hand, and as I had described them, and in the shape and design about which I had told him. You will receive the letter mentioning all that we need—because I told him to write everything down. Do not neglect anything that I mentioned in my letters, nor the other things about which I had told you, in person, while I was with you. When your India ship reaches you, send me many of the valuables it brings, for I had mentioned the ship to my Master, and he was very happy and praised you very much, saying, "Truly, you have the finest friend, O Bin Aisha; none is like your friend in the lands of Christians. Write to him and tell him that I have learned of all his honest dealings with you: indeed, he has earned my esteem."

Learn that a house was discovered under the ground here in our region in which we found three marble statutes, one in the shape of a man who was king of this land in past times during the period of God's prophet, Ibrahim al-Khalil [Abraham], may peace be on him, and two other figures. As soon as we discovered them, we sent them to our Master, may God grant him victory, and we thought to let you know about them, since we and all your Christian merchants here admired them. They confirmed to us that one of them is the statue of a king and is very old. Finished.

I return to the inquiries regarding your wife, the Madame, and her two sisters. Do let me know whether she has been delivered of her burden. Do let me know, and you will receive some cloth which our children want to send to her: we hope she will accept it. Meanwhile, do excuse me that I am obliged to remain in the court of Mekness to fulfill my duties, as your factor tells you [and therefore I cannot travel to offer my personal congratulations]. Since I came back from France, I have stayed in Mekness for two full months in the presence of my Master, God grant him victory. He did not cease from ordering me not to be absent and, God assist him, he gave me more responsibilities in the affairs of his dominion, whenever they occur. I ask God for the continuance of health and strength. At present, we await your reply and letter to find solace in it: for only letters can remove the pain in our hearts and cool the fires. May God grant that we hear good from you. Finished in the latter part of the month of God, Rabi' of the glorious Prophet, in the year 1111. May God bring us good and protect us from evil. Amen. Amen. Amen.

What has made this letter necessary is the need to insist very much on the pots. We wish to have a dozen of the shape and size we mentioned in our letter written by your factor in the Frankish tongue. These pots are for eating couscous, as you saw when we were visiting your country. We also urge you, friend Mr. Jourdan, to send us two dozen birds, known as *darraj* [pheasants], male and female, that Saint-Olon and La Croix had shown to us on the road [to Chambrot]. It is important that you send us two dozen.

You will be receiving, my friend Mr. Jourdan, five shawls for your wife and her daughters from you, and for her sisters. She also has a pair of shoes and a piece of cloth. Other shawls will reach you, two for Madame Saint-Olon and her daughter. Another shawl is for Madame Le Camus Melson. The name of each is written on each of the presents. Please give each gift to each. You will also receive a table cover that Mrs. Jourdan could put on her card table.

Written toward the end of the month of God, Rabi' al-Awal in the year 1111.

You will also receive a gazelle with which your children, whom I cherish as my own, will play. They were the ones who sent these small presents to your children for play, God willing. Amen. Amen.

Servant of the throne raised by God, Abdallah bin Aisha, may God be with him. Amen.

TO JEAN JOURDAN
November 15, 1699

Praise be to God alone. There is no strength except in God, great and almighty.

From the slave of God and captive of his follies, servant of him who has been royally elevated by God, descendent of the family of the Hashemite Prophet, may God ennoble him, Abdallah bin Aisha to our friend and *habib*, Mr. Jourdan. Greetings and peace on him who has followed the light and walked in the way of truth. My love [*hubb*] to you is a love beyond measure, and I inquire about you all the time, and remember you at home and in travel, you and your wife, the madame who is as dear to me as my daughter. I mention you to my children and talk about you always, and about your two charming daughters, whom I regard as my own. God is my witness that I do not remember you except as we were together rejoicing there [in Paris]. You are, more and more, in my conversations, as well as in the conversations of my children. May God send you peace, all peace.

What I wish to tell and assure you is that I am, thanks be to God, quite well, staying with my master, may God grant him victory. He, God grant him victory, continues to add to my dignity and honor, by the grace of God and His Prophet. As I talk about you, I always tell him about your good deeds, your support in all things, and about all the good you have done to us and the gifts you have given. I have not ignored mentioning anything of your worthy benevolence. My master, may God give him victory, rejoiced very much, more than you can imagine, and he charged me to write to you this letter and the ones I wrote you earlier.

Find enclosed with my letter the valuable letter of his majesty. You will find in it his words and the commission he gave me in regard to overseeing all your affairs, and at the same time, releasing you from the authority of the governor and council of the port so that you and your factors and ships and all your merchandise will deal with me, without anybody, of whatever quality or status, coming between us. This assurance demonstrates his *mahabba*, may God give him victory, to you and shows to all people the honor he bestows on you, for the love you have for me. Whenever you write to me, I show him your letter word for word; I read it to him and he retains the information in his mind and confirms that I should oversee your affairs and permit no one to interfere, whoever they are. Rejoice, therefore, and prepare yourself for this matter of which his majesty, God grant him victory, spoke from his heart and mind, and with which he has been preoccupied.

Listen, therefore, O Mr. Jourdan. By God, after returning from the land of France and reaching the court of my master, may God give him victory, I did not stop telling him about Sultan Louis, his court, his reign, his fame, his gracious manners and honor, his kindness to all people, and his power over all the kings of the Christians, until he absorbed all the information. He said, "Such a man deserves to be known and befriended." I also told him about the evening we were among your people in Paris in the house of Mr. Winser[?], brother of the Emperor, and there was Mr. le Dauphin, son of the same emperor, accompanied by the princess, his sister of the same mother, who is now without a husband, he having died. When I described to him her marvelous qualities and her modesty and high spirits, and how that night she had expressed happiness and gaiety at seeing us, my master remained deep in thought, and then said, "Tell me more." And I replied, "O majesty, the daughter of the king of France is someone who is the sister of Mr. le Dauphin of both father and mother. She has great qualities and modesty, which we saw that night in the company of her brother. We appreciated the respect and hospitality she showed to us, in honor of the servant of our master, God give him victory." He became very happy and said, "Go, O Bin Aisha, in this instant and hour, and journey to France for the purpose of asking for the hand of that girl [in marriage] whose qualities you have described to me. And do not return unless you bring a reply that satisfies me. If God wills, we will marry her in accordance with the law of our book and the law of our chosen Prophet, the peace of God be upon him. She will retain her religion and the customs of her predecessors, and she will not experience anything unsatisfactory in all her affairs."

When I heard this, and confirmed that he would not change his mind until he attained [his goal], I said: "My Master, may God be with you. It is difficult to sail in this time of year. The ships that had been here all returned when they saw the storms and tempests of the sea. If God wills, I can write to my friend Jourdan who will deliver our letters to the court of the King, with a letter to our friend Mr. de Pontchartrain.[15] He will be the intermediary and negotiator in this great matter." So he said, "Do it."

I have thus written a letter to the aforementioned minister about the matter and what it entails. I am sending it, with this letter, so you will hand him the letter and receive his answer. If he approves of the matter, let the afore-mentioned minister send me a letter in his own hand authorizing that I board one of your war ships. When they arrive, I will board in order to pur-sue the matter. If God brings success to this project, there will be *mahabba* and engagement between the kings, and the reward will accrue to him whom God has chosen to bring it about.

As you know, O Mr. Jourdan, I did not speak but good things about your king, his kingdom, his fame, his court and his ministers—saying all the good things that I confirmed to you when I was in your country, so that God would bring about the charitable release of the Muslim and Christian captives. But my letter addressed a matter that is by far more weighty in the court of great kings than the captives and all other issues. It is the mother of all great affairs, if God accomplishes it. So think about what it means to you, and try your best to fulfill it, and let me know about it, and all other matters that concern you in regard to traffic and commerce in our country. As for the love that is between us, it continues to grow in my heart and will appear in the future. It is strong and not diminished, may God bring you and me to fulfill His will.

You will receive another letter written by your factor about this matter. You will find what you need to do for my master, may God grant him victory, on the cover of the letter as well as inside. Be alert and circumspect in all matters, and reply to everything. As for the carpet for which I had asked you when I was there, do not forget to buy it for me at whatever cost, and send it to me on the first occasion and tell the factor the price, and he will be reim-bursed immediately. With these small services, the heart of my master, may God grant him victory, will be gladdened, and we will confirm the mutual promises between us and you in accordance with the law of the servants of kings. By God, by God, I entrust this matter to you: keep it in your heart, and pursue it until the will of God is fulfilled. Finished.

Also send to me, as I asked you in other letters, the small things and valu-able curiosities that arrive in your ships from Siam, and do not forget any of the knives/sabers and other things. Do not forget either that master crafts-man who makes water run and then watches it flowing. Send him with the first ship that comes to the Arab shore and enters our country and port. Fin-ished. Written on the twenty-second of the month of God Jamadi al-Awal in the year 1111.

Servant of the royal throne, Abdallah bin Aisha, may God protect him, Amen.

To J.-B. Estelle
December 23, 1699

Praise be to God alone. There is no strength except in God almighty.

From the slave of God and captive of his follies, servant of the high throne of God, Captain Abdallah bin Aisha, may God make him successful. To the Christian Estelle the French, peace to him who follows divine guidance and walks in the way of righteousness and finds truth. I always inquire about you and do not forget all that I said to you in affection and *mahabba*. I inquire about your wife, Madame, whom I have placed in my heart like one of my daughters.[16] Extend to her my sincere greetings, as much as it is permitted by divine and human law.

Know my friend, that I had discussed many matters with our friend Jourdan pertaining to trade and business—as you doubtlessly know. It is through you that I have come to know and befriend him. When I returned from my journey, I left him a few matters to handle for me. He was willing to do so, saying, "We shall do everything for our master, may God grant him victory and prolong his life."

The first thing was the carpet that I stopped to look at many times while you were with me. There were also other rare objects that I designated, each by its name, and he told me about his ship in India, that when it returned, he would send me what was suitable. When I reached the court of my master, may God grant him victory, I reported to him all that my friend Jourdan had said, repeating everything word for word. I also told him about his goodness to us [the delegation], and how he supported us and showed us a commitment of *mahabba*. Everything that I said remained in the mind of my master, may God grant him victory, and he frequently asked me, "Do you have news from your friend Jourdan?" and I would remain helpless, without any reply, as I had not had any word or letter from him. I was deeply disheartened for not hearing from him, and I became ashamed. I wrote to him more than once but did not receive anything at all, until lately I found in some captives' letters that you are coming here.[17] I have left you to prepare for your arrival. Because of your *mahabba*, I ask you to bring with you our friend Jourdan's answer, explaining the reason for his delay and his excuse.

This is what I wanted to tell you today.

May God be praised, my master has added to my authority and prestige and has handed me the government and command of the country and region, in order to bring good to it. He has given me power in all things, including the negotiations with you, for which [reason] I had traveled to your master. I am still empowered by his authority to negotiate and finalize what is good and advantageous, including all matters I had discussed with the ministers while I was there. Discuss with them what they want to see in my answer, but perfection comes only from God and from my master, may God grant him victory.

For the love of God and for the love I have for you, please bring with you a present, a few Muslim captives, foremost among them being Mohammad al-Sammar, whose brother, Qasim, was with us [in France]. Upon my return here, his old mother, aged and blind, came to me pleading, day and night. I had, in your presence, urged our friend Jourdan to help in this matter, and he had promised that I would not see the face of any of the factors unless accompanied with this captive. I have not heard from him regarding this matter nor any other.

I hereby charge you with this [captive's] affair. Do not let me see you except brining with you one of the captives, he [Mohammad] being the foremost; and if two, he would again be the foremost; and if more, he would be the foremost. I will not accept any excuse in this regard, for I have seen what happened to his brother when we were among you. Today, I am here with his mother in great sorrow, and what you will do for him will ensure for you my friendship and my commitment. You have known my commitment [to you] in greater matters. Peace.

The first day in the month of God, Rajab, year 1111. Greetings to all the captives among the Muslims. May God open for us the venue to ransom them because we still seek God, may He be praised, and may He grant victory to our master, and all goodness, joy and perfection, may He be thanked. Amen.

To Madame Jourdan
July 2, 1700

Praise be to God alone. There is no strength except in God almighty.

From the servant of God and slave of his follies, officer of the exalted throne who has been elevated by God, descendent of the family of the Hashemite Prophet, the imperial *Shareef*, may God make him victorious and exalt and cherish him, Amen. [From] Abdallah bin Aisha, may God help him with His generosity to serve his master, the prince of the faithful, may God grant him and his armies victory. Amen.

To her who is in our hearts and spirits, and on our tongues every day and night, with our children and friends, and even inside the court of my master, may God make him victorious, who is as dear to me as my daughter, and even more, and to Madame Marie Guillebon:[18] greetings to those who follow the straight path, and whom God guides in His ways.

I inquire about you repeatedly as I miss you very much. Your *mahabba* is firmly rooted, mixed with the sweetness of reciprocal accord; I have found in your letters and papers all the perfection that you had declared in the fullness of your heart. As I opened and read them, my children and I found great joy; we saw there the grace of God the one and only who gave you a child. We have rejoiced very much and we pray that God will give joy to you, to his father and his sisters. May you have long life and success in all your enterprises.

I am firm in the commitment I made to your husband, Mr. Jourdan, and I ask God almighty to help me reward him. Had I not been now committed to fulfill my master's commands, I would have been able to find the opportunity to fulfill what your husband had asked me to do.[19] Until your ship returns this time, God wills what He wants, and all his desires will be met. A little patience is needed: everything has its time.

Your friend, De la Clouzerie Manier, has seen with his own eyes that my excuse was valid; I did not conceal anything from him about my affairs, especially after I found him a reasonable and sociable man. I ask of you and God to speak favorably of him so that he will come to reside here, and for your husband to recommend him to Mr. de Pontchartrain so that he may obtain the consul's patent for coming to this country and overseeing the affairs of merchants. He will insure their rights and will serve as a mediator, fulfilling all my master's desires, may God make him victorious. And if any one has any concern about the captives or others who are in our country and in obedience to our master, may God make him victorious, let him communicate with me, and I will pass on the information to my master, may God make him victorious. We shall make sure that all things will be carried out fairly.

Greetings to your older and younger sisters, although neither of them is young, and to your two daughters who are the light of your eyes. Embrace them for me, three times each and ten times their little brother, and receive the *mahabba* of all my daughters and their mother, who miss you as dearly as I do. I assure you, only God knows how I miss you in my heart and cannot wait much longer: I never forget them. Night and day I think of them.

I know full well, Madame, that you do not forget me, and all that I have in my heart, you have put there. May God bring us together again in this world. Learn, too, that my daughters have made you the center of their conversations wherever they are, and only God knows what is in the hearts and intentions.

Completed in the middle of the Muharram month of God in the beginning of the year 1112 H.

Receive also the greetings of Mohammad Sousan, who wrote these lines, and who is ever grateful to your benevolence, and Mohammad al-Thughiry, both of whom send their many many greetings too to the translator, Mr. De la Croix and his son.

Praise be to God. I add to this letter the assurance that my master, may God make him victorious, urged me to write to your husband, my dear friend Jourdan, that he buy him three diamonds each for more or less 4,000 riyals so that the total does not exceed more or less 10,000 riyals; and to buy him a kilo of fine, expensive and precious pearls. It must be done for you are like my daughter; I give you authority to represent me in the affairs between myself and your husband. It must be done. It must be done. I ask of God that He give me life to see your face once more, and that He find the way. Amen. Amen. There is no happier day than the one in which I receive your letter. May God show me your face. Amen.

Written by the servant of his highness, Abdallah bin Aisha, may God be with him. Amen.

NOTES

1. For references to, and studies on, Aisha, see Charles Penz, *Les Captifs Français du Maroc au XVIIe Siècle* (Rabat: Impr. Officielle, 1944), chap. 7; Younés Nekhouf, *Une amitié orageuse: Moulay Ismaïl et Louis XIV* (Paris: Albin Michel, 1987), 334–40. There are numerous studies of Mulay Ismail, his relations with France, and his marriage proposal; see Eugène Plantet, *Moulay Ismael, Empereur du Maroc, et la princesse de Conti* (Paris: E. Jamin, 1912); and chapter 20 in Wilfrid Blunt, *Black Sunrise* (London: Methuen, 1951), which includes translations into English of parts of the letters included here, but rendered from the French, not the Arabic. For Bin Aisha's journey, see the detailed account in Philippe de Cossé Brissac, *Les Sources Inedites de L'Histoire du Maroc . . . Dyastie filalienne* (Paris: Paul Guethner, 1953), 5–10.

2. Cossé-Brissac, *Sources*, 5:321.

3. Ibid, 5:320.

4. Ibid, 2:427 and 4:507.

5. Ibid, 5:341. He so recalled the kind treatment he had received during his slavery that he started crying. His tears made the speech of his eyes more eloquent and effective than the words of his mouth, and drew tears from most of the people who were present there.

6. Comte Henri de Castries, *Moulay Ismail et Jaques II* (Paris: E. Leroux, 1903).

7. Cossé-Brissac, *Sources*, 5:338.

8. Aisha had used the same words in describing King Louis XIV: "dont l'amour estoit depuis si long-temps gravé dans son coeur, et qu'il faloit marcher sur la teste comme sur les pieds"; see Cossé-Brissac, *Sources* 5:325.

9. These are possibly daughters from a previous marriage.

10. Pidou de Saint-Olon was a French ambassador to Morocco who wrote an account of his travels, *Estat present de l'empire de Maroc* (Paris: Michel Brunet, 1694).

11. Jean Jourdan had asked for a license to export wheat and manufacture wine—which is the reason Aisha is hesitant.

12. The report consisted of a list of items Aisha wanted: powder flasks and mirrors (a large one for the house, a small one for his daughter, and a round one for the king); all the Barbary, German, or Damascene antique swords that could be found; two black ebony coffers; two dozen male and female pheasants; a dozen male and female turkeys; four dozen panes of glass for the royal coach; three or four crystal cups, similar to the ones already sent along with other crystal dishes and plates; four dozen ruby stones for rifles; and two ruby cups for the king. In return he would send three statues that could perhaps be of use in France.

13. This refers to the ship *Amphitrite*, which Jourdan had sent to China in 1698.

14. In the margin was written "for couscous."

15. The letter he mentions was written on the same day as this letter to Jourdan.

16. Eight months earlier, Aisha had attended the marriage of Estelle to Elizabeth.

17. Estelle's presence was important because it served as an assurance that the French would neither bombard the city of Salee nor blockade it. The year before, the French envoy there had been driven out by Aisha, and this had led to the deterioration of relations.

18. This is the name of Madame Jourdan's daughter.

19. Mr. Jourdan had asked him for goods, horses, and statues.

Index of Names

Index of Places

DATE DUE

JY 19 '07			

DEMCO 38-296

Please remember that this is a library book,
and that it belongs only temporarily to each
person who uses it. Be considerate. Do
not write in this, or any, library book.